IMMERSED
IN MYSTERY

En Route
to Theology

Enda McDonagh

First published 2007 by
Veritas Publications
7/8 Lower Abbey Street, Dublin 1, Ireland
Email publications@veritas.ie   Website www.veritas.ie

10 9 8 7 6 5 4 3 2 1

ISBN 978 1 85390 969 6

Scripture Quotations from the *New Revised Standard Version Bible* © 1993 and 1998 by the Division of Christian Education
of the United Council of the Churches of Christ in the United States of America.

'A Mayo Theologian? God Help Us!' was originally published in Gesa Thiessen and Declan Marmion (eds) *Theology
in the Making: Biography, Context, Methods*, Veritas, 2005. 'The Word in the World' was originally published in *New
Blackfriars*, March 2006. 'The Faith that Sets Free' was originally published in *The Furrow*, June 2006. 'The Golden
Echoes and the Leaden Echoes' was originally published in *The Furrow*, June 2005. 'No Habitable Grief: Spirituality
and Suicide' was originally published in *The Furrow*, November 2005. 'The Spaces of Our Grief' was originally
published in *The Furrow*, June 2006. 'Ethical Globalisation' was originally published in Lorna Gold, Bryan Hehir and
Enda McDonagh (eds) *Ethical Globalisation*, Veritas, 2005. 'Politics and Christology' was originally published in *Essays
in Memory of Alexis FitzGerald*, Dublin: Incorporated Law Society, 1987. 'Church–State Relations in an Independent
Ireland' was originally published in *Religion and Politics*, Mackey and McDonagh (eds) Columba Press, 2003. 'The
Reign of God: Signposts for Catholic Moral Theology' was originally published in James F. Keenan (ed.) *Catholic
Ethicists and HIV/AIDS Prevention*, Continuum, 2002. 'Love and Justice: In God and Church; In Sexuality and Society'
was originally published in J. Filochowski and P. Stanford (eds) *Opening Up: Speaking Out in Church*, Dartman,
Longman & Todd Ltd., 2005. 'Moral Theology and Transformative Justice' was originally published in Raphael
Gallagher and Brendan McConvery (eds) *History and Conscience*, Gill and Macmillan, 1989. 'Faith and the Cure of
Poetry: A Response to the Crisis in the Catholic Church in Ireland' was originally published in Andrew Pierce and
Geraldine Smyth (eds) *The Critical Spirit: Theology at the Crossroads of Faith and Culture*, Columba Press, 2003. 'Give
Beauty Back' was originally published in *Irish Theological Quarterly*, January 2005. 'Theatre, Tragedy and Theology'
was originally published in W. Jeanrond and DH Mayes (eds) *Recognising the Margins: Developments in Biblical and
Theological Studies*, Columba Press, 2007. 'The Tears of God' was originally published in *The Furrow*, December 2004.

Extract from 'Little Gidding' by TS Eliot from *Four Quartets*, courtesy of Harvest Books, 1968. Extracts from *Riders to
the Sea* by JM Synge, courtesy of Dover Publications, 1993. 'Quarantine' by Eavan Boland from *Against Love Poetry:
Poems*, courtesy of W.W. Norton & Company, 2001. 'Ceasefire' from *The Ghost Orchid* by Michael Longley, published
by Jonathan Cape. Reprinted by permission of The Random House Group Ltd. Extract from 'Ash Wednesday' by TS
Eliot from *Collected Poems, 1909–1962*, courtesy of Faber & Faber, 1963. 'Mysticism for Beginners' by Adam Zagajewski
(trans. Clare Cavanagh) from *Collected Poems*, courtesy of Faber & Faber, 2004. 'Death of an Irish Woman' by Michael
Hartnett from *A Farewell to English*, courtesy of Gallery Press, 1978. Extract from 'Healing' by Michael O'Siadhail from
Love Life, courtesy of Bloodaxe Books, 2005. 'Edge' by Sylvia Plath from *A Poetics on Edge: The Poetry and Prose of Sylvia
Plath*, courtesy of Peter Lang Publishing, 2001. 'Suicides' by Janet Frame from *The Pocket Mirror*, courtesy of George
Braziller Inc., 1991. 'Pied Beauty' and 'I Wake and Feel' by Gerard Manley Hopkins from *Gerard Manley Hopkins: The
Major Works*, courtesy of Oxford University Press, 2002. *The Instruments of Art* by John F. Deane, courtesy of Carcanet,
2005. *Swallows in December* by Jerome Kiely, courtesy of Trafford Publishing, 2006. Extract from *All in a Life: An
Autobiography* by Garret FitzGerald, courtesy of Gill & Macmillan, 1991. 'This Poem' by Elma Mitchell from Neil
Astley (ed.) *Being Alive*, courtesy of Bloodaxe Books, 2004. 'Refugees at Cobh' by Seán Dunne from *Collected*, courtesy
of Gallery Press, 2005. Extracts from 'A Disused Shed in Co. Wexford' by Derek Mahon from *Collected Poems*, courtesy
of Gallery Press, 1999. Extracts from 'The Oral Tradition' by Eavan Boland from *Selected Poems*, courtesy of Carcanet,
1989. Extracts from 'An Féar Suaithinseach' by Nuala Ní Dhomhnaill from *Selected Poems – Rogha Dánta*, courtesy of
New Island Books, 2000. Extract from 'Adam's Curse' by WB Yeats, courtesy of AP Watt Literary Agency. Quote by
Simon Goldhill from *Love, Sex and Tragedy: Why Classics Matter*, courtesy of John Murray, 2005. Extracts from *Faith
Healer* by Brian Friel, courtesy of Faber & Faber, 2001. Extract from 'From the Republic of Conscience' by Seamus
Heaney from *Opened Ground: Selected Poems 1966–1996*, courtesy of Farrar, Straus and Giroux, 1998.

Designed and typeset by Paula Ryan
Printed in the Republic of Ireland by Betaprint, Dublin

Veritas books are printed on paper made from the wood pulp of managed forests. For every tree felled, at least
one tree is planted, thereby renewing natural resources.

Contents

INTRODUCTION

Not Drowning but Waving

> Our world of clay was a fabulous boat
> floating out on an ocean of darkness.
>
> John F. Deane, *The Instruments of Art*, 2005

Mystery is the oldest word in the theological book. To some critics the oldest trick in the book. When all else fails in terms of explanation or justification, mystery is invoked and accusations of bad faith are frequently and sometimes justly riposted. 'Mystery's' exclusive attachment to religion has long vanished. Anybody visiting the mystery section of a contemporary bookshop will find no trace of religious mystery except perhaps by accident in something of Umberto Eco or Andrew Greely. Indeed the modern mystery book section is rapidly mutating simply into the crime section, this perhaps being the trivialisation of the religious mystery of original sin.

Whinging about the decline of great words from love to mystery is no help to their rediscovery and restoration. In Christian discourse and particularly in Catholic theology a valiant and often successful effort is made to maintain the power, the role and, as far as possible, the meaning of mystery. As far as possible is all one can say, as religious mystery and the mystery and mysteries of the Christian God far exceed the understanding of human beings, without excluding all such understanding or rendering the mystery utterly unintelligible or inaccessible. These are the difficulties that great theologians and religious thinkers and indeed great religious moralists and artists have had to wrestle with all their lives. And the understanding they gained, the light they shed, enhanced and encouraged all religious believers while leaving inexhaustible mystery still inexhaustible. The mysteries of Creator and Creation, originating and continuing, yield manifold insights to theologians and philosophers, to poets and scientists, without ever dissolving the primordial mystery of how there should be something rather than nothing or of how that unbridgeable gap was crossed.

In the older and broader history of religions, which cannot be pursued here, mystery was associated with particular cults, exclusive, even secret, societies and knowledge confined to the initiates or elite. In the Jewish and particularly the Christian traditions of concern here, mystery relates to the nature and activity of the Jewish Yahweh God and of the God and Father of Jesus Christ. Of course it would be foolish to exclude all wider religious influence and to pretend that the language, images and action models employed by Jews and Christians were not partly derived from human counterparts, or analogies, as they are more usually called. This must surely be true of Christianity whose central doctrine/mystery is of God becoming human in Jesus Christ.

The critical, and in this context, mystical opening of John's gospel speaks of the light coming into the world while the world did not comprehend (overwhelm) it. For generations of readers of John the echoes of Genesis' account of creation are overwhelming. But this was New Creation, as Paul preferred to describe it: the salvation of the original creation and the final coming of the Reign of God as the Christian scriptures and their early and late commentators regularly interpreted it. The *mysterion* of Paul hidden from all eternity in the mind of God, elegantly concealed and revealed to believers in the parables of Jesus and exploding from death to resurrection in God's crucial act of foolishness before men, is where these meditations start and where they hope to reach their final conclusion in the light that finally and definitively overcomes the darkness in the *eschaton*. Meanwhile we must be content with the half-light and suffer the occasional complete darkness in the various sections of this volume: in the celebration of the half-light and the struggle to escape from the threatening darkness in the secular but open reflections on education; in the sacred-secular wrestling of the divine word in the human world; and in the fruitful bonds of personal and academic friendship. Hence the titles of the three sections as they recognise our immersion in 'mystery' with its light and darkness, its revealing and concealing, in those powerful stages of at least my, and I would hope, many people's human life: In the Academy; In Word and World; Among Friends.

As the chapters themselves indicate, they were written to a large extent on the run over two or three years, in response to the demands of causes and friends which I was unable to refuse. For all that diversity of occasion I trust that the unity of my deeper, if often more aspirational engagements as a Catholic priest, Christian theologian, academic, friend, humanist and servant of the marginalized, may provide sufficient unity of theme and purpose for the volume as a whole.

In the writing of these chapters, as in most of my attempts at theology over fifty years plus, I have often felt lost and at sea. In facing honestly the ultimate mystery of God, the courageous human being is bound to venture out too far and to get in over a merely human head. Yet the resources of head as well as heart, of community as well as individual, of prayer as well as praxis may enable theologian and believer to hold on to the creative and saving hand of the mystery of God. In that hope as in this book the theologian may, to reverse the poet Stevie Smith's phrase, be 'not drowning but waving.'

Enda McDonagh, 2007

IN THE ACADEMY

The Mystery of Learning

Towards a Philosophy of Education in a New Era

It is perhaps ironic, but also encouraging, even exciting, that with philosophy now one of the poor relations of our university education and non-existent at first or second level in Ireland (unlike many of its EU colleagues), we should still want to explore a philosophy of education in the changing conditions of our society. And all the terms in the title of this lecture are disputable even in the absence of serious debate about them. Such debates as there are seem fearful of the kind of intellectual analysis which a stronger philosophical presence in our universities and public discourse might encourage and indeed enable. That this exploration should be attempted by somebody who has never been professionally a philosopher may be regrettable in some respects, but it may also permit a certain intellectual and experiential freedom derived from seventy years *in statu puppilari*, from the infant scholar to the Professor Emeritus whose university studies and interests ranged from philosophy and theology to science and the arts.

As Teddy, manager of the 'Fantastic Francis Hardy: Faith Healer' in Brian Friel's wonderful play, remarks: 'I'll tell you something, dear heart: spend your life in show business and you become a philosopher.' The education business is a kind of show business too, at least for those of us on this side of the podium. But education is much larger than education business. At least it was and is supposed to be, although the present signs are not always encouraging. And a philosophy of education, if such there be, obviously does not fit Teddy's type of dear heart or other barstool confidences, concerned as they may sometimes be with education rather than show business. For that matter the educational musings of politicians, editors and academic leaders may be much more focused on education business or what amounts to much the same thing, education for business, than on education itself. 'It's the economy, stupid!' has long since moved from the office of the would-be President of the United States to the education offices of governments, of university administrators and indeed of other educators. That business preoccupation may be the most telling threat of the New Era, of which this lecture's title speaks.

To concentrate on such a present danger, however imminent it may sometimes seem, would be to betray the search for an illuminating and coherent understanding of education, its purpose, process and product, in this or any other era. Paranoia in education, as in politics and personal relations, is the deadly enemy of the true and the good, two traditional and essential characteristics of that profound understanding of education we may label a philosophy of education.

In invoking the true and the good as essential and so continuing characteristics of western education at least, we must travel from fifth century Athens BCE, through the early medieval universities of the thirteenth and fourteenth centuries of the Common Era and on to at least nineteenth-century Dublin, with wide variations on these themes throughout twenty-five centuries and beyond. This is not the occasion and neither am I the expert who might guide you through the complex development and yet persistent identity of these primary university features. Suffice it to say that these features have survived in face of many intellectual, cultural and political upheavals. One task of this paper is to examine how they may not only survive but flourish in what may be fittingly called a new university era.

But this paper is not just another foray into the much debated role of the university today, despite its importance in itself and in any effort to consider in depth education at all stages in its formal and informal manifestations. It is worth recalling that those progenitors of philosophy of education such as Socrates, Plato, Aristotle also paid serious attention to the earlier stages of education, what we would call first and second level, and not just to the more advanced levels. In doing so they placed considerable emphasis on the educational role of parents themselves, a role being gradually diminished in our context.

The Aims and Principles of Education

The phrase is borrowed from John Henry Newman's famous discourses, although inevitably adapted, even translated, into language and ideas appropriate to this lecture and this lecturer. Attempting a philosophy of education in its life span and not just at university level or even through the school levels, I have to try to be at once more general than Newman, his illustrious predecessors and successors on university education, and peculiarly attentive to the very different era in which we live. Yet continuity with these masters, even to the point of facing the 'menace of metaphysics', is no less necessary to a genuine if general philosophy of education. How far the translations or variations and the continuities are successfully combined will be for people more expert than me to judge.

In the range of reading, immediate and remote, as well as in my near fifty years as a formal educator, while still a learner, I have had what I might call principles but more aptly poles before me. They were the individual student as person in his or her own right to whom I must personally respond and the context of the wider societies from class to school to university to civil or ecclesial society in which that response had to be made. Both teacher and student, and for that matter researcher at a different level, ignored at both their perils this dipolarity of education. Teacher and student as persons in community(ies) are the first principles (*principia*, starting-points) of any educational enterprise. And this applies to parents and children, to 'masters and apprentices', to lowly laboratory assistants and highflying research bosses as much as to regular classroom teachers and their students.

Here we touch on 'the menace of metaphysics', at least as a philosophical understanding of the human being in her dignity and basic equality as member of the human race, her right to personal development to the extent to which she is capable, within the confines of family, school and society. This personal development or education in the broad sense occurs as indicated above in the dialogical mode involving pupil and teacher, school and society, and more urgently now the physical environment in which all these exist. It is the existence of such realities not as projections of the mind but as subjects of encounter and dialogue which grounds education and makes its further examination and development essential to true and fuller human existence. Such true and fuller human existence may be adopted, in fidelity to Newman and other masters, as a simple description of the aims of education itself.

Autonomy and Vulnerability

In briefly discussing the aims and principles of education as adapted from western tradition, two notable deviations might be observed. The first of these was the qualification of individual autonomy, which in recent centuries certainly played a dominant role in social thinking and in educational theory and practice. From the child-centred emphasis in early schooling to the often isolated doctoral student at university level, the primacy of the individual prevailed in school as in society. And this was not without good reason. The dignity of the individual person as instanced earlier and the wide variation of learning abilities and interests all require specific attention to the individual at every level of education, and particularly at the earliest ones. The irreducible and irreplaceable individual person and learner has to be recognised and respected as such by teacher and system. She in turn is increasingly responsible for developing her individual gifts for her own sake and for the sake of the community who has provided her with these facilities and in the context of which she becomes a mature person.

Between Individual Autonomy and Social Determinism

That the individual person has all the rights and eventually the responsibilities in school and society has been in theory at least at the heart of our educational philosophy. The obvious failures to respect and protect these for the variously deprived, the poor, the travellers, those suffering from physical or intellectual disability and more recently in our country the new immigrants, have not negated the principles, still less stemmed the rhetoric. What is less clearly analysed and understood is that individual education is also committed to the good of the community, the common good, not as something added on from outside in return for what has been received in the educational process but as intrinsic to that process itself, as intrinsic as the community dimension is to the existence and growth of the person. This intrinsic connection of person and community and their mutual ethical demands provide some of the knottiest problems in a range of disciplines, and not just in philosophy. Education as a whole in the last century has experienced both extremes from sheer individualism to social determinism and with a lot of ineffective muddling in between, and with damaging consequences to person and society.

An apparently more small-scale problem is that of people with physical or mental disabilities. Yet their educational neglect might well give the impression that they were lesser human being or at least had fewer and weaker educational rights. This is not only an injustice to themselves but damages society in its practice of justice. It could be seen in our countries as a result of competitive individualism but the lessons of Romania and other former USSR countries reveal the other dark side of the educational coin.

Education and the Problem of Human Evil

From the Greeks through the Medievals but above all through the Enlightenment and its aftermath education was assumed to be the road to progress, to the formation of the good person and the good society. At a certain level of both abstraction and practice that is still a tenable proposition. Yet the mixed results, including downright evil caused by education and by the educated in every century and country, may not be dismissed. The petty criminals of petty schooling are not the problem. Much more serious are the evasions or encouragement of sectarianism, racism and sexism of which so many schools have been guilty. And in recent years, as the damage to the environment by human activity became more obvious, little effort has been made to combat it by education.

However, the utter destructiveness inspired and endorsed by some of the most highly educated in the most advanced countries over the last century more powerfully undermine education's claim to be the guarantee and vanguard of human progress. From Oxbridge to the rape of Africa, from the Free University of Berlin to the savagery of Auschwitz, from Yale to Abu Ghraib or Guantánamo Bay, the list goes on and on, reaching from past and present into a future bloated with educational and cultural expectations. The fault lies not in our schools but in ourselves and in our evil tendencies as well as in our educational, political and economic systems which may indulge these tendencies as much as they oppose and seek to correct them. In developing an adequate educational programme, humanity's destructive capacities will need to be taken into account together with its immense capacities for good, without transforming our schools into institutions akin to self-defeating boot camps or even prisons.

Purpose and Process at Elementary Level

Diverting into a rather long discussion of the evils to which all are heir may seem inappropriate in a search for a philosophy of education. Yet it is the real human being and the real human society with their mixed history of good and evil which must inform our search. With that mixture duly noted one is free to proceed along the more positive lines with which education has been traditionally concerned, from Plato to Augustine to Rousseau to Newman, Dewy and more recently Allan Bloom, to pick a list not quite at random.

Assuming with the ancients that the purpose of education is the good person/citizen in the good society does not immediately illuminate the task of today. Apart from the debated meaning of the good, personal and communal, in this as in other eras, the discrete goods to which contemporary education is directed are always complex and sometimes conflictual. At the elementary stage complexity and conflict may not appear so obvious or so threatening. Yet when you count in the role and desire of parents, and the increasing cultural and religious differences which even Ireland is experiencing, some difficulties are bound to arise.

In an important sense these difficulties are not entirely new. The mixed population of many schools hitherto while not involving racial or religious differences to any great extent did involve differences in personality and personal ability, in family and social background, which called for sensitivity to difference from teachers and pupils. Because they were less obvious they were often ignored, to the detriment certainly of the pupils. The much more obvious differences today in ethnic, cultural and racial characteristics offer much greater challenges to teachers and pupils.

The first challenge, however, is to see beyond the presenting differences to the basic and equal humanity of each pupil with the consequent rights to equal treatment in accordance with their special needs and capacities. Seeing beyond these differences may be claiming too much in that the basics in language, for example, will have to take account of each pupil's original language. It is exactly here for a multi-cultural society, such as ours is becoming, that the problems of unity in differentiation with the individual development, being at once respected in itself and integrated into society, become first apparent in school.

Reading and writing have long been the mark of the educated person. They face new risks today from the media multiplication, bearing innumerable and confusing sounds and images, half-words and pseudo-words. By crowding out regular and structured words and sentences they diminish language and communication, making it difficult for teachers to get past the mobile phone and the Ipod. Of course the judicious use of these ever-evolving media have their value in personal enjoyment, social relations and straightforward learning but they should always be measured against the more sophisticated and tested means of a broader educational tradition.

This corrective is achieved not by the reading and writing drill alone but by associated introduction to the arts and crafts of music and dancing, of drawing and making, where the pupils begin to learn some sense of style and beauty and creativity by doing for themselves rather than passively observing the work of others. Stages of development have to be aligned in these activities with the student's personal growth but it is hardly ever too soon once schooling has started to offer some creative outlet in at least a fun form to the young. The purpose of education will thus have an effective beginning, with one significant exception of course.

For reasons not always easy to decipher the third 'r', arithmetic and mathematics, are usually regarded as the bogeymen of early and sometimes later education. The distinction between the left and right sides of the brain or the newer concept of multiple intelligences do not seem to account adequately for the resistance some students display to learning both elementary mathematics and science. Both share many of the imaginative qualities of the more acceptable humanities. And both can be equally enjoyable in the right environment. And certainly both in varying degrees are essential to the developed citizen and society of modern times. It might also be remembered that it is the schoolchildren of today who are most likely to suffer the eco-damage now strongly predicted but hardly featured in early education. Where to begin and how to proceed with these reputedly difficult subjects require decisions from the experts, the teachers who may have to experiment with different pupils and subjects in search of the most effective methods.

A serious lack in discussing programmes for primary or later schools would be that of human relations between students themselves and between students and teachers. We have had plenty of examples of failures in this area recently. The first responsibility lies with the teachers in conducting their classes in that spirit of truth, goodness and justice to which all education is directed. Students must develop their own sense of responsibility partly modelled on that of their teachers but also endorsed by their parents and by the peers they choose as companions. In a fragmenting society breaches of good conduct will be inevitable and occasional sanctions essential without resorting to the physical or other injurious punishment so prevalent in the past. The building of supportive school community through team games, choirs and drama groups will help prevent some of the division and factions which may easily arise. Even in primary schools, but more so in secondary, student bullying can be a serious disciplinary problem as well as contradicting the very purpose and process of true education.

Building on the Elementary

The search for a philosophy of education seldom devotes much time and energy to elementary or primary education. The end product at university level is usually key subject matter. This may well be justified and is obviously congenial to many authors in this area who are themselves working in universities. However, a philosophy of education should endeavour to encompass and ground the whole process of formal education at least. This process has always included early schooling which up to recently in some of our countries was the only schooling available to the majority of our citizens. In a fresh turn of history university degrees no longer provide the end goal for all seeking further education. The fourth and fifth levels of education are emerging for post-doctoral students but more interestingly for a new back-to-school generation, whether second chance, retired or simply in search of new intellectual adventures. This movement may well confirm and deepen the philosophy of education sought after here.

The outline materials of elementary schooling provide the basis for more intense and specialised study at second level without losing the broad range of interests and subjects. Without therefore lingering on the detail of such programmes and their relation to one another and to the purpose and process of education, it may be more helpful to consider the transitional stage in which students find themselves as they move through adolescence into early adulthood. At the intellectual level many may be capable of the kind of abstract thinking more usually associated with university. So the great abstract values which have permeated education for millennia, of truth, goodness and beauty may become recognisable to them in their concrete studies of literature, science and art without reducing the potential delight which these concrete creations offer. Too often students come to these ideas and delights too late, a serious handicap in their further studies at university or elsewhere as well as in later adult life.

At the emotional level adolescent students veer readily between conformity to the dress and lifestyle of their peers, however attractive or unattractive these may be, and rebellion against the establishment, however benign or malign this may be. Both these moves to conformity and rebellion can play important roles in reaching adult maturity, although they can persist beyond the valuable growth stage to immature fixation, defeating the purpose of their education.

A more subtle and sinister, because disguised, enemy of true education at second level is the points race and the career obsession. Of course, one of the main purposes of education is to equip the student to make a satisfying life for himself with an adequate income in a career adapted as far as possible to his talents and qualifications, and as far as possible of his own choosing. This of course is rarely and simply available, although much more than it used to be. As entry into some careers and all university courses is based on examination results, and a less flawed method has yet to be devised, the pressure in the last years of second level is on acquiring maximum points in particular or all subjects, often without too much attention to the intrinsic value and delight of the actual subject. As recent research has shown that these results are a quite reliable guide to eventual primary degree results at university, they may be presumed to have much the same advantages and disadvantages: competence of a high standard without accompanying creativity and knowledge, without its traditional companion delight.

These conclusions may be much too harsh in not allowing for the flowering of students in a university atmosphere or for the inspiration of individual teachers at second or third level. We have all encountered late flowering students as well as students who followed brilliant examination results at second level with outstanding careers as university students and staff or in quite different contexts. Whether they or we have attained the traditionally final goals of education as good individuals and as good members of society is always more difficult to judge.

And finally to the University

In a later chapter I deal at some length with the reform of university education. However, some of the points made might be further developed here in a search for a philosophy of education. Not only is philosophy of education more usually treated by university people (perhaps other teachers are too busy educating to write about it), but as the culmination of the formal process, the university and its values influence, even shape, for good or ill preceding education.

Faithful to the great western tradition of philosophy and education one might summarise these values as truth, goodness and beauty. The earlier sections of this paper struggled with these ideas in themselves and their interactions and at least implicitly in discussing the particulars of elementary and secondary education. That discussion left aside at the time the explicit moral character of these values, at least of truth and goodness. Truth seeking and communication is at the heart of the educational process but is also central to human morality, both personal and social. While the example of teachers and the performance of truth in the activities of the school is the best education in it, truth also needs explicit discussion and instruction in the classroom. This becomes more urgent in multi-cultural and multi-religious society already with us. A key challenge in this context is how to combine respect for and commitment to truth with the respect for and care of people who espouse different views; how to combine attachment to the truth as one sees it with tolerance for other viewpoints. In a larger moral vision love of the differing neighbours could and should encompass love of truth. In the academic circles of university it might be taken for granted, (although frequently it cannot), that differences in academic conclusions would be native to the scene and never the source of personal animosity and quarrelling. In that connection the academic study of religion in university could provide the basis for amicable agreement to differ as well as restoring one of the great intellectual resources of university tradition to its rightful place. This university of Dublin, now joined by the Irish School of Ecumenics, deserves great credit for its promotion over the last decades of Inter-Church and now Inter-Faith theology.

After 'being' itself, goodness may be one of the most difficult philosophical notions to capture. However, in this context a certain clarity may be assumed both in regard to the general notion of the good person and, with more difficulty, in regard to the general notion of the good society. As the philosopher Alasdair MacIntyre might argue, such fundamental notions are rooted in a tradition, and, while capable and at times in need of development, maintain a certain consistency and clarity within that tradition. In a multi-traditional society (to coin another barbarism) the difficulties are intensified but may as in the case of truth yield to dialogue, practical compromise and tolerance. Again it is in the context of the university that these practices can provide the first draft at the intellectual level of social harmony in a diverse society. The university goal of the individual student attaining the intellectual roundedness and maturity which prepares him or her for a good life and livelihood, and to be a good member of the commonwealth nations, should take preference over the narrower professional interests which too often predominate.

The debates over the humanities and the sciences, the more general education and the specialised or the professional and non-professional cannot be properly treated here for reasons of space and time. They have been touched in earlier sections and received more extensive discussion in the paper referred to above. Besides they have been the subject of a great deal of public debate in Ireland over the last year or so. I believe in line with my approach to other divisive issues that mutually enriching compromises are available where the will to power does not prevail over the will to truth and goodness. And it hardly needs repeating that technical training should not take precedence over education and research in fundamental science or that the student confined to professional training is not a true product of the university any more than a humanities graduate ignorant of the fundamentals of modern science or a science graduate without some further study of the humanities is such a true university being.

The Ghosts of Beauty

Beauty is not commonly accounted a characteristic of education or the university. Yet it haunts all our great human achievements as they are penned in literature or limned in art or discovered in science and so the subject of study at all levels of education. More significantly still they characterise at their best human being and relationship, nature and its infinite variety. As with truth and goodness the sense of beauty is imbibed before it is formally learned. The learning is still extremely important if a deeper sensibility is to be achieved in relation to literature, music, architecture and the other human arts as well as to the human person, human society and the natural environment. My last thought then on education and its philosophy might be to adapt a phrase of Gerard Manley Hopkins: 'Bring beauty back.' It may be the surest protection against a ravaging utilitarianism at all levels of education.

Reforming the University

Idea and Ideals of University in Contemporary Ireland

The current debate about reforming Irish universities, while overdue, remains underdeveloped. A great deal of time and energy has been spent on the necessary issues of structural change and increased funding. They have not, however, been put in any deeper context of the developing meaning and purpose of universities and their longer term relationships to the kind of Irish society we might wish to foster. In this the debate has followed much the same lines as that in the UK and elsewhere. Few countries or universities have faced into these more difficult waters, leaving politicians with a rather limited view of university education as primarily an arm of economic development; leaving university heads to focus on managerial reform and funding requirements; leaving many academics unsure of the future integrity and prospects of their own disciplines and too many students and parents confused about the value and purpose of actual or proposed courses and degrees.

At the risk of sounding old-fashioned and irrelevant it seems important to raise again at least in summary form some critical issues in regard to the meaning, value and purposes of university education. The university, it may be said, is society's central and climactic intellectual institution both in its rigorous intellectual examination of humanity, its cultures and the world we live in and in its intellectual training of succeeding generations of students in pursuit of such tasks. To ignore the primacy of the intellectual in its critical and creative modes, in the topics it undertakes and in the methods it adopts is to fail the university vocation and its particular role and value in society. No amount of attention to personal short-term career advantages or economic social advance can compensate academic staff or students or above all society as a whole for neglect of this pioneering intellectual activity in the university's classic practices of teaching and research. Indeed it is by remaining faithful to the primacy of the intellectual, to the pursuit of truth at its most basic that the university as already indicated serves the wider society most effectively.

Truth is a crucial social good without which knowledge and understanding in personal terms and social trust and cohesion become impossible. As a university good, truth is sometimes and rightly described as a value in itself independently of the uses to which it may be put by individual or society. Holding on to that is essential to university integrity. But such acquired truth has almost always useful implications for person and society, as the great scientists and artists, creators, critics and technologists in a thousand fields have proved over the millennia, from Archimedes in his tub to Einstein with his $e=mc^2$. In the search for and communication of truth the university must set the national standard and inspire a truthful and truth-seeking society in every dimension of its life. This will always be its most significant and useful contribution to a society which sustains the university and which the university in turn sustains at its intellectual and moral core. How far the great or even good universities exert this kind of influence in their societies is a far better, if in the end immeasurable, test of their value than simple league tables or even list of Nobel Laureates. The fashionable tag of knowledge society reduces rapidly to knowledge economy and its perennial temptations to greed and exploitation if the knowledge is not put in a context of shared human resources and accompanied by the understanding and wisdom which the educated university graduate is always in the process of acquiring.

At the further risk of alienating even serious academics it is necessary to relate truth in the university to that other great dimension of human and university life – beauty. The discovery, creation and enjoyment of beauty is closely related to the discovery and enjoyment of truth, as the Greeks, St Augustine and a host of others appreciated well before John Keats. To understand the truth of humanity and the world, the purpose of so many university enterprises, it is necessary also to appreciate their beauty. Beauty is with intellectual curiosity or the desire for truth frequently the attracting force which draws scientists and others to explore both the circulation of the planets and the circulation of the blood. And the beauty of argument and conclusion often plays a persuasive role in accepting the results. All substantial university disciplines combine a sense of beauty with a sense of truth if staff and student are alert enough to appreciate it. In any proposed reorganisation of disciplines, departments and faculties such values will need to be taken account of ahead of the monetary cost-effectiveness, which may be so tempting.

Truth and beauty as belonging with the good in that classical trio are still far from out of date even if the terms seem lost to fashionable university discourse. And it is here that the concerns of current reformers may make the most immediate and fertile connections with the basic values of the university. The good, the overall enhancing of individual and of society should provide leadership in the discussion of how the university contributes to society's real development so as to merit its moral and financial support. Of course, that personal and common or society good must be subject to continuous examination as needs and circumstances change both within and without the particular society. It is both personal and common or shared. Persons reach their potential within a shared and sharing society; societies develop in relation to the growth of their individual members. A serious imbalance within society between individuals or groups in essential matters of shelter, health, education and human rights generally undermines not only the community and its common good but diminishes even the good of the more privileged individuals. The university, in its pursuit of truth in the social and other human sciences, will shed light on such limitations and in its associated professional training provide the skills necessary to rectify them. Such truth and skills will always be critical to the economic development of the society, always necessary to society's well being but always in need of direction to the fair sharing by all. The physical sciences in their broadest range are often treated as the crowning aspiration and achievement of contemporary university achievement but must always be set in a humane context not least by interaction with the apparently non-related humanities and social sciences. Professional education in medicine and the health-food sciences, in law, in engineering and technology, especially information technology – the new king on the block – remain central to the university tradition. With their colleagues in the humanities and sciences they have their proper context also in personal development and the service of the common good and in a just, informed and learning society, a more insightful and dynamic description than that of a knowledge society.

Such ideas and ideals may seem very remote from the immediate concerns of presidents and provosts, academics and students, ministers and civil servants as they struggle with the latest twists in university reform. They were also of very remote interest to the drafters of what is taken to be the ground plan of present Irish moves to university reform, the recent OECD Report on Irish Universities. Its authors might justifiably claim that their brief was much more restricted and that they concentrated as instructed on the managerial and funding needs to ensure the essential development in the competitive international field of research and teaching, while taking for granted the crucial ideas of university education as adapted to the twenty-first century and as they have been in continuous adaptation over so many previous centuries.

In Search of Reform

As one who has worked for over fifty years in universities in North America, the UK and Europe as well as Ireland and at so many levels of university life, I have lived through a variety of university reforms at home and abroad. Yet the need for such reform today I see as urgent and radical. What is and remains controversial is the principles on which it is to be based and the shape it should be given in service of the intellectual-academic purposes of the university.

The emphasis on administrative or managerial reform, which seems to have captured the favour of government, the headlines in the newspapers and the ire of many academics who are not necessarily opposed to university reform, has undoubtedly distorted the debate. To some extent the OECD report and the government's short-sighted cutting of university income beforehand, its acceptance of the OECD's demands for increased 'productivity' in undergraduate and postgraduate courses in service of the 'knowledge economy', while refusing to provide the funds necessary and recommended by their own commission, have obscured many of the real issues in administration. A reformed administration could no doubt promote better and quicker decision making but only if it is reshaped to ensure greater development within the university to enable academic departments and faculties to attend more effectively to their own teaching and research. At the same time the overall administration has to integrate more clearly the primary ideals and goals of the university, involve some serious members of the public in its composition and relieve the president or provost of chronic financial worries to enable him or her to give proper intellectual and academic leadership within and without the university. The limited positive impact which Irish universities have had on Ireland's limited public intellectual life may be in more urgent need of development than its impact on economic life. This will be a bold challenge to the reformers, administrative and academic.

How the administrative reforms are achieved in a particular university and what stable form they take will depend a great deal on the university's history, current structures, immediate priorities and needs. While much may be gained by studying structures and practices in the better universities around the world, much may also be lost by ignoring local resources and needs and by mindlessly imitating structures developed in quite different circumstances and to meet quite different needs. The attraction of the 'business model' of some of the larger corporations and the lurking suggestion of a kind of free market of universities sound naturally threatening to genuine academics and genuine academic purposes. To some people they might seem to provide a short route to solving universities' present financial difficulties but at what cost to the true idea of a university and to the society it serves. It is unlikely that such extremes will be attempted but not all the signs of due resistance to them at the top levels of government, of public service and of university are encouraging.

What may be clearly needed is some simplification of the administration at top level with a smaller, more effective and more representative board of governors working with a slimmed down administration to a series of devolved internal structures based on a reformed internal set of academic faculties and departments determined eventually by the intellectual ideals and nature of the university.

Reform within and between Universities

The needs and shape of internal academic structural reform must be in service of the particular academic disciplines and of the overall academic thrust of the particular university. Not every Irish university can maintain departments in every possible discipline to the required intellectual standard. Which existing disciplines are to be maintained and which new ones are to be initiated will depend on a variety of criteria: intellectual/academic, social and financial but primarily intellectual/academic. Disciplines which are historically recognised as essential to this particular university and in some cases to any university should be treated as core disciplines which fuel the intellectual life of society as well as university. Of course some of these have been abandoned not for intellectual or associated social reasons but for the fashionable ideological reasons which now threaten in economic guise. Theology was one of the first of these to go and its close associates, philosophy and ancient classical studies, three foundation stones of western universties and civilizations, are under regular threat in too many universities, here and abroad. That such rich heritages of scholarship and civilization should be treated so cavalierly in this economically wealthy but culturally deprived era is a sad commentary on our university leaders and their political and financial masters.

Yet there must be pruning if there is to be growth. That pruning might well take the form proposed for some universities in Ireland of merging departments and even faculties without simply eliminating any. Such merging would need to be by agreement rather than mandate and in accordance with intellectual rather than managerial criteria. It would not be an easy task but given good will and good reasons it could be completed relatively swiftly to the advantage of the disciplines, the university and society. In certain instance it might even be accomplished across institutional boundaries with a department shared between two or more institutions or integrated into one in a inter-university exchange to the intellectual advantage of all concerned. This could happen more easily within a limited geographical area such as the Dublin region and without diminishing the autonomy or integrity of an institution but it may become increasingly important to regard the territory of the Republic and eventually of the whole island as one university region with due respect for the authentic university character and independence of the diverse institutions. The latter (all-island prospect) may not be so unthinkable in the context of an integrating Europe and of the cross-border initiatives already in place. In the Dublin region and the west-south-west of the universities at Galway, Limerick and Cork some cooperative developments are taking place which could be jeopardised by heavy emphasis on internal competition as voiced by government, HEA and individual universities. Competition for students and staff, for buildings and other facilities in laboratory and library, for research and other funding is helpful, even necessary up to a point. Pursued in brutal business fashion it may easily destroy the fabric of Irish university education as a whole and do long-term disservice to the country. The health of society and of its universities depends primarily on cooperation with a lively element of competition to maintain and improve standards.

In the search for a more integrated and diverse student menu within limited resources the American credit system, which is now being gradually adopted in Ireland, may prove quite useful. Freedom to choose related or indeed different and challenging subjects in addition to one's main or major field of study could be a move in the direction of the broader education so strongly promoted by Newman. It does seem a shame that so many students graduate in the humanities and related cultural studies without any serious exposure to studying the great scientific and technological discoveries and advances of recent centuries. No less shameful is the lack of some basic education for science and other graduates in the great artistic, religious and other cultural achievements past and present. Some form of credit system over one or more semesters may help to remedy that situation. However, it will need to be expertly handled. Neat little packets of information are no substitute for the reflection which even a minimum knowledge of a serious subject requires. University-generated cocktail chatter on such subjects may be worse than simple ignorance. With wise guidance in choosing and proper teaching/tutoring a credit system does offer new dimensions to university education.

A more interesting mode of intellectual development for students specialising in a particular area may not be by add-on but by expansion of elements of other major studies contained within the first choice subject. In the study of any period of history, the history of its scientific ethos and developments could open the history student to the contemporary as well as the historical world of science. A scientist following the growth of his particular discipline should be enabled to relate to other cultural and political developments. A student of biology or cosmology could be opened up to the ethical, religious, anthropological or cultural challenges of his discipline. Some of the proposed credit courses could well emerge by the expansion of one discipline to meet questions posed by another. They are unlikely to provide merely packaged information and could promote deeper relationships between disciplines and departments.

At the local level the universities will also need to engage with the Institutes of Technology. The OECD Report was rightly insistent on the distinction between the two types of institution, although it clearly envisaged cooperation. This cooperation should be at teaching and research level where facilities, staff and students might be exchanged, or at least share some facilities. This is already happening in certain places if not to the extent it could. A significant area of cooperation could be in widening access for less advantaged students, some of whom might find it easier to begin in Institutes of Technology but would be well equipped to move to university later in their courses. Similarly some students who find university unsuited to their needs might go to the Institutes to complete their studies. A two-way system of this kind could enlarge and enrich the cohort entering third level and gradually help erase the snobbery often affecting staff and students.

The Need for an Equitable and Effective System of University Funding

Of course, university education is not the only educational game in town as university administrators and staff are generally well aware. However, they have legitimate grievances with government over the last few years which have been already sufficiently rehearsed in public. And it is not easy to see how these grievances can be redressed in the short term despite pious praise from the government for the essential role of the universities in economic growth in times past and still more in times future. The OECD report commissioned by government recommended the return of student fees, subsequently ruled out by government, and a general doubling of government grants with particular reference to scientific and technological research. Not much hope of that either. Some kind of task force will have to draw together minister, senior public servants and senior university people including some active academics if any long-term solution to the funding of universities is to be found and serious damage to their mission and effectiveness be avoided. There are a limited number of sources which can be tapped. Government remains the most important if only to ensure that the universities genuinely serve the common good of the society and not some private enterprises. Student fees, loans and grants will have to be reconsidered, perhaps when the next election is safely out of the way. Fees abolition did little to widen access, however good its intentions, and a more sophisticated grants and support system will be needed to help the disadvantaged. It is true that many of their difficulties begin in primary schools but unless there is continuous growth in access at tertiary level there will be little stimulus at primary and secondary level.

The suggested graduate tax may at this stage be better pursued through graduate associations and university foundations which can draw on a great deal of good will and good money (with no strings attached) if professionally pursued, as they are in most universities now, although it remains a small proportion of what is required. Major philanthropic organisations, particularly from the USA, have been generous to Irish universities in the recent past. More controversial have been arrangements with large multinationals on research into their particular products such as pharmaceuticals and genetically modified food, etc. Controversial not because of any irregularity in the arrangements but because of the public disputes about some resulting products and of the fear that the independence of scientists may be compromised by the interests and influence of donor corporations. No such scandal has emerged in Ireland as yet but if a large push towards such research funding were to be made as suggested by some spokespersons, it would be much more difficult to ensure scientific independence. In all these discussions and decisions wiser and more experienced heads are needed and the advantages and disadvantages weighed according to the kind of university criteria outlined earlier.

In this decade almost certainly major changes in Irish universities will occur but they need fuller and deeper discussion if they are to be truly positive changes. This paper offers one purely personal perspective on the need, basis and direction of such change.

Why the University Needs Theology

To many of the founders of the great ancient, medieval and much later universities, from Plato's Academy and the Schools of Alexandria, from Bologna, Oxford and Paris to Edinburgh, Tubingen and on to Harvard and Chicago, theology was a central and founding university discipline. To many but not all academics today that tradition is forgotten or ignored. Theology is too often despised if not excluded. And a combination of ignorance and arrogance is undermining the role of the humanities, including theology, in the intellectual enterprise of many universities, but that has already been canvassed in an earlier chapter.

In university terms the arguments for theology in the university may be summarised under four main headings with their own families of subheadings. These four headings of argument are: the historical, the cultural, the social and the intellectual, though not necessarily in any linear order of importance. As with so many so-called serial arguments these criss-cross and overlap. They might be better represented as a square with links between all the corners or as a circle with radii connecting various points on the circumference, any of which might be adopted as a starting point. However, the linear structure of writing compels one to choose a certain order and I have chosen this one with all these qualifications noted.

The Historical Argument

The easiest part of the historical argument is the study of the curricula of the universities themselves. From their earliest forerunners in the West, as indicated above, through to their major modern counterparts, theology was not only a recognised discipline but for long central to the structure of university study. Its decline, if not yet its disappearance, in the last few centuries was partly due to its own arrogance and its ignorance of the newly developing sciences but more significantly to the general secularisation process whose dismissal of religion theology proved unable to cope with. Yet explicitly and implicitly, as friend or foe, theology continued to influence major disciplines in ways the leaders in these disciplines did not adequately or fairly address. Even in the very latest anti-religious writings of scientist Richard Dawkins, the scientific arrogance and theological ignorance expose the need for a dialogue with university theology which he refuses or has no opportunity to address. In literature from Dante to Joyce a serious study of the theological background of so many great writers seems essential. And how does one understand and appreciate the great medieval and Renaissance artists or such moderns as Rouault or Rothko without some study of theology and spirituality. And this study does not begin or end with the university study of Judaism or Christianity. The Greek dramatists were deeply immersed in their own religious traditions. The great burial sites from the Egyptian pyramids to those of the Boyne valley have religious significance still awaiting further sympathetic theological exploring, as do most of the ancient archaeological finds of recent centuries. Perhaps more typical of university concern are the written remains of the great civilizations of the past and their religious connections. Without these scrolls and fragments and their later preservation in book form the origins of our own civilizations might be entirely lost to us.

The religious influence in almost every area of our ancient heritage is part of the business of university which pretends to offer some account of the descent of modern man and society. The scholarly study of that religious influence in theology is an equal partner with all the other disciplines which focus on aspects of that heritage. In western Europe and Ireland, where the Judeo-Christian heritage has been and still is so significant, no university is complete without a department devoted to such study in itself and dialogue with other disciplines in their historical development. The advent and influence of other religions will call for similar study of Islam, Buddhism and other major religions. However, the weight of the historical argument rests at present with the need for the introduction and development of Jewish and in Ireland particularly Christian studies while preparing the way in our rapidly globalising planet for the inclusion of all world religions.

The Cultural Argument

If cultural studies are not to turn into a shallow and shabby survey of certain lifestyles in their historical and current forms, they will need to engage with the religious beliefs, rituals and practices of past and present. And, of course, the best departments of cultural studies already do, if not always, with the intellectual underpinnings of the religions involved. The danger here is that they dismiss religion as a mere cultural product of other human-turned-cultural phenomena such as farming or marrying or dying without taking account of any deeper considerations. And such failure does not affect just ancient and perhaps extinct religions but may be thoughtlessly applied to religions living and influential in a university's own context. The presence in dialogue of a lively theology department could prevent any such shallowness.

Thus far the emphasis has been on elements of the common life of past and present generations, a basic constituent of social studies in many universities, although it may branch off into the more specialised disciplines of anthropology and archaeology, among others. The point to be stressed here is that all these branches of higher studies, whatever their classification, would benefit from dialogue with a vital department of theology or religious studies.

There is, however, another strand of culture which may be described, if with some misgivings about its presumption, as High Culture. This usually refers to the more significant human achievement in literature, art, architecture and music which form the core of humanity studies in most universities. In the past they were the natural allies of theology, not least because so many of these significant human achievements were inspired by and expressed religious belief and ritual. The mutual enrichment which a cathedral such as Chartres with its windows and the aesthetic and indeed biblical–dogmatic dimensions of theology have to offer one another is enormous. Eastern icons, medieval and Renaissance painting and sculpture are no less rich sources for dialogue with theology. Indeed, they are sources of theology in themselves. In a purely secular mode later painting and sculpture together with more obviously religious works reveal the creative, spiritual dimension of humanity which challenge and develop the traditional theology of the original creation stories and its contemporary theological exploration, human and divine (including work by, for example, Ireland's Imogen Stuart with its explicitly religious and secular themes, and John Behan who combines ancient Irish legendary themes with contemporary secular ones). The list of such serious artists across Ireland and across the world could be extended indefinitely and they would all have much to contribute in their artistic work to the world of spirituality and religion. Many of them, even near contemporaries such as Kandinsky and Rothko, have written insightfully of the spiritual dimensions of their own and of others' art.

I have left to the end the two art forms which have closest connections over the centuries with religion and theology, literature including poetry, prose and drama and music. Some of the literary connections have been mentioned in the earlier section and the danger is that theological may join literary scholarship in overwhelming all other cooperation between theology and the arts. Given the status of the scriptures in Judaism, Christianity and Islam and the dominance of written forms in most formal education this is not surprising and can clearly be of tremendous benefit to both literature and theology. Apart from their overlapping themes, religious and secular scriptures share much in the aesthetic forms and literary beauty which constitute them at their best. In more recent times methods of interpretation of texts, developed earlier in the Jewish and Christian scriptures, have been taken forward in more secular studies.

The bible as text with all the linguistic complications and the bible as literature have been learning from and teaching the wider world of literary studies, including the rich heritage of ancient, medieval and modern Irish.

Perhaps it is with music that theology's closest links occur. In his 2006 Reith Lectures on BBC Radio Four, the eminent musician David Barenbohm, in discussing music's universal appeal and its capacity to promote human unity, saw religion as its closest analogue (not necessarily institutional religion). The masterful masses of Beethoven, Bach et al. offer clear instances of the religious and theological resources which music of this high order offers. In the more scholarly and technical study of such masterpieces the creating and redeeming powers of Christianity find deeper significance and effectiveness.

The Social Argument

The overlapping or intertwining of the various strands of the arguments already advanced apply no less to the complexity of university disciplines grouped here under the heading 'social'. However their interaction with religion and theology operates for the most part on a rather different basis from those discussed earlier. That basis, morality including human rights, should itself be treated as a social as well as a philosophical science and under both categories had and still has strong connections with various religions. To clarify the argument university social sciences will be confined here to politics and law; psychology, sociology and anthropology. Technology and computer studies, which closely relate to the physical sciences, are crude classification for the final 'intellectual' section, but not as if those other sections were not also intellectual in intent and operation.

More disputable included in this social section are the professional disciplines of food science, engineering and medicine, not because of their lack of intellectual content but because they are such significant social practices and because as such they interact with religion mainly through the medium of morality. Many aspects of them will return in the fourth and final argument.

Tedious as it would be to consider each of these disciplines in relation to morality and so perhaps to theology, a couple of disparate examples must suffice. In politics and law the various kinds of justice, individual and social, are paramount. In the purely positive law tradition which prevails in so many modern states the consensus of the majority through agreed structures can provide justice and good order, if not always for the minorities and marginalised. However, the positive tradition leaves unanswered many questions about the dignity, beginning and end of human life, for instance, or about the foundation of justice, human rights and their unconditional demands. Here the debate turns on underlying culture and philosophy which is seldom complete without reference to the ultimate origin and destiny of the human being, questions of religion and theology. In particular it is difficult to found human rights on purely positive law. On the other hand, to speak of social morality only in terms of human rights language may narrow the range of such social concepts as solidarity and reconciliation, or such personal phenomena as friendship and marriage.

Economics is another area in which broader moral considerations such as social and distributive justice are necessary to prevent the wealth of the nation being dominated by the few. Economics as a science, at least as a predictive and productive science, has to face questions about the treatment of people and their environment, human and physical, which economics on its own cannot solve. The need for dialogue with the moral sciences is obvious and the connections with religious belief, while less direct, can be an important critical and motivating force. The justice and peace movements which theology underpins and promotes may help economists in their own analyses.

As a final but immeasurable example, technology in its various guises raises questions about the human condition and human behaviour which technology on its own cannot resolve. Nowadays very many of these arise as biotechnology advances at such a rapid pace. Public debates on these problems are not always conducted on an informed basis by moralists–theologians on the one hand and by scientists on the other. At least the moralists–theologians are not always willing to enter the world of the scientist in order to get a reasonable view of his intentions, arguments and actions. The same criticisms may be applied to many scientists, with both scientists and moralists fostering, not real dialogue, but that of the deaf.

At a more general level university administrators and their funders may easily exaggerate the longer-term value of narrow technological education, even for the economic development they wish to achieve. Technical skills are not always easily adapted to change in the technological world itself without a broader educational base. Many Irish proponents of increased and rather narrow technological education seem to forget that the Celtic Tiger growth of which they are so proud grew out of a much broader university education, in which the humanities, including philosophy, played a major role.

The Intellectual Argument

It scarcely needs to be stressed again that all the arguments advanced so far have a strong intellectual component. As I have emphasized elsewhere in this book, the university as a whole and in its diverse disciplines provides the intellectual dynamic of society. Every university discipline worthy of the name must have that intellectual substance which challenges student, teacher and researcher to seek truth and understanding of some significant aspect of humanity and the world. The disciplines enumerated earlier enjoy that intellectual substance. The arguments of the previous sections indicate how theology and religious studies share at least in dialogue the university validity of these disciplines. But religious studies and theology in themselves address significant aspects of humanity and the world which also challenge student, teacher and researcher. Beyond that they raise and pursue questions which elude other disciplines both in their historical origin and development and in their contemporary vitality and influence.

Closely akin to theology in its questioning, if somewhat different in methodology and source, philosophy is one of the oldest and most fundamental of university disciplines. It is a poor reflection on present university planning that philosophy is so neglected. Like theology it is a valuable dialogue partner to most other disciplines and often the potential mediator of dialogue, particularly in moral philosophy. Philosophy not only provides some of the most valuable tools of critique and creation for theology but must also address some of the basic questions with which theology is concerned, about the meaning and destine of humanity and the cosmos. In confrontation with a sometimes closed view of the physical sciences, for example about the world's origin and significance, philosophy and theology have questions if not necessarily conclusive answers with which science by its very methods is unable to cope.

There remain important differences between philosophy and theology. To attempt to reduce one to the other is another form of that reductionism so characteristic of the modern university. The origins of the great religions centre for the most part on charismatic or prophetic figures: Abraham, Jesus, Mahomet, the Buddha and so on. These religions are carried forward by living communities and traditions. They frequently involve sacred writings associated with the founder. They involve ritual and morality as ways of responding to the Ultimate Being or God who has made his presence and plans clear through the Founder, the Scriptures and the continuing life of the community. In these ways they attempt to answer the ultimate questions about human and cosmic life and death but they must be continually subject to critical intellectual exploration and scrutiny if they are not to lapse into mere self-deception and superstition. In the history of western universities, as alluded to above, this intellectual project of theology helped found the universities and will be needed to sustain them in view of the many threats they now face. The university's need of a strong and authentic theology may never have been greater.

A Mayo Theologian? God Help Us!

Irish Beginnings

In the Ireland of the 1950s one might aim to be ordained a priest but did not set out to be a theologian. Even if one ended up after ordination in postgraduate studies and then with a job teaching theology, such was the culture that one would be reluctant to accept the title 'theologian'. This was illustrated clearly in the comment of the subsequent Bishop of Kildare, Paddy Lennon, during his time at St Patrick's College, Carlow: 'I am not a theologian, I am a teacher of theology.' Although this remark was made in the sixties, even then Irish ecclesiastical culture and theological practice were changing under the increasing influence of visiting scholars and Vatican II. The establishment of the Maynooth Union Summer School in the late fifties gave a public platform to foreign theologians including Louis Boyer and Charles Davis from France and England respectively, the Germans Bernhard Haering, Josephs Fuchs and Joseph Ratzinger and a host of others like Raymond Brown from the US as well as theologians from the UK and Europe. The founding of the Irish Theological Association and the Irish Biblical Association in the late sixties provided formal indigenous structures for the professionalisation and mutual support of Irish scholars in these fields. Indeed the growing community of Irish theologians and scripture scholars, contemporary and younger, remain a constant positive influence. Such developments may seem old hat now but they had an important influence on many theologians of an earlier generation.

It would be ungracious to ignore the work and influence of still earlier teachers and theologians and of publications like the *Irish Theological Quarterly*, first established in 1909 and refounded in 1951. The later *Milltown Studies* followed a similar pattern. Influential journals such as the *Irish Ecclesiastical Record* and *Studies* would not have regarded themselves as primarily theological and neither would their later companions such as the *The Furrow* and *Doctrine and Life*. Yet all of these published important theological material in articles and in answers to theological questions from readers. The prestigious American quarterly, *Theological Studies*, frequently commented on such Irish material, particularly on the answers to moral questions in the *Irish Ecclesiastical Record*. Earlier still theologians such as

William Walsh, Walter MacDonald and William Moran, despite or because of their difficulties with some Roman authorities, produced significant work. In scripture too Edward Kissane, Patrick Boylan, Conleth Kearns and others were internationally recognised. So early twentieth-century Ireland was not a complete desert, even if theology as a discipline did not rate very highly in church, university or society. And the six years of theology at Maynooth, from BD through STL to DD, 1951–57, was not simply narrowly scholastic and provided a substantial grounding in the main disciplines which was often critical and occasionally inspiring. It proved a firm foundation for future theological development.

By the end of that six years a few lasting connections had been made with fellow students, theological themes, professors and publications. The themes might be given first mention as they continued to be influential, although, by one of these ecclesiastical accidents, they did not figure in my original teaching mandate of 1958 to teach fundamental moral theology, in the chair vacated by William (later Cardinal) Conway when he became Auxiliary Bishop of Armagh. My Maynooth doctoral dissertation had been on the Anglican doctrine of the church in the Tudor period and left me with such a serious fascination with ecumenism that my first full-length book was entitled *Roman Catholics and Unity* (1962), published at the invitation of the editor of a series on ecumenism, Bishop Oliver Tomkins of Bristol and chair, as I remember, of the World Council of Churches' Faith and Order Commission.

The second theme which took hold at the time was the relation between church and state and the issue of religious freedom. This was sparked by a family interest in politics and given shape in my postgraduate days at Maynooth through involvement with a group of young lay, intellectually vibrant and politically minded graduates concerned with the economic, social and political difficulties of the Ireland of the fifties. The group, which had been named *Tuairim* (Irish for 'opinion' or 'view'), opened me up to new ways of examining such issues, including the role of the church in our divided Ireland. It also left me with some very close and permanent friendships. A little earlier I had encountered the work of American Jesuit John Courtney Murray whose writings, which I found so liberating, led to his being silenced by Rome in the fifties, but he later provided the basis for the Declaration on Religious Liberty at Vatican II in 1965.

The third lasting theme was not, as I had anticipated, the relation between science and religion but that between the arts and religion. I had been an enthusiastic student of Theoretical Physics for my primary degree and had serious intentions of following it up. My archbishop decided otherwise and by then I was deeply involved in theology. However, an earlier (in primary and secondary school) and continuing interest in the arts, particularly poetry and theatre, became another intellectual interlocutor with theology and politics.

Travels in Theology

1. A European Education

After a year concentrating mainly on Aquinas at the Angelicum University in Rome but free to take in Stanislas Lyonnet at the Biblicum and Frederick Coplestone at the Gregorianum, I had an unexpected and irrevocable career change. I was appointed Professor of Moral Theology at Maynooth and requested to do a doctorate in Canon Law so that I could fill the portfolio of Professor of Canon Law as well. Diocesan priests at least were obedient fellows in these days and so back to Rome for Canon Law at the Gregorianum and a two-year licence to be achieved in one. No great satisfaction in that, but now that I knew my academic destiny I could look around a little for help and instruction to the Alphonsianum with Bernhard Haering and brilliant Irish Redemptorist Sean O'Riordan, also a Maynooth doctorate, and to that kindliest of theologians at the Gregorianum, Joseph Fuchs SJ, where one of my companions was friend and later colleague, Vincent MacNamara. Fuchs' seminar on the Law of Christ was one of the best I attended.

A year of Canon Law at the Gregorianum, despite the helpfulness of the Dean of Canon Law, Dutchman Piet Huizing, gave me a taste for wider horizons and after obtaining my licence I was accepted at the faculty in Munich for my doctorate. I had realised that my doctoral proposal on church–state relations was not very acceptable to the youngish Jesuit teaching Public Ecclesiastical Law in Rome, the area which dealt with church–state relations. So I was pleased to find that Professor Klaus Moersdorf at Munich was open to the proposal and so he remained, although he deeply disagreed with my views and those of John Courtney Murray.

Rome was more an ecclesial, historical and cultural influence than a theological one. That was due in part to the fact that I was not formally studying theology but philosophy, Aquinas- style, in my first year and Canon Law in the second. The death of Pius XII and the election of John XXIII deepened one's awareness of the history and universality of the church. And in spite of various restrictions on clerical leisure activity, the city and museums were there for the seeing and the concerts for the listening. For contact between religion and the arts one had only to look around: the monuments were everywhere. Yet, such theology as I heard from professors or students was not in any serious dialogue with the arts. The monuments themselves provided a continuing history of pagan and Christian Rome and its culture.

Munich, for all its cultural resources, could not compete at that level with Rome. For a student serious about the theological sciences in themselves and in dialogue with other university and secular disciplines, it was fresh and stimulating. Effective entry into the world of German theological scholarship in 1959 had deep and enduring consequences, although inevitably one began to appreciate the weaknesses as well as the strengths as the years went by and other intellectual and cultural influences, including the Irish, began to assume new importance.

In Schmaus (Dogmatics), Schmidt (New Testament), Egenter (Moral) and of course my director in Canon Law, Moersdorf, Munich had true scholars whose lectures and seminars I sometimes managed to attend when my Canon Law obligations permitted. Romano Guardini was in his last semester when I arrived and, although in frail health, was still attracting large audiences, including myself when I could get a seat. The completion of my dissertation on *Church–State Relations with Particular Reference to the Irish Constitution* was the main element in my theological/canonical development at that time. However, exposure to the German university and theological system as well as to the city of Munich and its culture had a marked influence. Theological and social exchanges with professors and other graduate students were part of a wider education and paved the way for deeper involvement in German theological life later on. Moral Theologian Richard Egenter was particularly helpful in introducing me to the Association of German-Speaking Moral Theologians in the sixties where I met many theologians from Eastern Europe, still of course under Soviet control. For a mixture of reasons my reading in German theology ranged far beyond the writings of contemporary moral theologians such as Bernhard Haering, Joseph Fuchs, Alfons Auer, Franz Boeckle, and a little later Bruno Schuller and Klaus Demmer, and into the earlier works of renewal by people like Fritz Tillmann, scripture scholar turned moral theologian.

However, dogmatic theologians and scripture scholars from across Europe such as Karl Rahner and his German successors like JB Metz, Hans Kung, Joseph Ratzinger, Dutch Dominican Edward Schillebeeckx, French Dominincans Congar and Chenu and their Jesuit compatriots de Lubac and Danielou, Scripture scholars like Lyonnet, Schnackenburg and Spicq, I regarded as essential reading for the reintegration of Moral Theology in theology as a whole. This was the first task confronting me as I began to teach theology in 1960. It remains a continuing and critical task.

Because of the strong Irish influence at every level in the Catholic Church in Britain one could, as an Irish theologian, easily miss its distinctiveness in theological terms as well as its European dimension. These were both cultural and ecclesial. Engagement with the Catholic Marriage Advisory Council and its leading members, Director Father Maurice O'Leary and medical-theological experts such as Drs John Marshall and Jack Dominian, helped provide the beginnings of a new vision of sex and marriage which moral theology badly needed. This was further developed at annual conferences convened by Cardinal Suenens in Brussels from the early sixties. A quite different process was initiated in the Ecumenical Moral Theology Group which Professor Gordon Dunstan of King's College, London, and I established in the early sixties and which included Scots and Welsh, Presbyterian and Methodist as well as Anglican and Catholic. A volume of papers from various meetings of the group was published in the late sixties.

Friendship and scholarship combined in both Oxford and Cambridge with Catholics such as Herbert McCabe and Nicholas Lash and Anglicans such as John Macquarrie and Donal MacKinnon and in the broader theological world with colleagues like Kevin Kelly. Through these interchanges broader and deeper theological concerns were at work than might be considered within the remit of even a renewed moral theology. God, suffering and salvation, ecclesiology and ecumenism, sacrament and society, secularity and religion, prayer and praxis were some of the topics which, although not regular in moral theological discourse, could and did, we hoped, enrich it.

2. Transatlantic Perspectives

The year 1963 was crucial in the history of the United States of America. In the high summer of that year there was the great Washington Civil Rights March with Martin Luther King's 'I have a dream' speech. In the melancholic late autumn the dream seemed more of a nightmare with the assassination of President John F. Kennedy. From June through August I paid my first theological visit to the US. Teaching summer school at the Catholic University of America in Washington DC in all that heat and humidity was far from pleasant but students and staff colleagues were delightfully refreshing. Although the Catholic Church in America was, in the recent judgement of one of its own significant historians, John Tracey Ellis, undistinguished intellectually if not downright anti-intellectual, there were exciting theological stirrings on the campuses and among the colleagues I visited on that trip from Washington to St Louis to St John's, Minnesota to Boston and New York. The energy and insight available wherever I went over the next decades have never ceased to amaze and, I trust, enrich me. The experience of teaching mature women students and a little later of having women colleagues of the highest calibre gradually connected very closely in my own development with the major lessons of that tumultuous year. Racism and its destructiveness, the possibility of overcoming gross and centuries-old oppression and injustice by peaceful means and under Christian inspiration, the ecumenical alliances and the imaginative strategies so courageously undertaken by Martin Luther King and the Civil Rights Movement, became lifelong intellectual and practical obsessions, particularly in relation to Northern Ireland and South Africa.

Over a period of forty years theological trips to North and Central America and the Caribbean yielded valuable fruit, both in what one approved of and in what one disapproved of. To a moral theologian increasingly preoccupied with justice and peace in the world, US political and economic power seemed more and more a negative influence. There were of course many notable personal and policy exceptions to this destructiveness over the decades. Many theologians and other academics, intellectuals and especially artists opposed the most negative of these policies. Many did not. Church leadership became entangled too often with single dominantly sex-related issues such as contraception, divorce, homosexuality, abortion, condom use even in face of the AIDS pandemic, etc., to give clear leadership on poverty, peace and other social issues even in their own country. Northern neighbour Canada was often a more comfortable place for the travelling moral theologian, while Central America and the Caribbean countries stuck world poverty and exploitation under one's nose. A continuing regret is that through a series of mishaps the theological travels never penetrated further south into the Latin American home countries of Liberation Theology. Meeting these theologians elsewhere and reading their work was only the next best thing, but still very helpful.

3. Africa, Asia and Australia

Without Africa where would any of us be? Indeed, would any of us be? If somewhere on that landmass humanity took its first faltering but upright steps, and home is where we start from, in Eliot's phrase, we are coming home when we land on African soil. That has at least been my increasing conviction since I first went there with Bishop Christopher Butler in the summer (our summer) of 1970 to offer the Catholic Churches in South Africa and Lesotho a series of winter schools in theology. Thirty-five years and more than twenty visits later, some of them quite extended, it would be an exaggeration to consider Africa as my most influential theological teacher, but influential it certainly has been. The sense of homecoming may have taken time to settle down, perhaps only really occurring during the summer stints studying the civil war/war of independence in Rhodesia/Zimbabwe between 1973 and 1978, and coming to full fruition during the working trips in the fight against HIV and AIDS sponsored by Caritas Internationalis and CAFOD, London, from 1990 onwards. In the very different contexts of theology workshops and of retreats, of war, famine and plague with their horrors matched only by the resilience of so many people, I began to find a God and feel a hope that had seemed lost in the shallows of my other home life. I began to find new reasons and perhaps new methods for theology.

The message of the gospels is a message of salvation and so a message of healing. The first impact of Africa on the naïve and vain European was that he was bringing the healing for all the ills of paganism and other religious distortions, of poverty, corruption and war, of AIDS and a host of other diseases and privations. And some of that was true, but could only be gospel truth and effective healing if the European began to recognise his own need for healing and his past and present roles in spreading and sustaining the many ills now afflicting African peoples. From colonialism and its political and economic exploitation through racism and apartheid to the surrogate wars promoted by the great powers of two centuries, the European and western record makes painful reading for the visitor, if not to be compared with the painful suffering of the indigenous peoples. Many Christian missionaries did their best to mitigate these sufferings but they did so, by and large and for a long time, under the shelter of the exploiting and colonial powers. It would be humanly demeaning of Africans to ignore their responsibility for some of the present distress. But politically, militarily and economically on their own continent, they have been an underclass for several centuries, deprived of power and of the responsibility that goes with it.

In the European tradition of theology, Anselm's 'Faith seeking understanding' was the classic description of a theologian's work. For a long time it seemed to me better to keep the Pauline triad together and speak of 'Faith-Hope-Love seeking understanding' where that understanding could not be achieved by intellectual effort only but also by the practice of love of God and neighbour, and through that love the birthing and nourishing of hope. As involvement in Africa grew, mindful loving service assumed a priority which helped to keep despair at bay for the visiting servant and sometimes as least helped develop hope for the local people. Faith still sought understanding but the faith and the understanding were dependent on the love and hope which the Christian community of locals and strangers was developing.

I hesitate to describe this as Liberation Theology, as if indeed there were just one kind of Liberation Theology. Yet in origin and in method it belongs to that family. This mainly African shaped practice of theology has also been partly responsible for my hesitation in describing myself as a moral theologian, in any conventional sense at any rate. Perhaps all theologians are now called to escape the pigeonholes of the traditional disciplines of scripture, systematic, moral, etc., and accept the call to the theologians in a broader sense with particular interests and experiences in which they acquire sharper skills with deeper knowledge and understanding.

My theological trips to Asia were motivated in much the same way as those to Africa, to be of practical educational help, particularly in helping the HIV and AIDS pandemic, and often followed similar patterns allowing for the cultural and religious differences. Yet these cultural and religious differences affected the theological visitor in some interestingly different ways. The remnants of colonialism still showed. The poverty, corruption and oppression, from within and without, dominated the areas of concern to us. And war or the legacy of war was often very evident. But just then the visitor was forced to consider also the legacy of Gandhi, the still active influence of the Dalai Lama and the Asian contributions to a civilization of peace as well as of war. Although it was mainly through the conflicts in Northern Ireland and Zimbabwe that I began to appreciate the horrors of armed struggle, it was in the few Asian countries in which I worked that I finally became convinced of the possibility and the necessity of alternatives to war in the twenty-first century. The theological campaign which Stanley Hauerwas, Linda Hogan and myself have recently been promoting owes something at least to Asian exposure.

The second significant shift in theological thinking after Asia did not of course originate there. But like the reaction to war it emerged much more clearly there. And to continue the reshaping of theology from 'faith seeking understanding' to 'love, hope, faith seeking understanding', the new shape would have to make much more explicit reference to prayer and to contemplative prayer without losing its practical and intellectual dimensions. The short-lived and mainly casual encounters with the contemplative element in Buddhism and other Asian religions which these visits to Thailand, Burma, Hong Kong, the Philippines and Japan permitted could only provide the stimulus for attempting the conversion of theology to a seriously contemplative activity. However, the challenge can no longer be evaded. An earlier discovery of the significance of the liturgy for Christian living and moral theology could not and had not neglected the importance of personal prayer and contemplation. However, the Asian experience renewed the sense of contemplation as essential to the theologian.

Beyond Asia's geographical, cultural and religious boundaries lay those paradoxical outposts of the West, Australia and New Zealand. One of the joke competitions of my postgraduate days in Dunboyne House at Maynooth offered a prize for the shortest possible theological work. One of the winners was *A Theological Analysis of Limbo* but the overall winner came from an Australian and was entitled *The Australian Book of Mysticism*. To young Irish theological snobs it sounded a winner. On my first theological trip to Australia I was presented with a beautiful book entitled *The Australian Book of Religious Verse,* edited by Les Murray. This was the real thing and a real winner. I was already familiar with some of the Australian poets, novelists and artists through Australian friends picked up along the way. But the impact of this book was amazing and a perfect cure for any residual Irish religious arrogance. It was hard to cope with the sometimes offensive pragmatism of Australian politics, the popular addiction to sport of all kinds and the conservatism of much of the hierarchical church. Yet the vitality and beauty of its artistic life with perhaps the Sydney Opera House as its key symbol plus the intelligence and energy of so much of its pastoral and theological life were very appealing. And one was not allowed by the people I mixed with to forget the unresolved problems of the Aboriginal peoples, their religious and artistic achievements. This was not something I was made aware of in the same way in the US, although it had affected the theological and ecclesial consciousness in Canada and still more in New Zealand.

The point of this theological travelogue, if it has one, is to emphasize that much as I love books and libraries, a great deal of what shaped my theological life I received from the people, events and places I encountered in my travels as a believer in search of the God of creation and incarnation, of passion, death and resurrection, of the God of the drunken variousness of people, places, ideas as well as things, as Irish poet Louis McNeice nearly but more neatly put it.

The End of All Our Exploring

Theology is never a single journey with just one destination in mind. There are incessant comings and goings, intellectual and spiritual as well as in this case the geographical, political and cultural changes which all these travels entail. Yet if home was where we started from, in the deeper sense as applied to all humanity, that for me was Africa. Yet in other Eliot words, 'the end of all our exploring/Will be to arrive where we started/And know the place for the first time'. And that for me was Ireland, Maynooth and Mayo. And of course most of my theological life from First Divinity in Maynooth was, despite all the travel, spent in Ireland. As I now look for distinctive Irish influences I mention only a few of the most important. The sense of the margins and of people at the margins of society and church began for me in Mayo and has only been reinforced by theological travels and reflections. The Irish imagination and its companion, beauty, particularly as expressed in literature, have made me receptive to other peoples and cultures and above all to ways of doing theology which are continually pushing one to transcend one's present self and one's present work. And for me and my theology the oft-quoted phrase of British Chief Secretary for Ireland c. 1900, Augustine Birrell, 'It is the Mass that matters', still applies. A Eucharistic (moral) theology combines liturgy, word and life in material–symbolic, personal–communitarian, transcendent and transforming ways.

Fortunately all those influences, Irish and global, are still active. Their impact has affected teaching and writing over the past fifty years. And as one lives in hope, the springboard of all fresh theology, there may be a little more to come. Yet as Maurya, the tragic mother in Synge's beautiful and great play *Riders to the Sea* puts it at the conclusion of her grieving for the death by drowning of her sixth and last son: 'No man at all can be living forever, and we must be satisfied.'

IN CHURCH
AND WORLD

Mystery and Morality

The Word in the World

In the beginning God created the heavens
and the earth ...
and God saw that it was good ...
God created man in the image of himself,
in the image of God he created him,
male and female he created them ...
God saw all that he had made, and indeed it was very good. (Gen 1:1,
10, 27, 31)

In the beginning was the Word:
The Word was with God and the Word was God.
He was with God in the beginning.
Through him all things came into being,
not one thing came into being except through him ...
The Word became flesh,
he lived among us,
and we saw his glory,
the glory that he has from the Father as the only Son of the Father,
full of grace and truth. (Jn 1:1-3, 14)

For this is how God loved the world:
He gave his only Son, so that everyone who believes in him may not
perish but may have eternal life.
(Jn 3:15, 16)

God was in Christ reconciling the world to himself, not holding
anyone's fault against them, but entrusting to us the message of
reconciliation. (2 Cor 5:19)

He has let us know the mystery of his purpose,
according to his good pleasure which he determined beforehand in
Christ, for him to act upon when the times had run their course; that

he would bring everything together under Christ as head, everything
in the heavens and everything on earth. (Eph 1:9-10)

He is the image of the unseen God,
the first-born of all creation,
for in him were created all things
in heaven and on earth ...
He is the Beginning,
the first-born from the dead,
so that he should be supreme in every way;
because God wanted to reconcile all things to him,
everything in heaven and everything on earth,
by making peace through his death on the cross.
(Col 1:15, 18b-20)

In the struggle to find a way into the rich and mysterious theme assigned to
me, I sought refuge in reflecting on some favourite and, I hope, relevant
biblical texts. The journey thence may not have turned out as I would have
anticipated and as you might have better appreciated, but at present it is all I
have to offer. And a word of apology for the language; although it is
pronominally accurate according to original text and the Jerusalem Bible
translation, I am not happy that it is politically or theologically correct in
relation to the World and Word we are discussing here. Corrections as
needed I leave to individual listeners and readers.

Creation and Reconciliation

Although there are many related biblical words and concepts for what is
here summarised as reconciliation, such as redemption, salvation and
liberation, each with its own nimbus of meaning and reference in
Christian scripture and tradition, the focus on reconciliation may be
illuminating in a way particular to our task of relating the character and
work of the Word to the character and need of the World. And
reconciliation can do this best perhaps, as the texts cited suggest, through
its close association with the work of creation for which, it seems, no
alternative scriptural words or concepts exist.

In recent theology sharp disjunctions between creation and
redemption or its alternatives like reconciliation, between nature and
grace, even between sacred and secular have receded, if not entirely
disappeared. This was also true of some much earlier patristic theology.
Without dissolving the real distinction in concept and action between

creation and reconciliation as process and product, I believe that they are best understood in this context of Word and World as aspects of the same originating and continuing activity of the creating and reconciling God. Reconciliation is not then an emergency measure introduced by the creator to counter human failure, although it performs that task in the course of sinful human history, but provides the necessary complement of communion to the differentiation intrinsic to divine creative activity. The connections between human 'creation', differentiation, communion and reconciliation form an analogous pattern, as we shall see.

The linguistic, theological and other difficulties associated with speaking of Creator and creature have a tangled and unfinished history. It is with great hesitation that I raise them at all in the present distinguished company. An old phrase of Nicholas Lash's returns to haunt and inhibit: 'Theologians are people who must watch their language about God.' That species of language-watching is developed still further in his recent publication, *Holiness, Speech and Silence: Reflections on the Question of God* (2004). To add to my hesitation, and to be fair, to my illumination, I have been reading *Sacred and Secular Scriptures* (2005) by Nicholas Boyle. For all the richness of their publications and that of many others studied in the relevantly recent past, my preoccupations with the Word in the World and my feeble attempts to speak of God and God's relation to creation reflect a different intellectual, practical and faith history, some of whose origins are now obscure even to myself.

In the crucial relation of Creator and creation we are continually faced with the temptation to think of God as another being outside, separate from but infinitely superior to creation if we are not to collapse creation into Creator in a form of pantheism. Conscious of these twin temptations I believe some differentiation between Creator and creation is possible and necessary although it is not to be identified with the differentiation between or within creatures or the distinction of persons within the Godhead. The non-identity with these realities rests on the peculiar differentiation in communion which relates God and creatures and which, as I have mentioned earlier, depends on the single dynamic of divine creative activity as being both differentiating and uniting or reconciling, in its original sense of bringing others together in unity as others, that is while preserving their distinction. It may seem premature to describe this as reconciliation, particularly in the light of the Genesis stories of creation and of St Paul's usage, as cited above. Yet it helps to see how the single continuous creative activity of God moves lovingly on as it encounters not just the difference of creatures but their willful estrangement in human sin.

And how that dynamic loving led to the sending of God's Son, to the overcoming of the differentiation of Creation now turned hostile and to the overcoming of that hostility in entering fully into the human condition to the point of dying at hostile human hands, only to be raised as the first-born among the dead. This is the final coming together, beyond estrangement, of Creator and creation, summarised, as noted, by Paul: God was in Christ reconciling the world with himself.

God's Faith in the World

God's faith in the world may seem an unusual, even unorthodox expression in dealing with a world which subjectively speaking evinces little faith in Godself, at least little Christian faith. It might be argued that to say God loves the world, a scriptural and clearly orthodox expression, implies God's faith in and hope for the world. Objectively in what we term the secular world of the West, and certainly, in its human structures and practices as in its physical structures and activities, the world betrays little of the psalmist's reading of it, as showing forth the glory of God. Cosmology, evolution and other physical and social sciences have occluded such manifestation and address. Yet in the absence of such address by the world to its Creator, the Creator–God has not abandoned the world or what has just been described as God's faith in the world, expressed through covenants and prophets and last of all by the New Covenant of the Word made flesh. Summarising all this as divine faith in the world reveals yet another dimension of the continuing divine creation-reconciliation activity and of the continuing dependency, fragility and contingency of human and cosmic existence. Nostalgic awareness of this condition/plight is often best revealed, explicitly or implicitly, by artists, especially poets, from Wordsworth, Arnold and Hardy in earlier English times to Irish contemporaries like Nuala Ní Dhomhnaill, Derek Mahon, Eavan Boland, Seamus Heaney et al. I will return to some of that Irish work later in a different context and assume for the moment that the English work is well known to the majority of this audience.

For now it is necessary to draw out some of the implications of Word as the divine expression of faith in cosmos and humanity through Creating and Reconciling, and reaching to its culmination in the Incarnate Life, Death and Resurrection of Jesus of Nazereth.

Globalisation and Reconciliation

In general discourse the fashionable feature of the world in which the Word of God is to be preached and discovered today is probably that termed 'globalisation'. Despite the term's recent popularisation, the phenomenon is not entirely new. Indeed a case could be made for its being as old as humanity itself. Only an arrogant, Eurocentric view could have claimed to have discovered lands occupied for eons. And perhaps only a similar view could have so happily settled for annihilation, enslavement or at best expropriation and exploitation of these lands' earlier peoples and their resources. Despite the adventurous, generous and courageous spirit of many of the early 'discoverers', it was from that narrow European political, economic and religious perspective the first phase of modern globalisation developed in the late fifteenth and sixteenth centuries. With the industrial revolution in Europe and particularly the innovations in transport of steamship and railways, a new political and economic phase began, more akin to the present one. However, with air travel and much more intensely with the computer and the internet a shift in kind, certainly in economic terms with the instantaneous transfer of capital and the easy mobility of goods and services, has emerged. But it is still by and large controlled for the present by the economic, political and military powers, who are therefore its real beneficiaries. For all the rhetoric about making poverty history or at least halving it by 2015, about fair trade and substantial increases in aid, injustice between and within countries has continued to grow. Such injustice seriously impairs the effects of the Word in the World. Globalising for all its pretensions to unifying the world is far from providing the differentiation of equals in communion, in justice and peace for all, which reconciling even at the human level implies. And God's faith in the world remains frustrated by the powers which control and exploit the majority of the world's citizens and resources.

One significant difference is noticeable in how the Word today relates to the present globalising World, as compared with earlier globalising periods. (I prefer the qualifier 'globalising' with its sense of process, past, present and future, to the substantive 'globalisation' with its sense of fixed origin and current completion, akin to that other recent misreading of our world, 'the end of history'; a digression too far in our context.) The significant difference to which I refer is that unlike earlier phases of globalising, the missionary cross-bearers no longer follow the sword-bearers and the traders, at once blessing them in their conquests, and seeking to proclaim the Word while enjoying their destructive protection and exploitation. Of course many missionaries rose above those entanglements, from Bartolomeo del Las Casas in sixteenth-century Hispanic America to Bishop Donal Lamont in twentieth-century British Africa.

As most Christians and their leaders in non-western countries are themselves of the indigenous (pre-European) peoples, preaching of the

Word and building of the Christian community must draw on their own native resources and no longer appear an exotic hangover from colonial conquest. For many African and Asian local churches this is made all the more difficult by the economic and cultural colonialism, even empire, from the West which has continued in new forms long after the era of political and military empire. The growth of such local churches and the reconciling creativity of the Word in their unstable, poor and sometimes warring worlds has been partly supported by the church's central authority and sometimes undermined by its refusal to take these churches as genuine local churches and not just Roman franchise holders. The Word cannot be truly creative and reconciling in a globalising world if, in spite of the rich diversity of its expressions in Bible and Tradition, it is narrowly and efficiently controlled through the major technical instruments of the globalising project, instant communications of Roman dictates with frequent and suspicious monitoring of local initiatives.

There are further and deeper differences arising for the proclamation, presence and power of the Word in this globalising world. The most challenging theological one may be the fuller realisation by Christians that the Word is present already, everywhere and among all peoples through the creating and reconciling activity of the one God. As much might be inferred from the biblical texts cited with others, as well as from the occasional theological insights of theologians ancient and modern. Preaching the Gospel to the whole world and baptising them in the name of the Father and of the Son and of the Holy Spirit remains the primary commission of the community of Jesus' disciples, the church. Even in the New Testament there are important nuances from Jesus rebuking the disciples for forbidding non-disciples to cast out demons in his name to Paul addressing the Athenians on their worship of the unknown God. The disputes over the admission of Gentiles without their having to assume the rituals and obligations of Israel is another indication of the broader reach of the Word. And such disputes and developments recur through Christian history so that 'extra ecclesiam nulla salus' never excluded other views of the saving presence of God without benefit of explicit Christian confession and baptism. Baptism itself had its own theological equivalents where the administration of the sacrament was not possible, such as in the pre-Christian era or for later peoples to whom the Word had been proclaimed. These trends were strengthened at Vatican II in ecumenical and interfaith terms as well as in the church's developing openness to the modern world. Even if the broad reach of de Chardin's vision of a developing Christosphere never received much ecclesiastical, or even theological approval and Karl Rahner's account of anonymous Christianity seemed to many theologians as at once too clever and too parochial, the Christian and theological world engaged in a new dialogue about both the universality and uniqueness of the Word made flesh, and so made universal, even cosmic, in Jesus Christ. The possibility and the urgency of these debates has been intensified by the intimate encounters between religious faiths and between these faiths and non-religious or secular faiths which the globalising process has accelerated. It is, I am sure, clear to this gathering that the various alternatives to religious faiths are themselves ultimately faith-based rather than simply rational positions.

In the multiple dialogues envisaged here, with their intellectual, imaginative and practical dimensions, the creative, reconciling and incarnate Word will encounter severe new challenges while developing in response rich new insights. It will not suffice to assume fullness of truth in Christian teaching or scripture which could in time supplement and complete the partial truths of the rest. Unless Christians are prepared to learn from and be changed by expressions of the Word in the wider human world, they will not engage in any real dialogue. More significantly they will have betrayed the Word in the World, which they believe they have been explicitly commissioned to serve. Service, humble service, to Word and World is the key practice here, the humble earth-bound practice of the One who emptied himself even unto death on the Cross. The Word, Incarnate and Crucified, is Lord not in any triumphalist, conquering and Constantinian spirit but in loving self-surrender, in the continuous letting be and letting go of creation/differentiation and in the simultaneous/continuous bringing together of reconciliation.

Creation and reconciliation are the global activities of God moving through cosmic and human history to eschatological fulfilment. So cosmos and the human race are, as indicated earlier the objects of God's faith and hope as well as of God's love. In that sense all human communities are faith communities, recipients of God's faith and trust, which to extend the vision of John are part of the world of God's own, to whom he came even when they could not comprehend him. The diverse human faith responses, sacred and secular, referred to earlier have their contribution to make to the recognition and understanding of the Word in the World. Even somebody as clearly hostile to all religion and particularly Christianity as Richard Dawkins expresses something, however closed and skewed, of the contemporary faith community of scientists which may provide a necessary challenge and corrective to our sometimes lazy understanding of creation and creator. With our own chastening history of theological imperialism and its distortions of the Word made flesh, we might be sympathetic to scientists' temptations to imperialism while seeking to continue the dialogue with them and so continue attempts at joint conversion to the fuller truth which may further liberate both of us.

As science and its partner, technology, are with commerce key forces in driving current globalising, discerning and proclaiming the Word in the World will involve discerning it in the scientific and technological world as the origin, presence, power and justification of values such as truth and goodness. The development of such creative and reconciling dialogue is for another time and place and people more expert than I. Let me turn instead to two areas of Word and World which have preoccupied me over much of my theological life, politics and poetry, in which latter I include the arts generally.

The Word in the World of Politics

While politics may have always been heavily influenced by and at times subservient to economics and commerce, it remains the key discipline in theory and practice for the successful management of the peoples of the world, nationally and internationally. By successful management of peoples I mean of course the just, peaceful and participatory organisation of society, in solidarity with all peoples at home and abroad, observant of human rights and under the rule of law, national and international. The list could of course be extended but I will have to abbreviate it here and deal mainly with national/international justice, peace and solidarity in their creative/differentiating and reconciling aspects.

It is in this confusing political world we must also look for the Word in its creative and reconciling if secular activity. The separations referred to loosely as those of church and state, of religion and politics, of sacred and secular, and which have been in many ways so beneficial to both sides, should not be taken as excluding the Word from the second of each of these duos. Such separation in practice based on differentiation in concept could enable each side to challenge, correct and enrich the other in their sacred and secular character and in their characteristic activity. The differentiation and equality in difference among citizens of the state is ultimately founded and powered by the creative presence of the Word among us. So wherever we find this differentiation and equality in dignity, rights and responsibilities being fostered and cherished, we may discern activity of the Word, even if the promoters and protectors of such politics are unable to make the connection themselves. Indeed in nineteenth and early twentieth century Europe it was the breaches between church and state and the other duos which facilitated the emergence of these political realities, even if with these breaches they could not eventually be given any firmer foundation than positive human law.

Differentiation and equality involve community, bonding, what we have been calling reconciliation, as in origin bringing and keeping the different, the others together in a mutually enriching way and in further development as bringing together, forgivingly and positively, the different who have been estranged, the hostile others. As I have sought to develop these ideas more fully elsewhere I will summarise such reconciling activity as the renewed and persistent act of bonding which every society needs to survive, including the entire human society, particularly just now in the throes of rapid and often unjust and exploitative globalising. Where the differentiation in equality and bonding in solidarity within a single state and between states are honoured and promoted, the creative and reconciling Word is at work in approval and support. Where the differentiation and bonding are abused by the powerful at the expense of others, less powerful or powerless, as is so frequent in our world, the Word is at work condemning and resisting. In the ambiguous situations in which we may often find ourselves, humble attention to and service of the Word in the suffering and excluded, and in personal prayer and the liturgy, may enable us to distinguish between the Word's approval and its condemnation, between its support and its resistance and turn these distinctions into action.

While reconciliation may seem more characteristic of human political activity, creativity and its associate imagination are also clearly necessary. What we call human procreativity confronts the procreating parents with a new and irreducible different human other and stranger. The bonding and formative process which the parents are called to involves creativity and imagination on a sometimes exhausting scale. The self-surrender of unselfish, caring and frequently reconciling parents betokens reconciling self-surrender of God in Jesus Christ. And all this forms part of the continuing sacrament of marriage for the couple and the family, the Word realised anew in the flesh of parents and children. In a related fashion the church, the explicit community of the Word's creative and reconciling presence and power, embodies, in the words of Vatican II, the sacrament of the one human community of God. This one community is always in the process of formation or creation by the gracious, creative power of the Word, mediated through creative human activity with the church exercising its sacramental role of effectively manifesting and recognising the Word at work in the World. Much of the church's recent teaching and practice in the fields of justice, peace and solidarity have been sacramental in this way.

Artistic Creativity and Reconciliation

As reconciliation seems more native to politics so creation and creativity have been regarded as native to the arts. Yet great major and even minor works of art have a reconciling role as Heaney hints in his Oxford lectures 'The Redress of Poetry', although we will not be pursuing his precise argument here. The sense of presence which serious art evokes and is, as indicated by Nicholas Boyle, developed by George Steiner in his book *Real Presences* (1991), is in ways at least supportive of the general argument here. The argument may be briefly stated. (Some further elaboration may be found in my recent book, *Vulnerable to the Holy* (2004).) Human creativity as expressed in artistic productions reflects and reveals a human capacity which transcends the simple calculating deployment of material resources, and resists simple reduction to arrangements of atoms and molecules or whatever. The work in turn takes the attentive reader or viewer or listener beyond herself into new dimensions of joy or sorrow which again resist reductionist explanations. This is perhaps most powerfully experienced through great music. As the creative productivity of the artist encounters the creative receptivity of the audience, one may speak of both transcendence and transformation. The Word is at least signalling its presence in the world as a creative, transcendent and transforming energy.

One of my favourite modern plays, touted by many knowledgeable critics as a modern classic, is John Millington Synge's *Riders to The Sea*. The mother, Maurya, faced with the last of her sons, Bartley, to be lost at sea, utters a final lament. Synge had by now abandoned the rather strict Christian faith of his Protestant mother and some contemporary commentators would like to interpret the lament as purely ancient, Celtic and pagan. Some such background as the Samhain reference may be there but Synge was too respectful a listener to the Aran Islanders to ignore their genuine Christian language and sentiments:

> They're all gone now, and there isn't anything more the sea can do to me ... I'll have no call now to be up crying and praying when the wind breaks from the south, and you can hear the surf is in the east, and the surf is in the west, making a great stir with the two noises, and the one hitting on the other. I'll have no call to be going down and getting Holy Water in the dark nights after Samhain, and I won't care what way the sea is when the other women will be keening. Give me the Holy Water, Nora; there's a small sup still on the dresser ... It isn't that I haven't prayed for you, Bartley, to the Almighty God. It isn't that I haven't said prayers in the dark night till I wouldn't know what

I'd be saying; but it's a great rest I'll have now, and it's time surely. It's a great rest I'll have now, and great sleeping in the long nights after Samhain, if it's only a bit of wet flour we do have to eat, and maybe a fish that would be stinking ...

They're all together this time, and the end is come. May Almighty God have mercy on Bartley's soul, and on Michael's soul, and on the souls of Sheamus and Patch, and Stephen and Shawn; and may He have mercy on my soul, Nora, and on the soul of every one is left living in the world ... Michael has a clean burial in the far north by the grace of the Almighty God. Bartley will have a fine coffin out of white boards, and a deep grave surely. What more can we want than that? No man at all can be living for ever, and we must be satisfied.

(She kneels down again and the curtain falls slowly.)

I have heard very similar lamentations in African villages, particularly at the burial of AIDS victims. The Word in the World today and perhaps in all days too often takes the form of lament. The women of Jerusalem weeping on the way to Calvary are joined by millions today in the face of the daily crucifixions of disease, famine and war. Must they be satisfied? Can the Word remain passive? Will the creative and reconciling powers which the divine artist inspires in the human enable the human to reveal and resist the tragic and destructive divisions of our time and so prompt the judgement and the healing so urgently required.

In the following Irish poems, none of them incorporating direct Christian reference, I try to surrender to the creative technique and rhythm of the poem while remaining alert to the internal reconciling of the language and deeper reconciling of persons, presences and world, sourced eventually, as I believe, in the Word of God.

'Quarantine' by Eavan Boland was published in the *Irish Times* literary page on the Saturday after 9/11. But it reflects her broader concerns with personal and social tragedy in history, and more particularly her frequent return to Irish examples.

Quarantine

In the worst hour of the worst season
of the worst year of a whole people
a man set out from the workhouse with his wife.
He was walking – they were both walking – north.

She was sick with famine fever and could not keep up.
He lifted her and put her on his back.
He walked like that west and west and north.
Until at nightfall under freezing stars they arrived.

In the morning they were both found dead.
Of cold. Of hunger. Of the toxins of a whole history.
But her feet were held against his breastbone.
The last beat of his flesh was his last gift to her.

Let no love poem ever come to this threshold.
There is no place here for the inexact
Praise of the easy graces and sensuality of the body.
There is only time for this merciless inventory:

Their death together in the winter of 1847.
Also what they suffered. How they lived.
And what there is between a man and a woman.
And in which darkness it can best be proved.

Michael Longley's 'Ceasefire' was published in the *Irish Times* on the Saturday after the first IRA ceasefire in 1994, but by accident, he says. His moving account of the creative preparation for the reconciliation act is beautifully portrayed.

Ceasefire

I

Put in mind of his own father and moved to tears
Achilles took him by the hand and pushed the old king
Gently away, but Priam curled up at his feet and
Wept with him until their sadness filled the building.

II

Taking Hector's corpse into his own hands Achilles
Made sure it was washed and, for the old king's sake,
Laid out in uniform, ready for Priam to carry
Wrapped like a present home to Troy at daybreak.

III

When they had eaten together, it pleased them both
To stare at each other's beauty as lovers might,
Achilles built like a god, Priam good-looking still
And full of conversation, who earlier had sighed:

IV

'I get down on my knees and do what must be done
And kiss Achilles' hand, the killer of my son.[1]

The artists' imaginative if obscure embodiment of the mystery of the Word in the World should not be left to 'secular' poets. Gerard Manley Hopkins and RS Thomas can be equally dark and difficult in struggling with a presence in which they certainly believe but occasionally seem to lose track of. There is so much more to be explored, analysed and recorded even in the restricted material with which I have been concerned. A major feature today is the dialogue between the major religions, although it certainly should not be separated from the political and artistic concerns which I have voiced. As a basis for all such exploration and dialogue I might combine two phrases from George Steiner and St Paul in describing us humans as Guests of Creation and Ambassadors of Reconciliation. And it is by the creative gifts we receive as guests of creation that we are enabled to follow our vocation as ambassadors of reconciliation in serving, revealing and proclaiming in our inadequate way the Word in the World.

The Faith that Sets Free

In church as in politics as in commerce, as in education and the media, and in a variety of other institutions and professions, there will always be more to expose and to shock. This requires, from the church at least, repentance, and from all some naming and punishment of the offenders. It would be tempting for a church official to claim that church offenders suffer more publicly and more painfully than their political or commercial or other counterparts. Although there might be some truth in this, the standards expected of bishops, priests and religious, as preachers of gospel morality and as trusted community leaders, are properly higher and their breaches of these standards are rightly seen as more scandalous. At this stage the exposure and punishment of church offenders might be confidently left to tribunals, secular and ecclesiastical, and to a vigilant and fair-minded media. That surely implies more explicit and public acts of repentance by church leaders right up to the level of the Vatican for their part in the scandal. However, the further challenge to all committed Catholics is to discover a way of reforming church attitudes and structures in a more authentic service of the Gospel of Jesus Christ.

There is much wisdom in the traditional saying that 'if you want to go there, you shouldn't start from here at all'. All this is compounded in the present instance by the difficulty of knowing where 'here' is and the still greater difficulty of knowing where 'there' might be. In the currently confused state of the Catholic Church at every level, hierarchical, clerical and lay, with fear and anger, defensiveness and aggression, afflicting and dividing so many of its members, no coherent picture emerges of the church's 'here'. The 'there' to which the church is summoned is not a matter of church choosing even if it had any foresight into its shape and location. Sensitive to history as they should be, church leaders and members can only marvel at the unforeseen and unpredictable changes which two thousand years have yielded. From supper room or upper room to catacombs and basilicas, from palaces to gulags, from royal advisers to royal executions, from universities to hedge schools, from first place at table to total exclusion from social life, the church has, sometimes to its honour and sometimes to its shame, hit historical human highs and lows. And the highs have too often been corrupting, leading from Constantinian-style emancipation to privilege and corrupting power. All this is not without relevance to the present condition of the Catholic Church in Ireland, even if the contours of that condition are mixed and muddied. The 'here' cannot be deciphered in purely human terms by the most expert historical, sociological and psychological analysis, useful as they may be for certain tasks. What might, arrogantly perhaps, be called theological analysis may be the most useful first step.

The traditional and still acceptable descriptions of theology from Anselm and Aquinas might be drawn on to give a rather different starting point to the journey ahead. For Anselm, theology was 'Faith seeking understanding', and for Aquinas it was the 'Science of God and of all things in relation to God'. Faith and science are taken here to be truly human realities although both theologians were well aware of the limitations of the human in face of the divine and that faith itself was primarily gift from God. A somewhat different reading of the Scriptures and Tradition might allow us to speak of the Faith of God in creation and humanity.

The Faith of God

The phrase is undoubtedly puzzling on first hearing. The love of God for the world and in particular for human beings, we take for granted. The hope(s) of God for his creation and humanity we might more easily read into the adventure of creation as process as well as product. As always we speak analogically in speaking of God but it would be unthinkable that the biblical God should create a world without intending some final good. Such good is implicit in the Genesis accounts of creation where God looked on creation and saw that it was good. Attaining that good could not however be guaranteed once God introduced free creatures who might or might not respond lovingly to their Creator and fellow-creatures. And if God did not wish to determine the outcome but truly to respect human freedom then it would be legitimate to say that God had hopes for humankind, had placed divine hope in the human capacity to return love for love. As we know, this hope was not realised much, perhaps most, of the time. That did not discourage God from reaching out to humankind in promise, covenant and action as recounted in the Hebrew scriptures. The story of Israel symbolises the continuing creative efforts of God to affirm the original goodness of humanity and to enable it to attain its true vocation, love of God and love of neighbour. The faith which God maintained in the goodness of creation, the trust which, too often betrayed, he continued to repose in human beings, reached its climax in entrusting Godself fully to the human condition in Jesus Christ.

The historical rejection and execution of the Son did not finally destroy God's faith and trust in humankind. The raising of Jesus from the dead and the sending of the Holy Spirit issued in the New Creation and the New Humanity, which the community of Jesus' disciples and their successors were to embody, and to preach and to promote to the ends of the earth. There is no reason to labour the obvious failures of the successive communities of disciples including the contemporary Irish one. The point to remember in the midst of all this failure both for disciples and all other communities is that the divine faith and trust in all human beings has not and will not finally fail. And the first obligation of failing disciples is to remember this, to be more worthy of that divine affirmation and to offer by word and example a reminder to all humanity that they too are the recipients of this affirming faith and trust of God.

Divine Faith and Church Repentance

The Gospel of Mark introduces Jesus' public mission as follows: 'Now after John was arrested Jesus came to Galilee, proclaiming the good news of God, and saying, "The time is fulfiled, and the kingdom of God has come near; repent and believe in the good news"' (Mk 1:14, 15). Thus began the New Creation in Pauline terms, the coming of the Kingdom or Reign of God in Synoptic Gospel terms. The faith and trust of God in Israel and humanity was reaffirmed but it called and always will call for a return of faith, for repentance and conversion to God and neighbour. Without the humble acceptance of such repentance as the situation demands, the faith of God is frustrated but not withdrawn.

The good news and the coming kingdom wait upon us, as they enable the first, often painful and certainly humiliating steps to letting the faith of God energise us once more. Despite many sincere expressions of apology to victims and congregations for the sins of clerical sex abuse and their cover-up, and the honest cooperation with enquiries such as the one which produced the Ferns Report, church leaders and members generally do not seem to be energised anew. Perhaps the repentance has been too shallow because it is mainly verbal and has not cost the pain and humiliation which would really set the faith and trust of God free in our hearts. Perhaps we are still too protective of the institution, still more interested in damage limitation to it than in the lamentation with sackcloth and ashes, which our complicity in such horrors calls for. Perhaps we need a lead from the Pope to whom we are often too uncritically and so dishonestly loyal. Whatever the true 'perhaps', we must find the courage to let go of our false allegiances, our mini-gods of self or superior institution, if the faith which God continues to have in us is to break free and renew the face of the church, and so enable the church to participate in renewing the face of the earth.

The Listening and Learning of Repentance and Conversion

And God said
Prophesy to the wind, to the wind only for only
The wind will listen.
(TS Eliot, 'Ash Wednesday')

The culpable spiritual deafness which afflicts all of us from time to time was rampant for many years, indeed decades, in the Irish and other Catholic Churches. The most notorious and destructive example concerned clerical sex abuse but it was not the only one. Spiritual deafness is rarely so selective.

The episcopal and indeed curial refusal to listen to any theologians except the favoured and conservative few has resulted in blinkered views on issued as diverse as intercommunion in certain circumstances, war, the role of Catholic politicians in a mixed society, cooperation between Catholic and other organisations on pregnancy care and counselling, and the continuing confusions about condoms in research, AIDS-prevention and indeed regular family-planning. Not all of these are of equal significance or subject to the same severe dispute or have the same serious, even fatal consequences. Yet they are areas in which with many others church leaders can manifest persisting deafness in face of the cries of the needy.

The first requirement of the listener, particularly the listener-leader, is humility. Getting down off one's metaphorical perch to sit in the humus with the least and the suffering ones calls for the kind of self-abasement that no one really relishes. Yet it is only by shedding his pseudo-protection of trappings and pretensions that the sinful disciple of Jesus, each of us in whom the faith of God reposes and is resisted, can begin to hear the other's prophetic voice in all its confusion of truth and error, of rightful indignation and stumbling self-pity. And without the voluntary or involuntary undergoing of such humiliation, the kenosis (self-emptying) of Jesus (Phil 2), the deep listening, which the faith of God in us calls for and enables, will not take place. Only that deep, continuous listening will open the painful way to understanding the other and so to self-understanding of one's previous deafness. The price of that listening and learning is the shattering of defensive mechanisms which prevented us from being sensitive to the true voice of God. Learning of this kind goes far beyond the receipt of information, too often filtered by courtiers.

Only the knowledge which disturbs, even angers at first, will find its way through the carefully built layers of protective self-deception to repenting one's errors and converting to God and neighbour. While the human protest of offended neighbour and the troubled conscience of the self may be the immediate stimulus of the conversion process, the Faith of God in self and neighbour supply the initiating hope and fulfiling energy. Because of the faith of God in each neighbour, however alien or difficult in our eyes, and because of that divine faith and trust in each of us, we may never despair of the possibility of mutual forgiveness and conversion even in the most desperate crisis. That applies to the present situation of the Catholic Church in Ireland today, although the application is bound to be very painful still. That faith of God, vested in all humanity and witnessed by Christian believers at least, provides the basis and the energy for peace and mutual enrichment between the different religious, ethnic, political and economic communities throughout the world, if only we have the humility to listen to and learn from the others in serious and so disturbing dialogue.

Mindsets and Structures which Resist the Faith of God in Humanity

There are many psychological, socio-cultural and theological reasons why Christians, adherents of other religions and of none might resist this vision of God as having faith in human beings, believers and unbelievers. In this context the theological reasons are clearly the most important and for some people may be the only ones worth considering. However, it may be useful to examine some of the other reasons briefly, although it should also be noted that all of these reasons overlap and do not operate in any pure form.

Psychologically people may be so rigidly formed that it may be almost impossible for them to open up to strangers of another culture, race or religion. Indeed some religious believers are unable to tolerate within their own community what others, equally committed in that community, consider legitimate difference. We have many instances of this within the Catholic and other Christian communities as well as outside them. It would be easy and counter-productive to write all these off as fundamentalist, the fashionable code word for conservative opponents. They lie along a spectrum both of psychological rigidity and conservative beliefs, although it must be hastily added that so-called liberals may have their own spectrum of psychological and theological intransigence. Few public debates on contentious religious issues lack examples of rigidity and intolerance from all sides of the debate. At present it is more likely that resistance to talk of God's faith in the whole of humanity will come from the 'conservatives', although liberals may be simply indifferent.

An individual's or even group's psychological condition is influenced by a range of social, cultural, economic and political factors. Ethnicity and its status as majority or minority group are usually very significant, given certain historical experiences. The Northern Ireland troubles, pale as they now seem in the light of Balkan disputes, Palestinian–Israeli confrontation and other middle-east divisions-oppressions plus a galaxy of other conflicts, illustrated very sharply how the ethnic-political-religious mix would resist very deeply a common vision of God's faith in both groups.

In seeking to understand the faith implicit in God's creative activity it may help to consider human creativity, limited analogy as it may be. Human creativity is not confined to serious artistic work but enters into every facet of our truly human activities and relationships. From making a sentence to making a marriage the creative capacity of human beings is at work. Otherwise these actions and relations become mindless and uncommitted, clichéd and empty. Only thus is the faith of speaker or marriage partner in self and other properly expressed by self-entrustment to the other. At the more intensely creative and artistic level of painting, literature and music the faith of the artist in the work and in the self of the worker/artist seeks to awaken the other to the beauty and truth of the work, to elicit a return in faith, in belief and trust without suppressing the other's critical capacity. Indeed the creative use of the critical capacity enables the other as critic to awaken in turn the faith of a wider audience. In sentence-making as in marriage-making, in painting as in music-making, creativity with its critical companion walk hand in hand with faith and trust. The reliable witness, the credible scientist and the faithful friend/spouse like the authentic artist depend on that combination of faith and creativity which in human terms reflects the divine creativity and faith in God's work in progress which Christians call creation-salvation.

The Centrality of Jesus Christ

> He is the image of the invisible God, the first-born of all creation; for in him all things in heaven and on earth were created, things visible and invisible, whether thrones or dominations or rulers or powers all things have been through him and for him. He himself is before all things, and in him all things hold together. (Col 1:15-17)

Although this is not the occasion to develop a Christology which deals with all the difficulties that theology faces in relation to other religions and non-religions, the centrality afforded to Jesus Christ by the Christian scriptures in terms of creation as well as of salvation is crucial. As indicated above the faith of God in creating and creation reached its climax in Jesus Christ. That faith does not supersede or invalidate the faith of God expressed in creation itself or in, for example, the Mosaic Covenant with Israel. The belated acceptance by church authorities and Christians generally of God's continuing commitment to and faith in his First People is almost a commonplace of Jewish-Christian dialogue and was endorsed by Pope John Paul II. The further extension of that openness and dialogue on the basis of a benevolent Creator and so saving God, to other believers and non-believers, initially developed at Vatican II and in Pope Paul VI's encyclical *Ecclesiam suam* (1964), is possible, without Christians renouncing the centrality of Christ or without others becoming pseudo-Christians. It is perhaps on this basis of the Faith of God as affecting all religions and peoples that the Irish church could find its energising place in the rapidly changing multicultural Ireland. It must, however, encourage the intellectual and pastoral work which such a project demands.

God's Faith in Human Sexuality

While still in the midst of the clerical abuse scandal with the recent added distraction of the *Vatican Instruction on Admission of Homosexuals to Seminaries*, an early if very difficult candidate for theological rethinking is that of human sexuality. The vision of human sexuality as a gift rather than threat emerged very clearly in the Pastoral Constitution, *Gaudium et spes* of Vatican II, although that was really a recovery of a tradition which went back to the Creation stories in Genesis and had been endorsed by other Hebrew and Christian scriptures as well as by later theologians. It had undoubtedly been obscured for theological and cultural reasons over the centuries prior to Vatican II.

In the immediate context of this essay, rather than enter into the details of how the gift of human sexuality is to be developed and expressed in a range of relationships, the emphasis will be on some understanding of how God's faith in human beings applies to their sexuality also. Such an approach may help in providing a new starting point and setting for more detailed discussion of sexual ethics in the future.

God's faith in creating humanity as bodily, 'of the earth' loving beings, in continuity and discontinuity with the animal kingdom, saw their sexuality also as 'very good'. 'Male and female he created them. In the image of God he created them.' The evolution of the human species as progressively understood does not undermine this faith insight of the authors of Genesis or invalidate the claim of God's faith in humanity as sexual beings. Scientific study and biblical study have still much to discover but they are not to be seen as enemies but as operating with quite different perspectives, asking and attempting to answer quite different questions. The divine creation and celebration of human beings and their sexuality in Genesis 1 and 2 is eclipsed as are all other human gifts in Chapter 3 by the human refusal of the divine order. Yet the earlier spirit is never entirely lost. Although the general patriarchal structure of relationships dominates, there is much evidence of loving and faithful relationships between husband and wife as equal persons.

The most powerful illustration of a loving relationship between equals is celebrated in the 'Song of Songs'. This might provide the basis for a new sexual ethic according to Rabbi Arthur Waskow in the Winter 2005–6 issue of the American journal *Conscience*. At least it offers very explicit and positive insights into the beauty, intimacy and intensity of sexual loving between two equal human partners. No traces of male dominance or patriarchy here. No trace of the shame culture either in the direct language, attitudes and actions.

The creative composition of the songs, the creative relationships and expressions recorded, the imaginative and creative inclusion of such an apparently secular hymn to sexual loving among the sacred books of the Bible, the Word of God, offer much food for theological thought. This is reinforced by later commentators' relating the Song's sexual loving to God's love for humanity, a theme more expressly addressed by the prophet Hosea and St Paul. The mystery of human sexual love in itself is another facet of God's creative faith in humanity. So despite sexual failure as an inevitable part of human fragility, the divine faith in human sexuality, empowering and forgiving, ensures its finally loving and life-giving capacities. The biological, psychological, social and cultural dimensions of human sexuality require continuous, detailed attention in understanding and practice. However, in the context of divine faith in this created gift, these details may be re-examined in a richer and more positive way.

Set Free to Preach the Good News Once More

Of course those without Christian faith will be unable to make sense of the ideas advanced here. This may be true of many Christians also. Yet the faith that sets free in Paul's terms is divine faith and increasingly this seems to be primarily God's faith in creation which reached its climax in Jesus Christ. With this God in Christ on our side who can be against us? Going beyond Paul's words but not perhaps beyond his intent we might also ask: with God on everyone's side whom can we be against? In such a context we are free to preach the good news afresh to all. It is for all and already belongs to all even if they do not recognise it in our terms. In failure and disgrace we may more easily attend to the good news now partly obscured in the Christian community but which may be available in the sharper sayings of perceived enemies. The faith of God in them may be part of our being set free to preach the good news and promote the Reign of God.

The Golden Echoes and the Leaden Echoes

A Theological Salute to the Maynooth Ordination Class of 1955

The title, adapted from Gerald Manley Hopkins, presumes to reverse his order of 'The Leaden Echo and the Golden Echo', title for his unfinished play on St Winifred of Wales. On celebratory occasions like this it seems more appropriate to begin with the symbol of victory, or at least of the victory of survival, human and priestly. All that survives is not golden or even occasion for celebration. The leaden which still persists has its own claims on recognition in the assessment of any priestly life, even if it has not the depth or weight of Hopkins' own late dark sonnets.

In the beginning was the excitement, the enthusiasm, the sense of privileged self-sacrifice for a splendid cause. It was not of course an uncritical enthusiasm. Maynooth mentors had made sure of that. The 'who-do-you-think-you-are?' school of formation was alive and healthy, even health-giving for those who might appear to be getting above themselves. For all the real weaknesses and subsequent caricature of seminary life in the forties and fifties, it did not encourage in one student's experience any sense of clerical superiority. Yet there was sufficient, perhaps too much, 'affirmation' (a word never used in those days) from family and friends, fellow students and priestly colleagues to enable one to accept enthusiastically priestly ordination and priestly commitment. Even fifty years on it is still possible (occasionally) to recall the excitement and the anxiety of the days leading up to and following ordination. The prostrate forty plus around the altar of the Maynooth College Chapel on 19 June 1955 appeared no doubt calmly wrapped in prayer to assembled family, assistant clergy and presiding Archbishop McQuaid. (There were fifty-six ordained from the Maynooth ordination class of 1955 but not all of them at Maynooth.) The calmness and prayer-profile could be at least partly deceptive although the day's Master of Ceremonies (in popular repute, master of the hunt of recalcitrant students on other days) had at rehearsal assured us that 'once we were in the sanctuary nothing could go wrong'. Trying to keep still and prayerful on the cold marble, one incongruously felt the surges of panic which were not allayed even by the laying on of hands by Archbishop McQuaid, followed by a line of priests, some of whom were friends, who spoke one's name and made their blessing a message from a more human and maybe spirit-filled world.

From College Chapel to Parish Church, in this instance Bekan Parish Church, for a first Mass in the rural shelter of childhood marked the next big step. More space and time and welcome for laughter and tears, for pride and purpose among neighbours and schoolmates, particularly that year and that same day as two sons of the parish and two former pupils of the local primary school who had been ordained together in Maynooth had their first Masses in the church of their first communion and confirmation. Unfortunately my old schoolmate, fellow student and fellow priest of the Archdiocese of Tuam, Michael Comer, did not live to celebrate the golden day of remembrance. I feel sure that he will be there as his humble, serving and appropriately glorified self, and joined by a number of others from the class of '55 who have gone before to help prepare a way for the rest of us.

Although ordained to the diocesan priesthood with the prospect of a proper pastoral role, I followed, not by my own decision, a quite different route from most but not all of my classmates. That mainly academic route has always had its pastoral opportunities which I have relished and I have always delighted, despite the inevitable pain and frustration, in the teaching and lecturing and writing. Yet I do feel some sense of loss in never having fulfilled a full-time parish posting. It also prevents me from speaking authentically for the priests from my Maynooth class and for so many others who have enjoyed, and I am sure, suffered the pains of parish priesting. So I must speak from my class rather than for them, not in any teaching role I trust, but out of a largely different experience of the priesthood we have shared over fifty years.

A short reflection on the Silver Jubilee occasion in these pages took as its title and theme 'The Priest as Christian'. To be a Christian is still the primary call. This call to all the baptised to share in the priesthood of Christ assumes its own distinctive form and responsibility for those called and ordained to the ministerial priesthood. Service of God and church and so of humanity and the world outlines that form and responsibility, and shapes now the golden and leaden echoes of fifty years of such priesting.

The echo-chamber of one seventy-five-year-old is by turns chaotically alive with the cries of joy and of sorrow, of victory and defeat, of reason and rant; and is by turns as quiet as death, sometimes with the silence of serenity, even contemplation and of course sadly at other times with the silence of death itself, real or metaphorical. Tracking the golden and the leaden echoes through that cumulative chaos is a matter of chance as much as of choice, so that what is discerned and recorded cannot be regarded as in any way complete or even representative, just the fragmented residue, golden and leaden, of a half-forgotten half-century.

Sacramental Echoes

Birth and baptism of the children of family and friends seem to have been particularly golden moments. Initiation of relative strangers, children and adults, into the Christian community has its own golden tinge. I like baptisms in their sacramental, ecclesial and social expression. At St Joseph's Church in Greenwich Village, New York, where I helped out at weekends for a year or more in the 1990s, baptism was by immersion and was celebrated in particularly splendid fashion by Pastor Aldo Tos at the Easter Vigil. There were many other enriching baptismal ceremonies for the children of parents whose weddings I had celebrated, for the children of those who had had no wedding or whose marriage had not survived. Moving me into a larger and more challenging Christian world were those baptisms celebrated in interchurch services where I was assisted by or assisted a minister from another tradition, rare occasions for the only partly pastoral priest.

One of the extraordinary aspects of baptism is that it is both inclusive and exclusive. I was just ordained when I discovered my mother's sadness that her stillborn baby could not be buried in consecrated ground and was by official teaching consigned forever to the no-god's land of limbo. Happily she lived to welcome the more inclusive vision of Vatican II. In that earlier time while so much argument had raged and so much blood had been spent in establishing the validity of baptism by heretics and schismatics, people entering our own church from another Christian denomination were usually expected to undergo re-baptism, a distinctly leaden echo which has not been entirely silenced. In the midst of the Northern Irish violence I once suggested that to distinguish the religious from the political hostility and to prevent the sacrament from being a tribal rather than a Christian initiation, baptism should be performed in an interchurch ceremony with interchurch witnesses in the church of the parents' choice. Needless to say the response was a leaden silence. Such divisiveness remains a continuing scar on the Body of Christ into which all are, by agreed theology and teaching, inserted at baptism. In personal and theological terms this remains a significant leaden echo.

Deeper related problems have emerged in recent years for the Irish Church although many Irish missionaries have long experience of them. The growing numbers of Muslims and people of other major faiths offer a fresh challenge to the religious exclusivity traditionally associated with Christianity. The explosive mixture of such new and sharp religious difference with race and, in the wider western world at least, with fears of terrorism, make inter-religious dialogue an urgent demand on Irish Christians. In that dialogue the foundation of baptism and the unique role of

Jesus Christ will need fresh attention by all Christians. This is not an entirely new task. In the course of its history, Christianity, from its Jewish origins to its first contact with the unknown God of the Athenians, has had to expand its religious and mental horizons as well as its language and practices to meet the challenges of other religious traditions and to do justice to its Creator and Redeemer God.

A faint echo of that future dialogue emerged from my local town of Ballyhaunis when the first Muslims arrived with their Halal meat factory in the 1960s and 1970s. It was a matter of some religious excitement to the new parish priest, Canon J.G. McGarry, founder and editor of *The Furrow*. McGarry, who had mixed success with the 1955 class at least in instilling in them the rudiments of good preaching, was recognised by his students as in tune with, and even anticipating, the spirit and achievements of Vatican II. It augured well for the future of interfaith dialogue in Ireland that McGarry was the first point of contact with Islam and with the first Imam to visit his people in rural Ireland. The auguries, as auguries will, proved misleading.

Vatican II's initiatives in promoting dialogue with other religions and Pope John Paul II's assemblies of such diverse religious traditions to pray for peace at Assisi are but two of the signs of fresh openness to the challenge and potential enrichment for the church from the significant presence of other major religions in the heart of what has been the traditionally Christian West. Indeed, without denying the virtues and achievements of western civilization, such 'eastern' presence may well help free western Christianity from its captivity to so much of the imperial politics, culture and economics still affecting so many western mindsets and power structures. An incipient golden echo may be heard emerging from the East through the leaden echoes of past centuries of western domination. Baptism may become a sign to the world and its religions of the all-embracing love of a God who offers salvation and fulfilment to all, if the community of the baptised so love the world as the God who sent his Son.

In training and in life the ordained priest was compelled to acknowledge the centrality of the Eucharist. Yet in most priestly lives there is so much Eucharist that they might easily feel overwhelmed and at times guilty at what must appear a routine and lifeless celebration. And the term 'celebration', for all its theological profundity, does not resonate easily with the priest or participant of the regular daily or even Sunday Mass. The echoes, my Lord, are leaden. Reiterating the words 'celebration', 'celebrating', 'celebrant', 'concelebrant' does not alter the tone of the performance. Neither does some of the gimmickry borrowed from stage or pop concert. Yet some radical developments in education and practice of priest and people are needed if the words and symbolism, the actions and mysticism of the Mass are to be truly celebrated and shared by priest and people.

Of course there are the golden echoes from half a century of Eucharistic leadership. Some of these originated in quite ordinary circumstances at a Sunday or weekday mass where priest and people, grace and nature rhymed, to alter radically Seamus Heaney's famous phrase about hope and history. But there were extraordinary occasions also, at particularly moving funerals, sometimes at happy and holy weddings. And at still more extraordinary occasions as when a priest-friend Fr Tom Stack and I concelebrated, and really celebrated, his last Mass with 1955 classmate Joe Dunn as he lay in bed a few days before he died. This was the second time within months that I had participated in such a deathbed Eucharist. Earlier that year Fr Ronan Drury and I concelebrated with our close friend Fr Tommy Waldron of the 1954 class.

Equally golden was the gift of presiding at the Holy Thursday ceremonies at Crossroads, Mark 3, outside Capetown, where the homeless migrants from city and hinterland had been forcibly removed by the Apartheid regime some years earlier. The only two white faces in the big, packed barn of a church were that of the parish priest who had invited me, Fr Desmond Curran, originally from Belfast, and my own. The ceremony was long and rich on music and song as well as on washing of feet and greetings of peace. My homily, not that long in itself, had to be interpreted sentence by sentence by the catechist, consuming more time but without any sign of restlessness in the congregation, male and female, young and old. However, when the pastor suggested, after a very long communion process and before the final blessing, that I should tell the congregation what my reasons were for being in Africa in these years, learning and teaching about HIV and AIDS, I was inclined to say no for the sake of the people who had such a long session and because of my own tiredness and possible embarrassment. Trusting his judgement and recognising the crisis all about us, I went ahead sentence by painful sentence with the interpreter. The pain was not caused by him but by my search for the suitable words in English to describe to a congregation so mixed in age and so culturally foreign how HIV was transmitted mainly by sexual intercourse and how it might be prevented, or the risks at least reduced. In their generosity and concern about the pandemic, as it was being called in English, they responded with a warm round of applause.

Most of the congregation had been by now four or five hours in church and had walked for a couple of more to get there. The ramshackle buses who might have taken home those who had come the furthest were not all operating so Fr Curran and myself had a few more hours on the dirt roads ferrying in his people-carrier the long-distance worshippers to their shanty homes. So it was a day focused on the most graceful and grace-filled Eucharist of the liturgical year and it frequently returns with a thousand echoes of (pure) black gold.

Golden and leaden echoes filter through from other sacraments but they were never as prominent in the life of the priest-academic. Attention to the word was more a characteristic of his life.

Teaching and Preaching

The priest-academic endures a particular tension in seeking to live his double vocation with integrity. He is not unique in this. Apart from the obvious and increasingly widespread tension of husbands and wives trying to combine outside job/career with parenting, there are other professionals from medical consultants who are both academics and clinicians to politicians who have legal, academic or other commitments and still more those who have to double- or treble-job to survive. For the priest-academic the tension may be most acutely experienced in his attempts to distinguish and combine his roles as teacher in the classroom and preacher on the pulpit. Many diocesan as well as religious priests spend many years teaching at second level, for example, and very often do a very good job in a range of secular subjects from mathematics and biology to Irish and history. Quite a number of the 1955 class had that experience in their earlier years as priests. There probably is not the same tension between priesthood and teaching where the subject is simply secular, although a certain pastoral care of the students is required. This also applies to lay teachers. In teaching religion in school and perhaps particularly at third level in teaching theology, the distinction between teaching and preaching, and still more dangerously teaching and indoctrination, becomes harder for a priest to maintain. Yet to fail to maintain it is to fail the students and theology itself.

In the 1950s, for centuries before and decades afterwards, theology teachers were taken exclusively from the ordained. In the 1960s as lay students and then lay professors of theology began to appear, there was quite a debate about whether the priest-theologian had a special charism as compared with the lay person. I remember a very friendly but intense argument with colleague Kevin McNamara, later Archbishop of Dublin, on this very point. He was able to quote Yves Congar, a hero to both of us, in support of his position that priests did enjoy such a charism. Despite the theological prowess of McNamara and Congar I was not convinced, particularly as the church was increasingly recognising the special charisms of the laity and, more particularly, as I became increasingly disturbed by the absence of women's experience and intellectual abilities from the theological tradition. It did seem rather absurd to have to depend exclusively on celibate males for a theology of marriage. Fifty years on it is very difficult to find a young theologian in Europe or North America who is an ordained priest. Most Ph.Ds in theology are lay and usually female, as indeed are most theology students, undergraduate and graduate. What impact this will have on the theological mind of the church and its development, it is too soon to say. In the short term these lay theologians will escape the traditional priestly pain of having to distinguish carefully the academy and the pulpit, their teaching and preaching roles.

The golden echoes of a teaching and writing career in theology crowd the ear and on occasion mist the eye. Despite or because of a hankering for the immediate contact with 'real' people in the 'real' world, the students and colleagues encountered and the books and articles studied over fifty years have disclosed realities cosmic, human and, dare one say it, divine which might not have entered into the heart of this man anyway. The scholarly dispassion and rigour which theological reading, reflection and communication demand impose a discipline, even asceticism, which bear their own spiritual fruit. There are plenty of dark and leaden moments in that process as one fails to understand or to communicate. However, the moments of light and insight echo more strongly in the memory without removing the sense of ultimate mystery. In so many of its information and analytic stages theology has a strong scientific cast. Although more akin to the human sciences than to the physical it cannot simply be equiparated to a particular example of either, any more that the study of literature can simply follow a sociological model or sociology a physics model. It is the distinctiveness of all these disciplines in method and content within a general horizon of rigorous examination of appropriate evidence and reflection on it that makes for a vital university. Without the presence of the serious discipline of theology other disciplines want for an important challenge to their temptation to hegemony as theology in turn suffers without their challenge. In its turn the university itself is impoverished. Within or without an immediate university setting theology has to recognise these challenges and enter into the public intellectual life.

The scholarly asceticism which ought to mark all academic work in teaching and research assumes its own shape in theology as seeking to explore, understand and communicate the ultimate mystery as manifested for Christians in the Jewish and Christian traditions. This response to mystery has its reverence dimension. This is not unrelated to the reverence for human and cosmic reality which all true teaching and research in whatever discipline involve. However, in theology, as it deals with ultimate reality, the reverence relates to religious worship and prayer on the one hand and to the exercise of the transformative imagination of the artist on the other. The theologian, therefore, works in a community of scholars who belong to a historical community of faith while remaining in serious dialogue with the broader scholarly community and their more secular concerns. The painful tension which is generated at times between fidelity to the community of faith and to the scholarly community should be seen as the growth pains of a living faith community, however mistaken the theologian may be on occasion. The care for truth which the leaders of the faith community carry must be sensitive to these efforts of the theologians in seeking fuller understanding, as theologians must be sensitive to the responsibilities of the leadership. Again there are limited parallels with the specialists in other disciplines such as medicine, where the current service to health may be questioned by new discoveries, which are however not yet fully tested for official public use. The recent authoritarian treatment of Irish theologians Sean Fagan and Linda Hogan does not suggest a healthy dialogue, rather some leaden echoes of the past.

The reverence, prayer and worship dimensions intrinsic to theology provide a suitable entrée to the priest's preaching role. Rigorous respect for the truth is still required but in a more explicitly prayerful, personal and pastoral fashion. The homily or sermon as part of a worshipping service should be prayerful for preacher and congregation in the sense that it addresses and expresses the elevation of minds and hearts of both parties to God. To achieve this it must be the fruit of the preacher's prayer-life with its immediate preparation based on prayerful meditation of scripture reading or chosen topic. The congregation has its own responsibility to listen prayerfully but not uncritically, admittedly a difficult combination. To foster such response, introductory prayer and careful reading of the scriptures is essential. In some situations, many more perhaps than is usually allowed, it may be feasible to involve the potential congregation in preparatory consideration of text or topic. This can occur easily enough in preparing for special services such as baptisms, weddings or funerals. It might also be built into the parish celebration of particular seasons of the liturgical year such as Advent and Lent. In these ways the educational dimension of preaching may be more effectively combined with its prayer dimension.

For preaching to be effective in terms of both prayer and education it has to be personal, reaching from the personal centre of the preacher to the personal needs and capacities of the congregation. In the usually mixed congregations of parish masses this must be an aspiration rather than an achievement. Yet the aspiration is crucial and the achievement, if always partial, important. By his own self-exposure as an aspirant rather than a successful achiever in the ways of Christian discipleship the priest-preacher places himself more fully in the community as assisting and being assisted by his fellow disciples. The personal character of preaching should not be confused with any kind of ego-tripping. One of the best safeguards against such 'I-witness' anecdotage and distraction lies in the preacher's knowledge of and care for his listeners, his pastoral sensitivity.

Preaching is an exercise of pastoral ministry, a caring mediation of the word of God to the people of God, local (parochial) branch. The priest as pastor cares for his flock, not in any patronising or 'I am the boss' fashion but as genuine and loving servant. To regard his people as inferior, mindless or sheepish would be a betrayal of his calling and an insult to them. So the caring has to be diligent, intelligent and skilful, as well as loving. And this applies to his preaching as much as to his sacramental ministry, to his counselling and other support activities, even if in some conceptions of ministry 'pastoring', as one verbal barbarism has it, may be reduced to action at the expense of thought and word. Some of the good priests we all have known may as far as act and word are concerned have been more effective, in the one rather than in the other but all strove to be effective in both, and the best were truly effective in both.

Pastoral Care, Friendship and Love

The caring priest is for clergy and laity in many ways the ideal priest. His preaching may be poor and his liturgical sense crude but such will be forgiven if he is recognised as genuinely caring about his people. The caring need not, indeed should not, be oppressively public or shrewdly political in any vote-catching sense. It does involve being with people, getting to know them in the course of their daily lives, so that in the crises of their lives he can accompany and support them without seeming an intruder. This is the ideal after which he strives. In past practice and increasingly with the shortage of priests the individual priest meets the individual in crisis for the first time. This calls for special attention and skills. As the shortage develops it calls for pastoral teams of trained and committed lay people who can extend the pastoral reach of the priest while transforming the community into a truly caring community or community of caring communities, where all members learn to care for one another in Christian fashion.

Pastoral care implies equality as persons as well as differentiation of skills and responsibility. Best practice results in mutual caring where the official pastor is cared for as well as caring. Parishioners including the sick, the grieving and the deprived have much to offer their pastor in care and consolation. Pastoral care of even the most vulnerable should never be patronising and the good pastor gains more than he gives. In such contexts true friendships emerge and neighbourly love flourishes. Not without its dangers of course, as other parishioners may resent the special care some neighbours receive. In the persistent and loving care which the pastor seeks to offer all such resentment may be gradually overcome but not always. The old advice that the priest should have the special friends he always needs both for support and escape outside his own parish or institution has merit but it is not always necessary or desirable. The friends developed in common projects within his own work context can be truly enriching without being threatening.

For the celibate priest, friendship with women has its own complexities and dangers about which our mentors fifty years ago did occasionally warn us. An almost exact contemporary and a prestigious moral theologian from Europe, Fr Klaus Demmer MSC, told me recently about speaking to his religious confreres on the occasion of his Golden Jubilee celebrations and discussing the importance of priests having friends. He said, a little tongue in cheek I suspect: 'Every priest needs women friends; the younger priest needs some older women friends while the older priest needs some younger women friends.' This may be the sage conclusion of a loving seventy-five-year-old priest and useful advice for others but it is unlikely to work as a deliberate strategy. Friendship is, to begin with at least, often a matter of chance, although many would interpret that chance as providential. What transforms the original contacts into a developing friendship and subsequently sustains it even in difficulty yields no easy explanation. Friendship is a prime example of human and Christian love and obviously applies to relationships between people of the different sexes or of the same sex. In all friendship there is likely to be an element of sexual attraction or at least comforting compatibility. In former days the attraction of a woman friend could be seen as threatening to the celibacy of the priest. Nowadays a priest's friendship with another man might also have come under suspicion. After the revelations of the last decades the most suspicious of all relationships might be the priest befriending young boys and girls. The paedophilia and other sexual scandals involving priests and young people have seen the greatest damage to pastoral trust of the people in priests and the greatest blow to the pastoral self-confidence and effectiveness of priest and bishop. The slow and painful healing through official church repentance and pastoral reconciliation, which is still required, seems fated to damaging interruption by recurrent ecclesial mishandling.

There is no doubt that over fifty years a priest may fall deeply in love with a friend and make mistakes in expressing that love as well as in suppressing it. There is no simple way to cope with such situations. Hurt to one or both parties is almost inevitable. Regrets, apologies and reconciliation can be slow and painful. Yet the growth in human and Christian understanding often matched with a deeper level of friendship may sometimes be the graceful outcome. Given repentance and reconciliation, the 'felix culpa theology' may be applied to many mistakes made in fifty years of priesthood in all areas of one's life including one's friendships. Golden echoes may even transmute the leaden.

One further and developing element in pastoral care concerns the treatment of lay employees. Half a century ago, sacristans and priests' housekeepers were, according to the gossip, very poorly paid. That has been largely rectified but a whole new set of lay employees as diocesan or parish secretaries, as youth workers, music directors and so on have emerged and sometimes without any clear terms of employment. There might be real problems of injustice here which no amount of Christian self-sacrifice by the employee could excuse. Strange as it might seem the first pastoral duty of the bishop or priest employer to lay employee is a clear and just contract in its initiation, conduct and termination. Despite recent improvements it does not seem to be the invariable rule. Leaden echoes remain.

Justice Seekers, Peace Makers and Community Builders

In the Irish parish tradition few priests have been what was known in Europe earlier as sacristy priests. Their pastoral instinct sought expression also in community activities of wide variety. In the 1930s and 1940s this search was given more formal and structured expression through organisations like Muintir na Tire and Christus Rex, which lasted down into the first decade at least of the 1955 class. Meantime there were individual priest-leaders engaged in community building promoting rural electrification and local water schemes as well as more ambitious projects to stem emigration and even attract back some who had left. It was about this time the Irish chaplains to Irish emigrants began, first in Britain, later spreading to the USA and the EU. These also involved community building among the emigrants themselves and keeping them in touch with their families and neighbours back home. The mixed success of some of these initiatives should not take from the courage and imagination which inspired and sustained them.

Particular priests broke through the social and economic fragmentation of these decades in a more public way, sometimes at considerable cost to themselves. The sharp criticism of priests like Austin Flannery OP and

Michael Sweetman SJ for their campaigns on housing needs in Dublin were echoed in the later prosecution of Padraig Standun for peacefully protesting road conditions in Connemara and in the nagging criticism of Fr Sean Healy and Sr Brigid Reynolds at the CORI Justice desk, of Fr Peter McVerry and Sr Stanislaus Kennedy working for the Dublin homeless and of Fr Sean McDonagh for his commitment to environmental protection. Mgr James Horan of Knock and Fr James McDyer of Glencolumbkille were perhaps the most persistent and in some ways most successful of the publicly known community developers among priests.

In less economic and more socio-cultural terms priests contributed significantly to parish community in helping drama groups, musical societies and sports clubs. Unfortunately so much of this has been obscured by the scandals of clerical paedophilia, the decline in priestly vocations and the general decline of church attendance and participation. There is practically speaking no new generation of priestly community builders on the horizon. The punishment and purification which the scandals involve for all priests and not just the few perpetrators exposed and convicted may have been needed in a heavily clericalised church. The absence of new male vocations to the priesthood may have the double advantage of enabling effective participation by lay people and opening up ordained priesthood to married men and to women. It would be nice to think that the class of '55 would welcome, even work for these developments and that some of the leaden echoes of the past would give way to golden echoes from the future.

In such developments justice seeking and peace making, those primary characteristics of discipleship, would move to a new level within the church and offer a lead to the wider society in Ireland and wherever the Catholic Church was active. The fifty years of priesthood celebrated here have been blighted in Ireland by the divisions and 'Troubles' which affected Northern Ireland predominantly but all of the island significantly. The justice and peace, which Christ's disciples are called to preach and practise, remained, despite the best efforts of many Catholics and Protestants, baptised and ordained, unattainable for at least thirty years. And they remain at risk. Physical and sexual abuse of the young, not only by clergy of course, and social divisiveness and war-mongering, not only by laity, will be leaden memories in the midst of golden celebrations.

The Prayer Circle

The oft-cited remark from *The Diary of a Country Priest* by George Bernano that 'all is grace' might be rendered for the same priest that all is prayer. However, it would be necessary to add: for that to be recognised and developed it would only apply to those who have also an explicit prayer life. As the diocesan priest is said to be called to the active rather than the contemplative life, the distinction may be pressed too far too easily to the detriment of both dimensions of Christian life. Individualist views of contemplative life and prayer ignore their traditional community context as well as everybody's reliance on community support for all fruitful human living, however isolated a particular person may feel or be. The Christian and human activist who serves community effectively must do it personally and so tend his personal internal needs as well as social skills and service. For the ministerial Christian these internal needs involve a meditative and persistent prayer life which nourishes and is nourished by his caring, pastoral activity. In that circle all is prayer and prayer is all.

In leading liturgy and preaching the word of God, the priest's private prayer seeks public expression. Not that private prayer lacks a community character or excludes consciously pastoral experience. It is in negotiating the inner connection between his daily ministry and daily prayer that the diocesan priest feeds the hungry sheep, one of which is always himself. Unfortunately the diet of office psalms as imposed or conventional spiritual reading as recommended in training does not always provide the nourishment pastor and sheep or pastors as sheep really need. If one could have a starting over of spiritual living, reading and praying one might in the light of fifty years attempt a quite different programme of prayer and reading. Of course, some starting over is always possible, even for golden jubilarians. Let us hope that the class of '55 are still open to that new thing which their God is undoubtedly ready to offer. There may be further golden echoes to come.

Epiphanies

The Beauty, the Hurt and the Holy

In both scholarly reading and personal experience, the interaction between religion and the arts has become increasingly important to theologians and other believers. In Irish scholarly terms Gesa Thiessen's theological study of modern Irish painters was an important pioneering work, and has received significant follow-up by herself in her *Theological Aesthetics: A Reader* (2004). Much more attention has been paid to theological reflection on Irish writing with the late Peter Connolly, formerly Professor of English at Maynooth, Mark Patrick Hederman, Una Agnew, Pat O'Brien and Michael Paul Gallagher, perhaps the most discerning of recent commentators. In a different idiom the works of John O'Donohue and John Moriarty provide further insight into relations between religion, human living and their artistic expression. O'Donohue's 2003 work, *Divine Beauty*, is clearly relevant to the discussion here. By an odd coincidence another Irish Donoghue, Denis, Professor at New York University and formerly of UCD, produced a work entitled *Speaking of Beauty* about the same time as John's book. Despite its literary preoccupations it is rewarding reading for any student of beauty. However, with that nod to a little of the influential Irish background reading, this chapter will follow its own idiosyncratic route through the late musings of a septuagenarian theologian. And the musings were not just influenced by reading but by a range of experiences of art and life and by a range of friendships with loving, creative and critical people, including happily some serious and yet amusing artists.

To start with beauty is to start anywhere and everywhere, with anybody and everybody, even with you and me. The beautiful is as universal as the good, the bad and the ugly and often more difficult to discern. That may be because we are not as well educated or initiated into perceiving human, natural or artistic beauty. We may, and I believe, do have an innate capacity for beauty but it has to be nurtured and that can only occur in a community and culture with their own traditions of beauty. We learn to speak, to hear and to see in a family and community context, where our language, aural and visual perception rely on a developing combination of personal ability and communal resources. It is no accident that the Irish were until recently more renowned for their sense of verbal beauty, oral and written, than for their sense of visual beauty, although this was part of their earlier tradition and culture. The innate capacity and even desire for the beautiful may be restricted in various ways or even frustrated but it usually finds expression, however inadequate. This occurs most obviously in human relations between friends and lovers, spouses, parents and children. The baby presented by proud mother may look to the outsider like most other babies; to mother it is utterly distinctive and beautiful.

To speak in this way must seem to some like an evasion of any definition of the beautiful, of any rehearsal of the classical or at least conventional definition in terms of integrity, harmony, proportion and radiance. And indeed it is. Whatever about radiance, which correlates with the epiphany of my title, harmony and proportion are much more problematic in the last hundred years or more in relation to human/natural as well as artistic beauty. And there is no readily acceptable alternative on offer. So one must proceed indirectly in theoretical terms but in practical terms quite directly, by considering what someone experiences as beautiful or what by a much broader consensus is accepted as beautiful, while seeking in this context to give some verbal, even theoretical justification for such a judgement. This is not to endorse a purely subjective approach to beauty, 'whatever is in the eye of the beholder!' Beauty like intelligibility is a universal characteristic of the universe and like intelligibility it emerges in the interaction between human beings and the world, meaning the world of humanity, nature and art(ifact). The justification for this stance rests on the convergence of human experiences and cultures and is deepened and transformed for Christians in the doctrines of creation and salvation, perhaps better in the personae of Creator, Saviour and Sanctifier.

For all their undoubted, if oft times veiled, beauty, human, natural and humanly created beings are fragile, vulnerable to hurt or damage and destruction. In the human observer/interactor the fragility of the beautiful will always be a source of unease and in the limit case of hurt or destruction a source of pain. Yet the hurt of interacting with the beautiful has deeper roots and innate effects. The very appreciation of the beautiful reaches beyond the joy towards the exquisite suffering, to adapt a phrase of Welsh poet RS Thomas, which overcomes the observer in the presence of certain beauty. Like my friend who wept on first seeing Rembrandt's *Prodigal Son*, or so many parents who have wept with painful joy on the birth of their child, or the theatre and concert audiences who surrender in ecstasy and agony to a superb performance of Shakespeare or Beethoven or of many a lesser dramatist or composer.

Most ecstatic and in its turn most painful of all is the beauty discovered on falling in love and the further reaches of that beauty as the relationship matures over a lifespan. Love, another of these great and indefinable words, belongs with beauty in any complete description of human reaction to the beautiful. One may indeed speak of a cold beauty and a coldness to great beauty as Robert Browning does in his powerful, painful but beautiful poem 'My Last Duchess', but there is a hint of the wonder of love in the calculating description of its absence.

WB Yeats' 'The Cold Heaven', despite the terror of its opening lines, 'Suddenly I saw the cold and rook-delighting heaven / That seemed as though ice burned and was but the more ice', recalls 'love crossed long ago' for which he feels the guilt and fears the punishment 'stricken by the injustice of the skies'. It is difficult to find another poet, ancient or modern, who devotes so much of his work to the interrelation of human beauty, human love and human suffering and does it in such beautiful poetry. From 'Had I the heavens' embroidered cloths' through 'There is grey in your hair', Yeats sought perfection of the work of love-poetry even if he never quite managed perfection of the love-life. But that imperfection and its pain helped make the poetry work so beautifully.

All of which brings to mind Yeats' aphorism of women and poets, the central characters of his life and work, that they 'must labour to be beautiful'. As if with this line from the poem 'Adam's Curse' in mind, WH Auden in his poem on the occasion of Yeats' death observed 'Mad Ireland hurt him into poetry'. The labour pains of the artist giving birth to the beautiful carry their necessary hurt and for Auden originated with Yeats' engagement with or love of Ireland and, as one can easily read in so many poems, his engagement with and love of women. Beauty in human or artistic form comes forth from mother or artist in pain and involves its own pain for companion or observer. Hurt into creating beauty artists as painters of Christ's Passion or writers of war poems may be, so are their viewers and readers hurt in turn, as they allow the creative process and product of the artist to enter their minds and hearts. Beauty and hurt often belong together in the activity of the artist and the receptivity of the audience.

The creativity which issues in beauty is a gift, human certainly, but to believers in Christian and other great faiths divine also. The original creator is Godself from whom the world and humanity in all their complexity and beauty proceed. Creation as observed by God in the Genesis poems was looked on by the Creator–God and seen to be very good, very beautiful in God's eyes. It reflected the beauty or glory or radiance of God as the psalmist, and others remind us. That word 'kabod', glory, radiance or beauty is a key Hebrew term for the great unnameable mystery from which all proceeds and to which all returns. The beauty of this world shows forth the kabod or beauty of God. To appreciate this beauty properly, to let it enter one's very being, is to offer a gateway to its creator and origin, to let oneself be touched by the holy one of Israel. 'Qadosh', translated as holy in later languages, denotes the transcendent, utterly other dimension of Israel's God of beauty and radiance. In the story of Moses and the burning bush as in other biblical episodes kabod and qadosh come together as epiphany of the divine in the midst of the cosmic. From awareness of kabod to openness to qadosh is one way to holiness, to transformative spiritual experience as proposed in this paper and it will involve hurt and suffering en route.

The serene narrative sweep of the first two chapters of Genesis with the Creator–God looking in appreciation at the divine work of creation and resting on the seventh day prompts us humans with our human eyes to view that creation as reflecting the good and beautiful creator. It also suggests that by God's friendship or grace we may see God's work at least partially through God's eyes. The vision of God which is available in the half-light of faith is in part our sharing in how God views the world and everything in it as well as our own graced vision of that world as revealing the radiant, transcendent and creating presence of Godself. The lilies of the field, the birds of the air, the heavens in all their majesty and the least of humans, the hungry, the sick and deprived, reveal the glory and beauty of God, the divine kabod to those with the eyes to see. Epiphanies as the peculiarly intense emergence and perception of that divine kabod may be rare in most lifetimes but they can occur to anybody at any time in any circumstance. In the end it is a grace and so a decision for God but human preparedness helps in recognising the significance of whatever happens as well as moving us towards holiness or qadosh even if the drama of epiphany is never experienced and kabod as divine beauty and glory remains at a remove.

In that preparation, tutoring by the beauty of nature and art plays an important role. For the remainder of this paper I will concentrate on the tutoring role of art, particularly but not only in literature, not as instrumental in religious or faith development but as spiritually, that is humanly, transforming in its own right. And of course the encounter with many artistic objects includes the possibility of fresh encounters with nature, 'with the dearest freshness deep down things', in Hopkins' phrase.

In the process of transformation by poem or painting reader or viewer is attracted by and then, given time and affinity, captured by the beauty of the work. Captive to the work, inhabited by it, the reader/viewer/listener undergoes a change of consciousness, spirit, emotion, even body as the person surrenders to its unifying and transforming power. As the passion of the work, subdued or thunderous, embraces the listener/reader something of the passion of the author in heart and mind, in the process of composition enters the listener/reader to allow her to share the passion not only expressed in the end product but also in the act of composing and of the suffering which that usually involves. Both author and reader are hurt into the beautiful and in the classic work at least taken beyond the simply controllable pleasure and attractive object to the finally unreachable. The gifts of the act of composing and of the composition suggest something of that uncontrollable and therefore hurtful process for both composer and audience, which may prepare one at least to be aware of the transcendent radiance of the God immanent in the radiance of our 'earthly estate'.

For many people music would be the most powerful of the art forms in this transformatory process in itself and in the work preparatory to prayer or awareness of the transcendent. However, I do not feel competent to develop the argument in this area. With the technical know-how and equipment it would be illuminating almost to the point of epiphany to examine some paintings and sculpture of artists and art work I am familiar with: the Good Friday paintings of the late Tony O'Malley; the Passion series of Hughie O'Donoghue; a range of pieces by Imogen Stuart. Even without immediate visual AIDS it is worth reflecting for a moment on their work, particularly that of O'Donoghue (as I have dealt with that of O'Malley and Stuart elsewhere). In analysing some of his own paintings, O'Donoghue has drawn attention in retrospect to the layered character of much of it. So a typically elongated Passion image of the Christ reveals to him later his earlier fascination with the Tollund Man as discovered in the Danish bog well before he began the painting. Further reflection on his part reminds him of how the local river where he played as a child in North Mayo has entered into his imaginative creation of the Christ figure. At least in some artistic work we can follow with such expert guidance the unconscious transformation of human experience into a finished work which confronts us with one of the great sacred images of our tradition, the suffering Christ. How O'Donoghue himself may have suffered the agony, even the crucifixion, of producing such work, only he and perhaps not even he can finally tell. In contemplation of his paintings of the Passion we may also be drawn into the painful experience of their beauty in its process and product.

The Passion of the Christ and the paintings and other art works it has inspired in music and literature return us to the theme of Creation by God and thence to what Paul calls New Creation. The self-giving of God in creation of a world reflecting his glory and beauty and its climax in the creation of human beings in the divine image and likeness reached a new pinnacle in Jesus Christ, God become human. Self-giving becomes in another Pauline phrase, self-emptying, kenosis, at the appropriate time, the kairos. Creation reaches towards crucifixion. Loving the world into its true beauty is no cheap labour for the artist Creator–God or for the artistic, creative and saving Word of God, Jesus Christ, God's Son. As the evangelist St John notes and so many subsequent artists and theologians dimly perceived, it was on the Cross that Jesus was to be lifted up and glorified to reveal the beauty and glory of the loving, creating and saving God. In attempting to render this divine work into however imperfect human words or paint or music, human artists are following, unconsciously or not, the way of the Cross and proclaiming that their Redeemer liveth. It seems a very large claim to make for artists who may not themselves be believers or who as with most modern artists may not be concerned with Christ or religious topics at all.

In the most secular of artists there lives the spirit of creativity which is difficult to reduce to sheer materiality or the accidents of evolution. These free-standing art works may not in their insight and beauty be simply commodified as useful possessions without undermining their intrinsic value. In 'Guernica' by Picasso as in a Passion painting of Christ there is as well as a kabod-beauty, indeed through the kabod-beauty, a redemptive thrust seeking to overcome man's inhumanity to man. And it was surely some of the great modern landscape painters such as Monet and Manet who enhanced our vision or even cured our conventional blindness to so much of the natural beauty hitherto veiled from us. New vision of the world could well amount to epiphany under the tutoring eye of our great artists.

As Heaney's phrase 'the redress of poetry' reminds us, in the work of so many poets and novelists there emerges a renewal, a new creation of language and image as they seek to render anew the verbal beauty of the language and the imaginative beauty of their world. By their works you shall know them and it is to some of their works we must now turn in search of re-creative and restorative human words and verbal visions which could, where human spirit encounters Holy Spirit, prompt Epiphany and our being hurt into kabod-qadosh, the Beautiful and the Holy.

My strategy here is to quote a number of poems mainly by contemporary poets which, without any specific religious reference, illustrate, as I believe, the theme of this chapter. I begin with a poem from the *Selected Poems* of the Polish poet Adam Zagajewski. It is called 'Mysticism for Beginners' and is translated by Clare Cavanagh.

Mysticism for Beginners
The day was mild, the light was generous.
The German on the café terrace
held a small book on his lap.
I caught sight of the title:
Mysticism for Beginners.

Suddenly I understood that the swallows
patrolling the streets of Montepulciano
with their shrill whistles,
and hushed talk of timid travellers
from Eastern, so-called Central Europe,
And the white herons standing – yesterday? The
day
before? –
like nuns in fields of rice,
and the dusk, slow and systematic,
erasing the outlines of medieval houses,
and olive trees on little hills,
abandoned to the wind and heat,
and the head of the Unknown Princess
that I saw and admired in the Louvre,
and stained glass windows with butterfly wings
sprinkled with pollen,
and the little nightingale practising
its speech beside the highway,
and any journey, and kind of trip,
are only mysticism for beginners,
the elementary course, prelude
to a test that's been postponed.

The test of epiphany that has been heralded but postponed in Zagajewski's
poem is realised dramatically and unexpectedly in that of the late Irish poet
Michael Hartnett's 'Death of an Irish Woman':

Ignorant in the sense
she ate monotonous food
and thought the world was flat,
and pagan, in the sense
she knew the things that moved
at night were neither dogs nor cats
but pucas and darkfaced men,
she nevertheless had fierce pride.
But sentenced in the end
to eat thin diminishing porridge
in a stone-cold kitchen
she clenched her brittle hands
around a world she could not understand.

I loved her from the day she died.
She was a summer dance at the crossroads.
She was a card game where a nose was broken.
She was a song that nobody sings.
She was a house ransacked by soldiers.
She was a language seldom spoken.
She was a child's purse full of useless things.

For a slightly older contemporary of Hartnett's, the poet's loving her from the day she died has its natural reference to the love that often surges anew at the moment of loss, particularly death-loss but with echoes also of the loss of a culture, a language and a faith. Only then may the epiphanies generated by the beauty, the hurt and the holy finally emerge.

Micheal O'Siadhail's recent collection, *Love Life*, dedicated to his wife, Brid, has many examples of how human love, beauty and even hurt suddenly illuminate writer and reader. 'Healing' is a particular favourite of this reader:

Think that I might never have happened on you,
Mate and match;
For all the works of genes so many ifs.

Supposing the behop and noise of youth,
In turns and riffs,
In fumbled serendipities of time and place

I'd faltered or somehow failed to recognise
My counter-face
Or Eros hadn't led across the Rubicon?

Imagine we weren't ripe for one another –
Me blundering on,
Strung up, burning the candle at both ends –

Or if I hadn't suffered breakage underway?
The broken mends.
Burnt not shy. Wounded enough to heal.

Epiphanies may be rare but all the richer for that. They reflect religious and secular images and experiences, yet always seem to carry traces of transcendence or *Rumours of Angels*, as Peter Berger's book has it.

No Habitable Grief

Spirituality and Suicide

I have adapted, perhaps maladapted, as my title a phrase of Irish poet, Eavan Boland, who speaks of language as 'a habitable grief'. The inability to communicate, which so many suicides display beforehand in their depression, and the numb and dumb condition of so many of their bereaved, suggest something of the unbearable, uninhabitable grief which they both have been or are enduring. At least as a label for the spiritual torment which so frequently surrounds suicide, 'No Habitable Grief' seemed apt.

As we travel through the stark statistics of Irish and global suicide and parasuicide, as we try to assimilate the dark data of the sciences of medicine, psychiatry, biology and sociology, we are drawn ever more deeply into the dark labyrinths of human mind and body, of human relationships in their personal and social, even planetary and cosmic dimensions. The spirit-body which constitutes the individual human person does not come into and endure in existence in and of itself, and its relational character is not confined to its immediate family or even to people. Increasingly we are becoming aware of how interdependent we are, not only with other human beings but with the animate and inanimate environment in which we live, both on planet earth and within the wider cosmos, including and transcending our vital solar system. The old belief of how some people's mental well-being could be affected by the phases of the moon, hence the word 'luna-tic', may have been put behind us, but both poets and scientists are alert to how human health, including human mental health, may be influenced by the natural, human and cultural environment in which people live. All that is primarily matter for the relevant sciences but a holistic or integrated vision of human beings as persons, in communities and in cosmos, as body-spirits, will seek to integrate intelligently, honestly and lovingly the findings of the sciences. I say intelligently and honestly to do justice to the scientists' work, and lovingly to keep us alert to the humanity and uniqueness of the suicides, the parasuicides and the bereaved as primarily persons and not just cases, still less mere statistics.

This is a spiritual task in that larger sense of the human spirit's capacity to recognise and relate to another human being in a loving, caring, intelligent and honest way. The capacity to know and love are regarded traditionally as distinctive characteristics of human beings; with their self- and other-identifying capacities, their truth-seeking, relational-caring and community-building dimensions. Together these constitute what we may call humanity's spiritual character.

The inspirited flesh and enfleshed spirit forms a mysterious human unity which continually challenges us to further understanding but continually eludes our final grasp. So in trying to come to grips with suicide in its prediction and prevention, in its attempts or completion, in post-mortem explanation or impact on the bereaved, fresh questions tend to outrun the most up to date answers. We have many examples of this in the scientific literature as a whole. What might be called the spiritual dimensions of the present day suicide crisis, in the broad terms in which I am using the word spiritual, operate at every level of human investigation of that crisis, at the biological, psychological, sociological and religious levels. The fact that such investigations occur at all in the search for truth about the prevalence of suicide among diverse subjects, its predisposing factors, associated illnesses and risk behaviours, demonstrates the vitality and concerns of the investigators, their spiritual capacities and engagement. Without seeking to rehearse once more the remarkable scientific results already achieved, which I would be unable to do anyway, I merely wish to underline the spiritual connections of all human responses to suicide and to anticipate the danger of a spiritual response being seen as something simply separate and added on for those who might wish to have it.

My reflections on spirituality and suicide, however, are more circumscribed because all these 'spiritual' activities of the scientists are treated elsewhere. In the more restricted arena I have chosen, the spiritual concentrates on morality and on spirituality in its ultimate or religious sense.

The Moral Tradition

The moral judgement on suicide has varied over different cultures and religious traditions. In the great formative traditions of western morality, the Hebrew or Jewish, the Greek and Latin, and the Christian, there are variations within these traditions themselves both in regard to moral judgement and social response. Little moral attention is paid to the rare cases of suicide mentioned in the Hebrew scriptures or Old Testament although subsequent Jewish tradition condemned suicide as a violation of God's commandment 'Thou shalt not kill'. In Greek and Roman traditions suicide was regarded as not only justified but honourable in certain circumstances. Yet their dominant moral position treated suicide over long periods as wrong and shameful for victims and their families. Suicides themselves were often the subjects of posthumous degradation.

The Christian traditions followed the mainstream of regarding suicide as violating God's prohibition of killing with further arguments about God as lord of life and death, suicide as sinful refusal of love of self and indeed refusal of love of neighbour in abandonment of the community. The refusal of church burial and other expressions of condemnation of such acts have been very much part of the response of all Christian Churches until very recently. In the nineteenth and through the twentieth century such condemnatory attitudes and practices changed very significantly in western society and church, although remnants of them still remain in the shame, stigma and fear which relatives and others experience on the occasion of a particular suicide.

The psychological insights of recent times emphasize how major diseases such as depression, manic-depressive illness and schizophrenia, sometimes compounded with alcohol or other drug addictions, play powerful roles in completed and attempted suicides. This has altered the moral as well as the diagnostic treatment and preventive landscapes. Church burial, for example, is now the rule, the individual victim is seldom treated as unrepentant sinner and serious pastoral efforts by priests, people and more specific organisations seek to console and support the bereaved, not least by trying to prevent the traditional stigmatization of victim and family. As much of this stigmatization was and still is associated both with the harsh judgement of suicide as a particularly serious sin and with the threat to individuals and community which suicide at least unconsciously posed and poses, much more may be demanded in corrective religious, moral and social education than is at present available.

Taking the sin out of suicide or at least removing any notion of moral wrongness from it presents its own problems. (Sin is a theological word, involving culpable rejection of God and may be better left aside for the present.) I say this not to restore stigmatization of victim and family or reinforce their suffering. Neither do I believe that maintaining the objective (as it is called) immorality of the act is more likely to restrain the individual bent on taking his or her own life. Yet in our search for causes, for preventive measures, for appropriate family support we make it clear that there is something wrong here which should not happen and that when it does those most closely involved suffer grievous loss and need special care and attention. If it were simply an accident or could be construed as such we would not react in the same way, although fatal accidents can also be very traumatic for survivors and preventive strategies for such accidents are always in need of improvement.

We might then best describe suicide as a particular form of human tragedy, but does that relieve us of the duty of trying to understand and prevent it? Obviously not. Are we reducing it to the old, and in its time, consoling coroner's tag, 'self-killing while of unsound mind'? From all we read, serious psychiatric illness is present in perhaps 90 per cent of suicides but most analysts agree that other factors enter in, including sometimes a triggering context or event. Yet the evidence for people making an apparently sane and clear decision to end their lives is also strong. The tragedy may lie in a despairing but yet sane decision which sees no other way out, as some suicide notes seem to indicate. There is clearly further work to be done here involving various human and moral sciences. Insights into the complexity of such situations may be gleaned from a range of artists, especially poets. According to some commentators, suicide occurs disproportionately among artists and some have left us highly charged and insightful accounts of their despair, of their suicide attempts or of their pre-completion days. Here I take the liberty of quoting one of these.

Sylvia Plath's 'Edge', written some days before she took her own life and according to A. Alvarez, her fellow poet and friend, is 'specifically about the act she was about to perform'.

> The woman is perfected.
> Her dead
>
> Body wears the smile of accomplishment,
> The illusion of Greek necessity
>
> Flows in scrolls of her toga,
> Her bare
>
> Feet seem to be saying:
> We have come so far, it is over.
>
> Each dead child coiled, a white serpent,
> One at each little
>
> Pitcher of milk, now empty.
> She has folded
>
> Them back into her body as petals
> Of a rose close when the garden

Stiffens and odours bleed
From the sweet throats of the night flowers.

The moon has nothing to be sad about,
Staring from her hood of bone.

She is used to this sort of thing.
Her blacks crackle and drag.

One could go on quoting numerous other poets and artists who took Plath's way out but for balance I take a poem by Janet Frame in which she describes the position of so many of us outsiders desperately trying to understand.

Suicides
It is hard for us to enter
the kind of despair they must have known
and because it is hard we must get in by breaking
the lock if necessary for we have not the key,
though for them there was no lock and the surrounding walls
were supple, receiving as waves, and they drowned
though not lovingly; it is we only
who must enter this way.

Temptations will beset us, once we are in.
We may want to catalogue what they have stolen.
We may feel suspicion; we may even criticize the décor
of their suicidal despair, may perhaps feel
it was incongruously comfortable.

Knowing the temptations then
let us go in
deep to their despair and their skin and know
they died because the words they had spoken
returned always homeless to them.

The Moral as the Spiritual
I have made the point that all the work of scientists, doctors, nurses, carers and friends in their attempts to prevent beforehand, diagnose later and support potential victims and already bereaved families, clearly make moral responses in the search for truth and in respect and care for their suffering

fellows. And these moral responses may and can also be called spiritual. It is in these activities and values of truth seeking and respect and care for self and others that the human spirit expresses itself and so transcends, moves beyond a simply determined material unit to become a body opened by the spirit to the world, cosmic and human, open to become a real person in the wider community and universe.

Suicide poses serious challenges to this moral inspirited body, to this and every person, to the would-be suicide or victim, to the would-be preventers and healers, to the bereaved and their supporters. It is the activity and awareness of this moral–spiritual community from the scientists to the family that should provide the medical resources and skills, the loving and enduring care and support, which may hope to reduce the numbers of those who despair their way into suicide and at the same time help to share and heal the sufferings of those left behind.

While these challenges may be met in a particular case or in a small number of cases by highly motivated professionals, family and friends, the crisis we face now with almost a contagious epidemic among certain age groups requires a more coherent social development. From the nineteenth century classic study of French sociologist, Emile Durkheim, to the more recent personal remarks by many social commentators in Ireland today, such as President McAleese, John Lonergan, Governor of Mountjoy Jail, and the Irish Catholic Bishops' Conference, there are social as well as personal elements at work in the increasing resort to suicide or parasuicide among Irish people. And of course not only among Irish people who increasingly share what Durkheim might have also called 'anomie', the collapse of shared moral and spiritual values in a community. Where the 'me' becomes the centre of the world, where profits and personal wealth take priority over people, where material and professional success is the major test of the worthwhile person, where individuals lack any real community setting or commitment and where consumption flourishes at the expense of communion, the lonely, the unsuccessful by our famous/infamous Tiger standards, and, above all, those marginalized by serious psychiatric illness, still bearing some of the stigma of earlier times, are at further risk of seeking the ultimate escape. In moving to stress the need for a more moral and spiritual society as the context in which the personal needs of potential suicides might be more effectively addressed, I am not suggesting a return to any kind of repressively religious society but a rediscovery of the worth and dignity of all human beings, particularly the vulnerable, and the capacity for organised, skilful and loving care for and even by the vulnerable in peer support groups. It will not be feasible to respond effectively to suicidal persons and their immediate circle, if they still have one, without a serious education of the society as a whole at school and adult level, and a moral transformation from a 'me and my family/cronies only' to a society that values truth, justice and loving compassion in service of society's least ones.

From the Moral–Spiritual to the Spiritual–Religious

In face of the passionate distress leading to and deriving from suicide and parasuicide, the moral reflections offered may seem at times cold and detached. Yet some detachment is necessary on an issue like this in laying the groundwork for effective analysis and discussion and still more for effective planning and action. The passion is at least equally necessary and, given my own background, I find that passion best nourished and guided by my Christian faith. There are two main strands of such passion which are integral to Christian faith and which at least shed some consoling and perhaps preventive light on suicide and its suffering surrounds.

Let's begin with creation and, as we Christians recognise now, the continuing creative process, involving in Christian faith a loving creative God who, creating human beings in the divine image, shared the divine creative capacity with them also. I realise that is quite a mouthful and in teasing it out in relation to our concerns here we must unfortunately leave aside many difficult problems about more immediate human origins and development.

Assuming for the moment that they can be solved to the extent humanly necessary and possible, and I believe they can, I wish to concentrate on the human being as creature, and so contingent, as not self-originating but contingent in existence, who might or might not have been, might or might not be in the future and is finally mortal. Returning to the poetic language of the Book of Genesis, man and woman are created by God from the dust of the earth. They come as divine gift into the world, which is also divine gift to them. In a brilliant recent adaptation of the Genesis poem, philosopher, literary critic and general polymath, George Steiner describes human beings as Guests of Creation (and of Creator) and as Guests and Hosts of one another. It is in those gracious and gift images of Genesis and Steiner that we may recognise both the dignity and responsibility that we enjoy in and for our own lives and that of the others, as well as the respect and gratitude we are called to show for the whole of creation. The gift of human life in particular summons to grateful and loving care of our own lives and those of others in the knowledgeable, skilful and creative ways which we have already discussed in regard to the network of professional skills and moral commitment. As guests and hosts of one another, of creation and Creator, the passion of the joyful guest and gracious host will fuel that support and passion for one another and especially for those who are in particular need. The last shall be first in our vision of society as community of host–guests in celebration. The self-destruction of one of these host–guests will appear all the more tragic in such a vision and leave abandoned the particular hosts and guests to whom she was closely bonded. Yet such self-destruction happens despite the closest bonding and deepest celebration. It too has its roots in the moral–religious understanding of humanity that originates and develops in the Hebrew, Christian and other moral–religious traditions.

Creation and Destruction

The creativity which humans share with the divine creator is allied to a freedom without which it could not operate and yet is vulnerable in that very freedom to a destructiveness of self, human others and the world about them, as the whole of history bears witness. It is in that mystery of the creative–destructive character of humans (it includes all of us in varying degrees), that the origins of suicide lie. Although suicide is mentioned in passing in the Old Testament or Hebrew Scriptures it does not, as noted, evoke any particular condemnation. In the New Testament the only reference to suicide is to that of Judas in remorse at the betrayal of Jesus and again without judgement. It is, however, in the broader accounts of human joy, creativity and grateful dependency, of human arrogance, destructiveness and misery that we glean some real insight into the ambiguities of the human condition and the passion of the Creator's response.

Among the many celebrations of divine and human creativity are what are sometimes called the creation psalms, for example, Psalm 104 from which I quote:

> Bless the Lord, O my soul! ...
> Who hast stretched out the heavens like a tent ...
> Thou didst set the earth on its foundations ...

Yet the psalms also provide many instances of human suffering and destructiveness as the psalmist weeps for his sins, feels himself oppressed by his enemies, abandoned by God and angry at that God. Anger at God is a powerful feature of Jewish religion and psalmist response to human suffering. It is clearly an acceptable spiritual response to the God who seems uncaring or ineffective. It could express what many despairing victims or survivors of suicide cry out today. In Psalm 50/1, the sinful psalmist confesses his sins and cries for healing: 'Have mercy on me, O God, according to thy steadfast love; according to thy abundant mercy blot out my transgressions ...' In Psalm 86 the psalmist attributes his misery to fellow humans: 'O God, insolent men have risen up against me;/a band of ruthless men seek my life.' The great cry of abandonment in Psalm 22, 'My God, My God, why hast thou forsaken me' is placed on the lips of Jesus on the Cross and we must return to that.

Of course, despite the frequent cries of protest and even sometimes of desperation the psalms and the Hebrew scriptures generally carry a message of hope and healing, of salvation when a Saviour–Messiah will renew and restore Israel and indeed all peoples. However this takes a very unexpected turn with the prophet(s) of the Book of Isaiah where the saviour is pictured not as a triumphant King of Israel and of the world but as a 'suffering servant'.

As we move, or rather the Creator–God moves, to confront the destructiveness that becomes more rampant, the promise of a divine saviour takes on the paradoxical shape of the suffering and powerless servant in the prophecies of Isaiah. The Book of Isaiah chapters 52/53 is the classic example: 'He was despised and rejected by men; a man of sorrows and acquainted with grief' (Is 53:3).

It is, however, in Jesus Christ that the Creator–God enters fully into human creativity and destructiveness in order to affirm and transform the creativity and overcome the destructiveness. In preaching the good news or the gospel and in enacting its new creation potential from the wedding at Cana, with which Jesus begins his ministry, to the healing in Gethsemene of the ear of Malchus, slave of the High Priest, which had been cut off by Peter's sword at ministry's end, the incarnate Son of God at once endorses continuing human creativity. By undergoing human suffering and oppression, even to the death of a criminal on the Cross, he destroys human destructiveness. Calling out in despair the opening words of Psalm 22, 'My God, my God, why have you forsaken me?', he still prays for his enemies and for all human destroyers, 'Father, forgive them, for they know not what they do', before echoing the final hope of so many complaining and angry psalms with his 'Father, into your hands I commend my spirit'.

It is with this background that Christians may hope to be co-creative and co-suffering, compassionate guests and hosts of their human sisters and brothers in celebration, protection and mourning. By sharing the creative potential of those vulnerable to suicide as well as their self-destructive potential, they may be motivated and enabled to accompany them from destructiveness to creativity once again. Even should they fail on a particular occasion they may have conveyed something of the ultimate consoling love of a neighbour, and of the transforming mercy of

God in those very last moments. Such neighbour love and companionship will at the same time express and expand the creative capacity of the compassionate companion, despite the immediate trauma of loss or of feelings of anger, failure and guilt. The angry 'why', the disappointment at the others, victim and survivors, even the temptation to judge may eventually be overborne by the mysterious richness of our human fellow guests of creation and of the final mystery of the God who is love and mercy, forgiveness and new life. By becoming a fellow guest, God in Jesus Christ leads the way through the most horrific of human deaths to new life in resurrection. While the call to prevent suicide and to support survivors is intensified in face of the mystery of Jesus' death and resurrection, our efforts at providing exact moral analysis may finally have to bow before the creative–destructive mystery that is the human being.

I will conclude if I may with the work of a poet who, while rejoicing as a guest of creation in so many of his early poems, suffered many of the extremes of despair in his later ones, and that despite his firm formation in Christian faith and spirituality. Gerard Manley Hopkins (1844–89) was an English Jesuit poet who became Professor of Classics in the nineteenth century at what is now UCD. Here are examples of his early and late poems, of his times of celebration and of abandonment.

Pied Beauty

Glory be to God for dappled things –
For skies of couple-colour as a brinded cow;
For rose-moles all in stipple upon trout that swim;
Fresh-firecoal chestnut falls; finches wings;
Landscapes plotted and pieced–fold, fallow, and plough;
And all trades, their gear and tackle and trim.

All things, counter, original, spare, strange;
Whatever is fickle, freckled (who knows how?)
With swift, slow; sweet, sour; adazzle, dim;
He fathers-forth whose beauty is past change:
Praise him.

I Wake and Feel

I wake and feel the fell of dark, not day.
What hours, O what black hours we have spent
This night! what sights you, heart, saw; ways you went!
And more must, in yet longer light's delay.

With witness I speak this. But where I say
Hours I mean years, mean life. And my lament
Is cries countless, cries like dead letters sent
To dearest him that lives alas! away.

I am gall, I am heartburn. God's most deep decree
Bitter would have me taste: my taste is me;
Bones built in me, flesh filled, blood brimmed the curse.
Selfyeast of spirit a dull dough sours. I see
The lost are like this, and their scourge to be
As I am mine, their sweating selves; but worse.

His return to hope is signaled in a poem from the same era, 'That Nature is a Heraclitean Fire and of the Comfort of the Resurrection', from which I quote the concluding stanzas:

Across my foundering deck shone
A beacon, and eternal beam. Flesh fade, and mortal trash
Fall to the residuary worm; world's wildfire, leave but ash:
In a flash, at a trumpet crash,
I am all at once what Christ is, since he was what I am, and
This Jack, joke, poor potsherd, patch, matchwood,
Immortal diamond,
Is immortal diamond.

Here the uninhabitable grief of deep depression, which affected Hopkins so severely in his final years, could at least occasionally yield to the beacon of the eternal beam. It may provide an utterly human example of how the spiritual and creative, even with enormous pain and difficulty, may triumph even in this life over the destructive, especially the self-destructive.

The Spaces of Our Grief

There is so much joy in all good poetry, even Irish poetry, despite Chesterton's shallow comment that all our songs are sad. Yet the joys are often bracketed by profoundly tragic people and events. This is certainly my experience in reading and re-reading the two recently published collections of poetry by Irish authors John F. Deane and Jerome Kiely on which I wish to reflect here. My superscription is taken from a poem by Deane in his collection 'The Instruments of Art' but it might also be aptly used to describe Kiely's collection, 'Swallows in December'. The affinity is deeper still in that they are both religious poets, or perhaps more accurately poets whose religious insights underpin and transform some of their best poetic achievements, feats rare enough in current Irish poetry. Beyond these affinities lies a whole difference in form and style; the more complex forms of Deane contrasting with the simpler but no less profound forms of Kiely. Here the poet as priest of Achill Island and West Mayo plays quite different melodies from the priest as poet of West Cork on sometimes similar themes.

The titles of these two collections already hint at the differences in mood and melody. Deane's 'The Instruments of Art' not only picks up on his other artistic interests, painting and music, but signals the labouring to be beautiful which all artistic creation involves. Kiely's title 'Swallows in December' flows more easily although the theme suggests the unusual experience of beauty out of season. The better way for the non-professional critic may be to reflect, prayerfully as the occasion demands, on some of their more powerful and beautiful poems.

As Deane was the first to hand I will begin with a few remarks on his collection as a whole and then concentrate on some individual poems. On the cover is a detail from a typical, complex and moving painting by the late Tony O'Malley, entitled 'Shadowy Carvings of an Ancient Execution, Good Friday 1992'. O'Malley's paintings have always resonated with Deane's poetry and he has a particular relationship with those paintings which O'Malley did every Good Friday. However, the blurb on the back cover points out: 'The guiding spirits [here] are Edward Munch and Vincent van Gogh.' Informed of this, the reader–reflector may still have to wrestle with the language and images, the rhythms and the references which these profound poems present.

As happens frequently with Deane's collections (cf. his recent 'Manhandling the Deity'), he interweaves natural, narrative and explicitly Christian themes while mediating in this volume the unsettling ways of his guiding painter spirits. This is must evident in the title poem, 'The Instruments of Art', with its subscription: Edward Munch. The opening stanzas describe Munch's working conditions with an underlay perhaps of the poet's own:

> We move in draughty, barn-like spaces, swallows
> busy round the beams, like images. There is room
> for larger canvases to be displayed, there are storing places
> for our weaker efforts; hold
>
> to warm clothing, to surreptitious nips of spirits
> hidden behind the instruments of art. It is all, ultimately,
> a series of bleak self-portraits, of measured out
> reasons for living. Sketches
>
> of heaven and hell. Self-portrait with computer;
> self-portrait, nude, with blanching flesh; self
> as Lazarus mid-summons, as Job, mid-scream.
> There is outward
>
> dignity, white shirt, black tie, a black hat
> held before the crotch; within, the turmoil, and advanced
> decay. Each work achieved and signed announcing itself
> the last. The barn door slammed shut.

The spaces of the artist's grief are creative 'in larger canvases to be displayed' and even in the 'series of bleak self-portraits' and 'outward dignity' until 'The barn door slammed shut'. The making and unmaking of love and beloved, of would-be priest and artist are depicted through the poem with 'patience in pain / mirroring creation's order'. But not all in vain:

> everything depends on where your eyes
> focus; when
>
> darkness comes, drawing its black
> drapes across the window, there will remain
> the stillness of paint, words on the page, the laid down
> instruments of your art.

'The Old Yellow House' as title for group of poems and for individual seems an obvious reference to Vincent van Gogh's 'Yellow House at Arles' which he hoped to turn into a community centre for artists. His previous religious and social engagement may have played some role in the ambition and elicited Deane's sympathies much later. Van Gogh and Paul Gauguin lived there together for six months amid increasing argument. After Gauguin left it ceased to operate as a centre while Van Gogh and house deteriorated. At this stage he cut off his left ear and presented it to a prostitute. Mental instability increased but in the institution which cared for him he continued to do some of his best work. In the group as well as in the title poem there are some faint echoes of Van Gogh but most of these arresting poems seem more redolent of Achill than of Arles.

More echoes of Van Gogh in Provence, his painting and his suffering, recur in the final sixth section, 'Seasons in Hell', with the Redemption coming through implicitly and explicitly in the moving poem with that title. This section, focused on Holy Saturday and the Christ-like artist, reaches back to section II, entitled simply 'The Artist'. This consists of fourteen sonnets meditating on the traditional Stations of the Cross in different church settings from Bunnacurry, Achill through Canterbury, Toledo and back to Bunnacurry. Here we are at the heart of Deane's artistic and religious faith: Christ as artist and his instruments of redemptive art.

For Deane, despite the suffering and death, creation in nature remains a prominent, beautiful and even miraculous theme. In its Hopkins-like precision, 'The Gift' offers a splendid example and is worth quoting in full:

> And did you catch it then? That offered flash
> of brilliance across the gloom? There by a curve
> of the river, by the salleys and ash-trees, a brash
> iridescence of emerald and blue –
> kingfisher! Skulking you were, and sulking, astray
> from sacrament and host, with your dreary
> dwelling on the ego. Pathetic. Pray
> grace in that sacred presentation, the high
> shock of what is beautiful leading you to betray
> this self-infusion for a while. And then that cry –
> its piping chee-chee-chee, secretive by the stream's drift
> and you step closer, cautiously, grace being still
> easily squandered, till you have it before you: the gift!
> Loveliness, and a dagger-like poised bill.

Jerome Kiely's 'Swallows in December' is divided into five sections, including People; Creatures; Places; Living and Partly Living; Stories. I list these at the beginning because it is impossible to do justice to the rich variety of his poetry in its joys and sorrows, in its celebrations of people and nature, in its grieving at the blindness and selfishness of his fellows, priests and laity.

The People whom Kiely remembers, enjoys and weeps for are the characters, unusual and marginal, who brought so much humanity to those with eyes to see, ears to hear and hands to touch. Jimmy 'The Funeral Man', who 'walks in front of every hearse/from church to burial place.' The lives and deaths of the whole village are led by 'Our sole egalitarian', who 'does equal honour /to the iridescent casket/moulded in a bank vault/… and to the white deal coffin easy gnaw for maggots/foetus from a tree/at the back of a council house.' In this and in other 'People' poems Kiely beautifully and movingly captures the generosity and pettiness of Irish life and death, rural and urban. The poem 'Why?' carries forward the death theme as it begins:

> We found him hanging stiffly
> like the pendulum
> of a stopped clock.
> The mechanism of habit
> had finally run down.

Only in 'The Cyclist (1936)' when the waiting poet–child is scooped up by his father on the father's return from a cycle do we find much of the spaces between the people's griefs:

> Reunion was another name
> for the crossbar where he lifted me;
> and in the cuddled circle
> of arms and handlebars
> I gauged the heat of scorching tyres
> as we freewheeled to the town a mile away …

Another joyous poem in this section is 'Beachcomber', a man with a metal detector in search of lost treasures on the beach, who 'bows profoundly/when a miracle occurs, and thereupon/the monkey on his back chortles'. The saddest for poet and priest–reader may be 'Brother Priests'. Only quotation can do it justice:

> They stood together on multiples of tees
> from where their eyes got bunkered on a hill
> and fairwayed down a lake.

They preached from one another's lecterns
to put their hobby horses out to grass
for one week of the clichéd year ...

They were like brothers till the gospel put
A fratricidal weapon in their hearts.
'I was in prison but you never came
to see me'; were Christ's killing words,
and when one of their own was locked away
they let him quote them, and they never went.

'Creatures' is the most joyful and musical section of Kiely's collection. 'Caterpillar' may not be his most favourite insect or mine, yet it is worth quoting his elegant correction of Richard South on the 'ELEPHANT HAWKMOTH CATERPILLAR ... in repose/giving the creature/a very wicked look':

I beg to differ, Richard.
Not wicked.
Baleful, rather.
There is a wizard world
of difference.

'Ladybird', 'Messages for Gatherers of Leaves', 'A Lucky Robin Gives an Interview' and many others combine the close observation, the imagery and music with a puckish humour and deeply religious sense.

'Places' develops the poet's sense of people and creatures in terms of beloved places with 'Garland Sunday' as typical of the poet's ability to combine past and present, Christian and pre-Christian as the first stanza indicates:

The wells are where the ancient gods –
once openly and nationally ours,
long hidden in their fear of croziers –
show their heads,
and once a year we bring them wreaths of flowers.

The section 'Living and Partly Living' is the climax of the book in its celebratory opening nature poems and in its heart-rending later prison poems. 'Route to the Butterflies', among the earlier poems, is a nature and religious poem, and provides a stunning narrative, summarised beautifully in the final stanza:

Now I've told you where the butterflies are,
so go to Donovan's Castle by car
and walk grasseasy up the middle of the road
and you'll come to the shimmering mind of God.

The heartrending comes quickly after that. Heralded in the touching 'Loneliness', it enters the reader's soul in 'First Cell':

Shrapnel of newspaper nudes
bursting from explosive walls
Two saucepans without handles
for pissing in the swollen night.
Refuse squatting
in the only corner not claimed by huddled clothes.

And in 'Prisoner':

Never before have I walked
under a geometric sky.
I watch the others scurry round the yard
impotent as mice
in an empty biscuit tin.

The humiliations mount from having his watch removed, his letters opened, even his shamrock destroyed. The fantasy in 'Deus ex Machina' of being rescued by a helicoptered God brings unexpected presence and peace:

… He has stepped
out of the harness straps
and come to my astonished cell
where we will share a single fetter
which is, Paul the apostle says, far better.

The last bitter offering of vinegar comes with the episcopal permission to say Mass, 'but never again in a church'. 'The Leper Mass' is the closest we get to Calvary in this wonderful and heartbreaking book. You must read it for yourselves.

In Deane and Kiely in their very different life experiences and poetic gifts we have holy scriptures for our age. May they be read, meditated on and prayed over by all who would wish to get beyond the tabloidery of our current media and their clichéd critics.

Ethical Globalisation and Globalising Ethics

Introduction

In these reflections I would like to notice the distinction between the terms 'globalising' and 'globalisation' to grasp the challenges in moving towards the vision of a more ethical world. *Globalisation* suggests a completed condition, a fixed vision of the world, the 'end of history' as Francis Fukuyama famously stated following the collapse of the socialist regimes. *Globalising*, on the other hand, with its suggestions of a continuing, variable and contested process, is one with space to shape a future yet unknown. For the sake of consistency and convenience globalisation will be retained as the usual term for the empirical reality although it is important to remember that it is as yet unfinished and so subject to human shaping and influence.

This globalisation proceeds in many distinct spheres of life such as the economic, the cultural and the political, but its nature and pace as well as resistance to it vary enormously. What is clear is that in all the critical spheres of human living, planet-wide interactions and influences are at work. In this basic sense, globalisation, however far it may be criticised, resisted and indeed shaped by such critiques and resistance, affects all, everywhere and always. This does not mean that a particular kind of globalising is inevitable even in the economic area in which it is most advanced and most criticised/resisted at present. Neither does globalisation necessarily mean the disappearance of the local and particular into some universal homogenised economic, cultural and even political system. To ensure that simply negative globalisation does not occur, criticism and resistance will always be necessary, just as local cooperation and creativity can contribute to a type of globalisation that endorses and enriches the local and particular instead of erasing it. Resistance and cooperation, critique and creativity expose the choices which have to be made if the globalising process is to be a truly humanising process. In so doing they expose the ethical dimensions of the debate.

Ethical Globalisation and Globalising Ethics

In recent discussions on ethics and globalisation two distinct approaches are discernible – ethical globalisation and globalising ethics. The more theoretical or intellectual of these approaches, *globalising ethics*, emphasizes the need for a globally shared ethics in which the foundations or principles of ethical decision making are shared as a prerequisite for shared decisions on global issues and practices. Such a shared global ethic may be the best, indeed the only way to ensure agreed and correct ethical decisions on the multiple complex problems arising from the current phenomenon of globalisation. Critics of this approach fear it may never be feasible to construct or discover such a set of shared ethical principles in face of the actual ethical diversity of the world or that it could be achieved only by the suppression of such diversity in favour of some single imperial model, in present circumstances, of western provenance. And of course many others have not the interest, the energy or the time for such debates. They prefer to adopt the second approach, *ethical globalisation*, looking to the practices underpinning globalisation as they or their constituents experience them and seeing how far these practices are 'good' for themselves and those they profess to represent.

Of course, what is good for any particular group may not be immediately evident to that group and so need further ethical discussion. In such matters intellectual debate can never be entirely avoided. Under this second approach the debate will first and foremost centre on the debaters' own principles as they seek to evaluate morally the particular effects of globalisation on themselves. The tension between these two approaches, ethical globalisation and globalising ethics, is not necessarily destructive, and their interaction is as inevitable as the spread of globalisation.

1.   Ethical Globalising

Economics and ethical globalisation

Globalisation is frequently defined or at least described in terms of the free movement of capital, goods and services across international borders accelerated by the rapid and continuing advances in the technologies of production, transport and communication. In the dominant politico-economic system in which we live this does not involve a similarly free movement of people. Yet for all the technologies and their virtual worlds of cyberspace, even economic globalisation begins and ends with people. At each stage of the production–consumption process, as at each stage of the most sophisticated technology, there is a human hand and a human face. Those human hands and faces demand treatment as human. They deserve a morality that respects their human dignity.

Of course, these may not be the exact words and concepts used in different cultural contexts but treating humans as humans, however differently envisaged in practical terms, remains a recurring aspiration, ideal and demand. In employment, the treatment of human beings as slaves or like animals or machines may be disguised as culturally acceptable or argued to be an economic necessity, but in today's world it almost inevitably raises moral questions for employer as well as employee. For powerful transnational corporations, whose headquarters are almost invariably located in developed industrialised nations, with their liberal and, at another remove, Christian background, the economic exploitation of employees and consumers, however disguised, must be judged ethically by the legal standards on the rights of the person, developed largely in the corporations' home countries. These are the standards such corporations claim to espouse. Such standards should especially be applied to the behaviour of industrialised country corporations in regard to their operations in developing countries where many workers, producers and consumers are often powerless in face of northern economic, political and military dominance.

The basic requirement of ethical globalisation is respect for all people, especially the weaker, and as so many analysts now insist not just free trade but fair trade. Criticisms of agreements reached by the World Trade Organisation (WTO) or other international bodies are justified in so far as they favour the strong as opposed to the weak. Thus, limited responses to campaigns on debt cancellation for the world's poorest countries, restrictions on imports from the developing world, imposition of destructive structural adjustment programmes and exploitative intellectual and plant patenting, all demonstrate how far the economic and political forces of the developed countries are violating their own ethical ideals.

Neither do developing countries lack their own moral or ethical compass or act merely as passive participants in the relationships underpinning globalisation. Some persistently and destructively violate their own moral standards at the expense of their own peoples. Many have a political and wealthy elite who exploit their people with corrupt and violent practices, at times in collusion with the political and economic powers of the North. The corruption allegations frequently brandished by the North as signs of political and economic weakness in the South too often originate in the North's search for profitable markets or cheap labour and commodities. Some of the commodities heavily and corruptly promoted are directly destructive, such as weapons, while some are more subtly so, such as baby milk powder or drugs no longer safe enough for consumers in the North. Yet those living in developed economies can also be exploited by their own, as jobs are suddenly transferred to cheaper labour centres overseas or social compacts to invest in health care or pensions are rolled back.

Ethical Globalisation and International Law

Ethical globalisation in the economic sphere depends on respect for others and their needs, on just rather than exploitative interactions between parties of such unequal resources and power and on fair rather than simply free trade. This could not be assured on the basis of economic activity alone with its over-riding concern with profit maximization. Economics, in its globalising mode, is even more in need of ethical standards or benchmarks and political regulation. Such standards and regulation are needed at both national and international levels with due regard for the valuable and valid traditions in the different countries.

An other, just world may seem an ambitious slogan, at present more attractive to the participants of the World Social Forum which met in Porto Alegre, Brazil, in 2005 than to the participants of the World Economic Forum which met at Davos. The Porto Alegre participants and their associates around the world may have no single vision of this other, just world or of how to achieve it, but they do have a strong moral sense of the primacy of politics in relation to economics and the primacy of local decision making and local democracy over grand centralised decision making at so many removes from the people most affected by these decisions.

Human Rights

Major instruments aimed at protecting and promoting the dignity of the human person have derived from the 1948 United Nations Declaration of Human Rights. The covenants, conventions and laws which developed over the intervening decades and the more recent United Nations Commission for Human Rights as well as flourishing national and international non-governmental organisations (NGOs) which advocate and protect such rights, have had an enormous impact in promoting a more ethical national and international political order. Their impact on economic globalisation is also real but limited as policy rhetoric lags behind policy practice. In part, this is due to the fact that the social and economic rights listed in the Universal Declaration are not all taken seriously, despite the enormous efforts by Mary Robinson in her time as UN High Commissioner for Human Rights and others. Western individualism, at once a source and consequence of western economic systems which greatly influenced the formulation of the UN Declaration and now influences its interpretation, has tended to give secondary consideration to socio-economic rights. In contrast, many developing countries, especially in Asia, have prioritised such rights with scant attention to civil and political rights.

This dichotomy, imperfect though it has been, has been weakened with the end of the Cold War and the agreement of conventions that award more balanced weight to all rights, such as the UN Convention on the Rights of the

Child. Unfortunately, the United States is one of the very few countries not to have ratified this convention. Rather than the concept and practice of human rights being somehow alien within different cultures, it can be enriched by reference to various traditions. Indeed, Mary Robinson saw the scope for this when she invited scholars from Muslim and other religions and cultures to investigate both connections and critiques between western formulations of human rights and other moral and legal traditions.

Ethical Globalisation from below

Approaching the subject of ethical globalisation requires multiple conversations within and between the different partners and their particular spheres of activity. Both Northern and Southern partners, to use a simplified polarity, should each recognise and accept the other as equal partner in the conversation, a dynamic conversation that involves mutual enrichment through a continuing process of conversion on both sides to the demands of their actual situation in both its power and its privations. A complement to this process of conversation is the need for peaceful resistance to the impositions of the unhearing or unheeding and for creative alternatives to unacceptable and destructive initiatives. In such diverse ways, unethical patterns of globalisation must be ethically reshaped.

Much of this reshaping will come from pressure from the powerless as they experience the pain of the process adopted by the powerful to serve their own interests. This globalisation from below must go beyond the resistance generated by pain to the imaginative and humane alternatives which their creativity can devise. The captivity of the economically and politically powerful to their own structures of profit and convenience will only finally be overcome by the resistance and creativity of the weak. Globalisation from below can provide a type of ethical and liberating globalisation for all.

Tackling Discrimination on a Global Scale

In tackling inequalities in power, it is important to recognise that such power is mediated by racial, class, gender and other factors. In these discriminations there is usually more at stake than economic privation, although that is almost always part of them. Ethical globalisation which is really from below must attend to the most deprived and excluded in different societies. Culture and tradition may play a large negative role in these discriminations, in the refusal to accept certain groups or individuals as proper persons. In fighting such prejudice and oppression their cultural dynamics need to be understood but they also need to be challenged and fought as far as possible from within each particular cultural and political system.

HIV and AIDS

A very destructive kind of globalising is at work in the spread of HIV/AIDS. This global pandemic, with its most extensive and intensive hold on some of the poorest countries of the world in Sub-Saharan Africa, is a striking instance of how the local so rapidly becomes the global and how an analysis of a very particular local phenomenon such as an AIDS-afflicted village in Tanzania, reveals all the interwoven negative realities as well as the positive potential of a globalising world. The global reach of HIV/AIDS from its first identification in California in 1981 reflects the intimate interconnections of our shrinking world. It also emphasizes the vulnerability of the poor and deprived to something as apparently neutral as this virus. HIV and AIDS are now dominantly diseases of the poor and oppressed.

A closer examination of our mythical Tanzanian village would expose the fault lines which connect it to its local district, region, country and the wider world, the economic and political relationships which leave its inhabitants deprived of health care, education and employment if not also such basics as clean water, food and shelter. The global relations impinging on this village are at best ambiguous and destructive. While local resilience can often harness the meagre local and national resources available, often with the help of NGOs and faith-based groups, to provide palliative care for people living with AIDS there is little left for those still uninfected, but deeply affected and socially vulnerable in so many other ways. In any consideration of ethical globalisation, the equitable global sharing of preventive and therapeutic measures in relation to this pandemic, and to other endemic diseases of the poor such as malaria and tuberculosis, must be high on the agenda.

War and Peace

The globalisation phenomenon applies to that age-old vehicle of human destruction – war – and its younger sibling, international terrorism, if indeed these can be so easily distinguished in age and character. While there are many civil wars, almost all of them have international consequences and many have at least partial roots in international politics, trade and military security. Indeed the arms industry, so significant in the economic life of the major powers, could not survive and thrive as it does without the continuing threat and the recurring outbreak of military hostilities. As part of the global justice and peace agenda so urgently needed and so eminently possible, a much stronger commitment to the abolition of war as a means of resolving political and economic disputes is required, particularly from the major political, economic and military powers.

A global movement involving all churches and religions and other civil society actors as well as governments and international agencies could achieve that abolition over the next decades. Like the struggle for the abolition of slavery, such a movement will not yield immediate results. Indeed, if war were outlawed internationally it is, again parallel to the case of slavery, likely to continue in some disguised forms. However, it will no longer be permissible to speak of just war or for reputable political leaders to have recourse to arms to promote their own or their country's interests. Lest this seem utterly utopian one should remember how the United States and Canada have been free of internal war for a century and a half, how the endemic warfare in western Europe has been abolished for over half a century, how the tyrannical rule of the Soviet Union collapsed without a shot being fired and how peaceful negotiation overcame the cruel apartheid regime in South Africa despite expectations of a bloodbath.

Of course, any commitment to the abolition of war as an instrument of conflict resolution will have to be accompanied by effective alternatives. These will include the promotion of international law, courts and security measures as well as the creation of imaginative and globally acceptable methods of resolving the most entrenched disputes from Israel and Palestine to Kashmir to the Democratic Republic of Congo to Colombia, to pick an arbitrary list. But the search for global peace must always include and be built upon the search for global justice. Despite and because of the present global injustices and widespread military conflict it is possible to imagine a just and peaceful world. Such an imagined world can become a reality through effective ethical globalising.

Technology
A critical feature of contemporary globalisation is rapid technological advance. An ethical evaluation of the development and commercial control of this technology is therefore a critical element when considering the ethics underpinning globalisation. For many of those engaged in the development and marketing of such technologies no particular moral issue seems to arise. If a particular technology can be produced and if it can be marketed profitably then it will be produced whatever the real need for it. Thus, the technological imperative is closely allied to the profit imperative. Perhaps legal restrictions on technological research and development, except in very unusual circumstances such as human cloning, are undesirable and impractical. Yet without legal restrictions ethical restrictions may appear futile. Of course, it is sometimes ethical considerations that influence consumer, producer and in some rare cases legislative responses to technological innovations, for instance in relation to biopatenting and food security.

A rather different ethical problem is posed by the need to ensure access to those technologies suitable to poorer countries such as agriculture, health care and education. Without the economic or political power of the advanced industrial nations these countries sometimes depend on the moral support of consumers, producers and politicians across the world to attract the interest and investment to prioritise their particular technological needs. In a globalising world such support based on ethical values is possible but it must face and face down the vested interests of the economic powers and their political supporters and clients. Once again the argument must be made for the priority of people over profits and the priority of ethics over economics.

2.   Globalising Ethics
The Need for Conversation
In the preceding discussion it was impossible to discuss any particular problem solely in terms of local ethical evaluation from the ethical–cultural standpoint of either consumer or producer, of the economic powers in the West and North or of their weaker correlatives in the South. Both standpoints were continually interacting and the call for conversation between them remains a permanent necessity. Yet in such an intensely globalising world there is also a need to consider the possibility of globalising ethics. Much of the reflection and writing on these issues has given priority to this approach. In practice the promotion of international human rights standards and law has assumed that such a global ethics already exists, although some leaders in the field have been sensitive to the ethical and cultural differences in which respect for persons and peoples should be understood and developed. The need for conversation continues at this level also, that of seeking some shared ethical values which could sustain a set of global ethical practices in an increasingly interdependent world.

This conversation itself will be relational with its own internal and ethical dynamic. No single partner to the conversation may dictate its terms or conclusion. Yet the different partners must try to outline a position which each believes comprehends enough of the others' positions to continue fruitful dialogue as well as practical and ethical cooperation. What follows is an attempt to provide such an outline in the hope of encouraging fuller dialogue and cooperation. Inevitably it will reveal the dominantly western and christian perspectives of the author.

Principles, values, norms and rules involve diverse ways of approaching ethical issues in the western tradition. They constitute different, if at times only slightly different languages of morals. Any one language might be used in the global conversation on ethics proposed here. The choice of value-language as the primary one does not preclude recourse to the others and has both advantages and disadvantages. A further specification of the interactive and relational character to the globalising phenomenon and any ethical conversation suggest that globalising ethics should concentrate on the ethical values inherent in the human relating between persons and peoples in all their different spheres from politics and economics to culture and religion.

Truth and the Recognition of Difference

A first requirement of any conversation is the recognition of difference, of the other person and people as other. The value of truth and truthfulness emerges in the persistent call to recognition and acceptance of difference or otherness in all human relating and interacting. The western tones of such language require deeper dialogue but the value of truth for the western partner contains a self-critical corrective which challenges that partner patiently but persistently to move beyond her current understanding to the fuller truth of the other and of the other's self-understanding. The search for truth and mutual understanding will never be complete. Such an ethical stance permits the kind of dialogue and cooperation which a sustainable global ethic implies whatever ethical language and tradition may be its starting point.

The Global Value of Freedom

Attending in truth to the reality of the other, even if that can only be partially achieved, involves letting the other be other. It involves respecting the freedom of the other just as the other is called to recognise the truth and freedom of the self. Personal freedom, the capacity and space to make one's own decisions and one's own life within the limits of equal respect for the freedom of others, may be a primary value in a strongly individualist sense for many in the western tradition. In other traditions the freedom of the individual may be more readily subordinated to the identity and good of the community. Yet personal freedom is emerging strongly as a desirable good in societies of these other traditions. They may be able to avoid the fragmenting individualism of the West which permits the more powerful to restrict and exploit the weak too easily. It is self-contradictory to speak of personal freedom for those excluded from effective participation in society by reasons of poverty, race, religion, gender or other discrimination.

Globalising, Ethics and Religion

The focus of this chapter being Christian perspectives on development, with such a strong ethical element integral to Christianity, and where the interaction of religions is a notable feature of globalising, dialogue between religions is as essential as between various ethical and cultural traditions. Indeed it is difficult to separate these three dialogues between the different religious, ethical and cultural traditions. From the Christian standpoint, sufficient encouragement and guidelines are available for such dialogue stemming from Vatican II's document on interfaith dialogue through the statements and action of popes, bishops theologians and of engaged priests and laity.

Pope John Paul II's prayer meetings for peace at Assisi, replicated on its own scale by Cardinal Connell in Dublin, were powerful symbols of the ethical role of religion in a globalising world. In an early study of the need for a global ethic, theologian Hans Kung declared there could be no peace between nations without peace between religions. Many other religious and civil leaders echoed this in a book which Kung later edited. In the past the great peacemaking potential and obligation of the major religions have too often been perverted; unfortunately, such perversion still persists. If we are to take seriously the ambitious call 'War – never again' by Paul VI and John Paul II, the Catholic Church certainly, its leaders, agencies and members, must commit themselves anew to the flourishing together in communion of the whole human race, to the tasks of ethical globalising and of globalising ethics.

Contemplating the Global Mystery

In Christian perspective, analysis, evaluation and their summons to development derive their origins and nourishment from contemplation. Meditation on the central events and truths of the Hebrew and Christian traditions can provide individual insights, motivation and indeed the outlines of an overall structure for the global enterprises of human development and planetary protection. In the globalising context attention might be drawn to two significant, recent works of Jewish and Christian provenance. In his book *The Dignity of Difference* (2002), Chief Rabbi Jonathan Sacks draws on the Hebrew Bible and tradition in this contemplative way in his extended analysis and evaluation of a world in the process of globalisation. While Pope John Paul's 2000 Apostolic Letter, *Novo millennio Ineunte* (At the Beginning of the New Millennium), offers a contemplative vision of Christ, church and world, calling for the dynamic transformation of the relationships and structures essential to a truly unified family of God enjoying together the gifts of divine creation.

In both Hebrew and Christian traditions, creation is the gift of the one Creator–God in whose likeness and image humans are created. By invitation and command of the Creator they are both the guests and the stewards of creation. On a shrinking planet the caring and sharing behaviour of the rapidly increasing number of guests and stewards towards the planet and each other takes on a fresh urgency. That caring and sharing is rooted in and nourished by a sense of dignity of every creature, with the dignity of the human creature as self-conscious, free and responsible and given by the Creator the moral privilege of ensuring respect for the dignity of difference among themselves, their cultures traditions and religions in their search for global unity in peace with justice.

The rest of creation with its rich differences in a unity which is also in process merits from the human stewards its own respect and care. While endorsing such contemplative insights and their practical implications developed in the Hebrew tradition by the Creator's First People, Christians turn to Jesus Christ and the tradition and people that he inaugurated for further contemplation, insight and guidance. Pope John Paul II stressed that further dimension of the whole human family whereby we are sisters and brothers of one another in Christ and so children of the one God. In the promotion of that final goal which Jesus announced as the coming of the reign of God, the community of disciples of Christ, the church, is to play both a symbolic and an active role. It is as sacrament of the unity of the whole human race, created, loved and redeemed by God through his son, Jesus Christ, that the church fulfils its symbolic role. That role will however only be credible, worthy of the Creator-Redeemer God, if it is implemented in practical love for all, particularly the poor and oppressed, the stranger and the enemy.

The God who is love must be embodied in deeds of love, personally and socially. The clash of civilizations to which Rabbi Sachs also refers a number of times can only be avoided by cherishing difference in the loving manner of the Creator of difference. The symbolic and active roles are more fully illustrated by the relationship of the particular and local churches/Christian communities to one another and to the universal church. The diversity in unity to which a globalising world aspires may be illustrated in an authentic, loving communion of distinctive, vibrant and ecumenical local churches.

As the contemplation deepens for Christians they discover that love is no abstract name for God. Neither is it just a characteristic of God's creative, redemptive and transformative action in the world, overwhelming as that idea is. The personal god of earlier traditions emerges for Christians as a tripersonal God. The Trinity in its unity and diversity, in its divine relationships of utter loving, becomes the template and driving force for a world created in that image and with that destiny of loving unity in diversity. At its deepest level a truly globalising world should carry the thrust of trinitarian, creative love.

The Reign of God

Signposts for Catholic Moral Theology

Faith in a creator–redeemer God, a God of love and power, may be more readily threatened in the face of human or natural disaster. The Lisbon earthquake in the seventeenth century became a classic occasion for a renewal of the old-Job debate about evil and the existence of a Christian-style God. The twentieth century has provided more than its share of such catastrophes, natural and human, raising the same basic questions. Doing theology after Auschwitz proved too much for certain Jewish and Christian thinkers. Recurring genocide and ethnic cleansing combined with devastating famines, floods, earthquakes, and nuclear disasters continue to trouble believers to the point where they may feel like a Samuel Beckett character, that God's only justification in the face of such evil is that 'the bastard doesn't exist.' In that tradition the theological impact of the pandemic of HIV/AIDS is first of all to reopen or, better, to reinforce the questioning of the very existence and certainly the nature of the God of the Christian faith. It is a questioning that is always valuable to the health of theology and of faith. Even if it does not elicit any new light on the issue, it keeps theologians and believers from complacent security, alert to the risk and vulnerability of believing.

One of the early reactions within the Christian community was to regard HIV/AIDS as divine punishment for human sinfulness, particularly sexual sinfulness and more particularly homosexual sinfulness. The widespread dismissal of this response by pastors, theologians, and other Christians did not entirely remove either the suspicion of guilt attached to many living with the virus or the social stigma incurred, sometimes with violent consequences. Deeper understanding of God's ways and more effective love of neighbour are required to overcome the prejudice and neglect which too many people with the virus still have to endure.

Apart from its precedents in the Hebrew scriptures such as the story of Sodom and Gomorrah with their New Testament echoes, the interpretation of AIDS and other human disasters as divine punishment has at least the merit of taking God's involvement in the world seriously. And this is a God who takes the world seriously. Attempts to distance God from the evil in the world to protect God's goodness and omnipotence can easily result in distancing God from the world entirely. The whirlwind God

116

of Job insisted on God's involvement in the most intricate aspects of world-making. If the divine response did not explain in human terms the mystery of human suffering, it both rejected the conventional view that it was a matter of divine punishment and refused to distance God from the reality of the world and its suffering. With Jesus' ministry and teaching, suffering and death begins a new phase of divine involvement and of human understanding.

The disciples' question about the blind man in chapter 9 of John's Gospel, 'Who sinned, this man or his parents?' is rendered superfluous in the new manifestation of God's glory, the healing mission of Jesus and his solidarity in suffering with the least ones. Only when Jesus is lifted up on the cross will he finally be glorified, will the glory of God be fully manifest. The paradox of Job is transcended in deeper paradox as the power and commitment to heal of the creator–saviour (healing) God is realised in undergoing human suffering and death. God's involvement with the evil in this world, God's promise and power to overcome it are revealed by solidarity with humanity in suffering that evil. So shall the kingdom or reign of God be achieved which Jesus announced at the beginning of his mission and ministry.

The Reign of God: Christian Symbol and Moral Imperative

In this history of Christian thought and practice, the kingdom, or as it is now more usually termed, the reign, of God has followed an erratic course. Even in the New Testament, the frequent usage of this term by Jesus in the synoptics contrasts sharply with its sparing use in John and Paul. The debates still continue both about how far in its synoptic usage it refers to the present (already, among you) or to the future, a future that is imminently and mistakenly expected or simply unknown, and about its invisibly, internal and eternal character (not of this world) as opposed to its visible and historical realisation. These debates and others such as the one about how far it is uniquely the work of God and how far it involves human cooperation are clearly relevant to any discussion of Christian morality or moral theology. The description of the reign of God as Christian symbol is not intended to short-circuit the debates, still less to remove the reality of Jesus' announcement from the contested terrain of contemporary history. To do so would be to make it irrelevant to the crisis provoked by HIV/AIDS and to the whole enterprise of moral theology.

In its origin, symbol (*symballein*) signals a drawing together of diverse, even conflicting ideas or realities. In the Christian tradition it declares and realises some compound of the divine and the human. The sacraments are primary instances. Creeds like the Nicene or individuals doctrines like the incarnation could in this traditional usage also be described as symbols. The reign of God as Christian symbol calls attention to the complex nature of the presence, power and activity of creator in creation, of God in human and cosmic history. The presence, power and activity of God in creating and sustaining, healing, transforming and fulfiling humanity and creation combines much of the elusive material suggested by references to the reign of God in both Old and New Testaments, while leaving the manner and timing of the divine presence and activity open to more precise determination. The more precise determination manifests in Jesus by divine solidarity with the suffering and excluded reinforces the description of divine reign as distant realities, the all-powerful creator and the most powerless of creatures, not in some simple alliance or even mercy mission but in genuine solidarity, in com-passion, in suffering with.

The key, then, to interpreting the saving and moral significance of the reign of God is the climatic presence of God with the poor and deprived Jesus Christ. The call of the poor and oppressed is the call which God hears and responds to in such radical personal terms.

It is the call to which those who follow Jesus must also listen and respond. For disciples the moral imperative of God's reign focuses first of all on the least ones, on those oppressed or ignored by the mighty in their seats of power and privilege, even episcopal or clerical. In this vision the moral thrust is toward recognising and seeking to overcome unjust structures and relationships in solidarity with those suffering such injustices. In this analysis, justice would seem to be the primary Christian virtue and not charity.

The justice-seeking of Jesus Christ, exemplary and efficacious as it is, was a supreme instance of the primacy of the charity he preached. 'Greater love has no one than that somebody lays down his life for his friends.' 'Out of love in search of justice' might be a useful summary of many saints and heroes inspired by the teaching and example of Jesus. Political heroes of our own time, from Gandhi and Bonhoeffer to Martin Luther King and Nelson Mandela, plus thousands of the unknown and unsung, have followed this Christian pattern, out of love in search of justice for the oppressed even to laying down of one's life. The anger and indignation of Jesus' prophetic predecessors in Israel at the injustices of the powerful and wealthy against the powerless and poor had its roots in love also and was frequently voiced at serious risk to the prophet's own life or well-being. Attacking and even slaying the prophet would be the Hebrew equivalent of attacking and even killing the messenger.

The Reign of God and the Shape of Catholic Moral Theology

The moral imperative of the reign of God requires some systematic expression. This might be developed in a variety of ways. In the manualist tradition of moral theology, the reign of God did not figure. The law of God as formulated in the Ten Commandments or as interpreted in natural law was the dominant model. The return of moral theologians to Scripture in the fifties and sixties offered some theological modifications, although most revisions retained the underlying law model, particularly some version of natural law. Only one serious attempt was made to use the reign of God as starting point and leitmotif by a moral theologian, Johannes Stelzenberger. (See his *Lehrbuch der Moraltheologie, Die Sittlichkeitslehre der Koenigsherrschaft Gottes,* Paderborn: F. Schoningh, 1953.)

This essay proposes one possible framework for moral theology based on analysis of some aspects of the reign of God as announced and inaugurated by Jesus and attempts to incorporate some of the excellent insights of natural law and biblical morality. For Christians, the God who reigns, would reign and will reign is first of all the creator God of Genesis, Isaiah, the psalms, Job, the synoptics and Paul, to take some quick biblical soundings. A moral theology which takes creation seriously is capable of integrating 'natural law' insights derived from an investigation of (created) human nature (in person and community) by (created) human reason (personal and communal). The historical and dynamic dimensions of human existence and natural law find a place in the reign of God's moral structure along with its personal, social and ecological dimensions. Creation includes cosmos and (human) community. The creator God is also the (Mosaic) covenant God of the dialogue. Creation itself is the original covenant. Later covenants from Noah, Abraham and Moses through the promised New Covenant of the prophets to be realised for Christians in Jesus offer critical biblical data on the continuities and discontinuities in the reign of God and in the human responses to it. Recurrent crises in divine–human relations, frequently manifested in the breakdown of human–human relations, prompted fresh initiatives from God and fresh covenants. God's growing involvement in human and cosmic history was directed to the sustaining, healing and transforming of humanity and cosmos, to the development of the divine reign.

What is of immediate significance for understanding the moral imperative of the reign of God is the divine strategy pursued in the progress from creation (covenant) through crisis (in human response) to *kairos* as the opportune time perceived by God for a new loving initiative. This strategy is far removed from the imperialism often attributed to God and more often appropriated by God's called or 'chosen' people. The anti-imperial character of God's reign only becomes fully clear in Jesus, the culmination of humanity's crisis and of God's involvement. 'Last of all he sent his son, saying they will reverence my son.' The recurring human crises and the continuing divine responses in loving surrender to human need have reached their climax as the divine Son emptied himself, taking the form of a servant and entering the human condition even to the point of suffering and death (Phil 2).

This self-emptying (*kenosis*) of which Paul speaks so eloquently was no masochistic search for suffering, but the fateful consequence of unconditional loving. Through this moral surrender of God in love of humankind, death itself was overcome as if creation, history and the tomb could no longer contain the 'dead' God. The bonds of history were broken and a new covenant and a new community were established. In that other piercing phrase of Paul in 2 Corinthians 5, a new creation emerged. The journey from creation (*ktisis*) through crisis (*krisis*) becoming *kairos* and involving a radical divine self-emptying (*kenosis*) reached its destination in the new covenant and new community (*kaine koinonia*), and more comprehensively in the new creation (*kaine ktisis*). In the great K words of (biblical) Greek, the God of *ktisis* confronted *krisis* as *kairos* and engagement of *kenosis* achieved *kaine koinonia* and *kaine ktisis*. These are the real signposts of the reign of God which human beings are called to follow in their imitation of God and in their discipleship of Jesus, the framework for a moral theology of compassion and inclusion, of seeking justice and peace out of love.

The more systematic structure of moral theology can and should take seriously this saving strategy of the divine reign. The more detailed analysis of particular moral cases and the direction of particular decisions will observe the same pattern. Whether story or virtues or law provide the subsidiary structures, the great K-pattern will provide the crucial shape.

Catholic Moral Theology and the HIV/AIDS Pandemic

HIV/AIDS has precipitated a serious crisis for humanity with devastating cosmic and community dimensions. The rapid spread of the virus with its devastating biological consequences as it develops into AIDS has presented one of the most serious public health hazards of the century. Creation as cosmos and as good, the human body as God-given and as good are radically threatened. Creation in its human and loving personal and community dimensions faces a major crisis. The reign of God faces total eclipse by these breakdowns in the illness and death of the many infected by HIV and AIDS, and by the immoral exclusion and neglect which they encounter from the healthy, wealthy and powerful. Compassion or 'suffering with' remains the divine strategy's first imperative. It ought to be followed by the allocation of all the resources available in a movement of justice and inclusion on the model of Jesus' own promotion of the reign of God.

Such a moral response, where the crisis *becomes* kairos, will involve sacrifice by the powerful. It will have to follow the kenotic line of God and of God's Son, the surrender in compassion and loving service of the reign of God. In terms of personal caring this may be very difficult for many family members, partners, friends and neighbours as well as for the professional physicians and paramedics. But is is at least understandable in the love-of-neighbour kenotic terms of the Gospel. The structural demands of justice in the allocation of resources and of inclusion in community are not always so evident. Yet they are the deeper and more far-reaching demands which members of the Christian community must strive to promote themselves and strive to persuade, more by example than word, the broader community to emulate. Crisis as *kairos* demanding *kenosis* at this socio-economic level is more difficult to make manifest and to implement.

In the world of HIV/AIDS the poor, the weak and the excluded are the most vulnerable to infection and the least likely to be attended. In the steps of Jesus, attention to these people above all enables *kairos* to issue in *kaine ktisis* (new creation) and *kaine koinonia* (new community). It is the way to ensuring that the reign of God is emerging among us, however partially. Catholic moral theology must be structured to give precedence to this work of compassion, justice and inclusion, characteristics of the Reign of God.

The Risk of God and the Reign of God

The reign of God as adumbrated in scripture and particularly in Jesus Christ might be rewritten as an account of the risk of God. Creation itself could be seen in this way, including the creation of potential partners for God, created in the divine image, risks that proved failures in many ways, drawing God into further *kenosis* – that is, into greater involvement and heavier risk. Crisis and *kairos* leading to *kenosis* in the incarnation, suffering and death of Jesus showed the growing risks God was prepared to take. The final return in resurrection, new creation and new community is still far from complete.

The disciples of Jesus are called to follow the risk-laden example of Jesus in seeking the sick and the poor, the stigmatised and the excluded. They have to be prepared to be stigmatised and excluded themselves in challenging some of the orthodoxies of their time in serving the deprived. Healing or plucking ears of corn on the Sabbath may be near blasphemy to certain 'orthodox' leaders, but they illustrate the priorities of the reign of God: people before rules, the needs of the sick and the hungry before the concerns of the comfortable and powerful. In the face of HIV/AIDS Christians and Catholics, the Catholic community and Catholic moral theology, must be prepared to take risks with their own rules. The divinely inspired risks of Jesus or of the reign of God might shed new light on such disputable but secondary issues as the use of condoms and the exchange of needles in attempting to prevent or reduce the spread of HIV/AIDS. Such practices are indeed secondary to the practices of compassion, justice and inclusion needed to turn the crisis into *kairos*. They are secondary, too, to the *kenosis* required of all Christians for the new creation and new community of the reign of the God of Jesus Christ.

AMONG FRIENDS

Celebrating the Mystery
of Friendship

Politics and Christology

In Memory of Alexis FitzGerald

In December 1981 when Alexis FitzGerald was at the climax of his political involvement as personal advisor to the Taoiseach, I published an article in *The Furrow* on relationships with Jesus Christ, an exercise in Christology as it is known in the trade. Within a week I had a long thoughtful letter from Alexis about the issue to which he added a typical wry, self-mocking p.s.: 'I am, disgracefully, more interested in the problems of Christology than I am in the grave political and economic problems facing our country.' This essay will examine some possible relationships between his life-long passion of politics and his more recent interest, theology and Christology.

The theme itself is very large with a long and tangled history, stretching from the New Testament to some of the latest statements of John Paul II and other Christian leaders. It has become a matter of intense interest to theologians in the last twenty years, inspired above all by the development in Latin America of Liberation Theology. Titles and works like *Jesus Christ, Liberator* (Leonardo Boff) give something of the flavour of this form of Christology as compared with the more traditional and conventional *Jesus, God and Man – an Essay in Christology* by Wolfhart Pannenberg. This development has been a source of enormous controversy among theologians, within and between the churches, with immediate political spin-off to the left and right. Nicaragua is only one, although a critical example, of how Jesus Christ may be claimed for or against a particular political position, Sandinista or Contra.

This essay could not hope to deal with even the current controversy in Christology in any adequate way. Instead it proposes to pick up some of the great themes of modern politics as they have developed in the West over the last two hundred years, since the American and French Revolutions basically, and to explore their relationships to the person, message and mission of Jesus Christ as recorded in the New Testament and interpreted in the subsequent Christian tradition. It is simply not possible to separate these political developments from the deep-seated influences of Christianity on the western tradition as a whole. And this will be evident in the discussion. In this later period, however, politics began to assume its own autonomy and became sharply distinguished, if not always separate, from religion and church. The emergence of such secular politics, although with quite different relations to religion, particularly in the American and French models and with subsequent qualifications, offered a new challenge to Christian faith and theology which has only been partly met.

To politicians it might appear that the challenge was to church leaders and theologians to recognise and accept politics as secular and autonomous. Many observers believe that this remains a continuing challenge and reproach to Irish church leaders and theologians. These church people in turn may believe that politicians cannot or, at least, do not grapple with the most urgent political problems of our time because they lack the inspiration, guidance and empowerment which the gospel brings. For problems ranging from abortion to nuclear war to mass starvation, poverty and unemployment, many Christians believe that more than the usual political calculus is needed to move beef mountains or to turn the nuclear arsenals into power ploughs. At least there is sufficient dispute and confusion among politicians and theologians to justify a further consideration of some central political themes in relationship to faith in Jesus Christ.

The old slogan of the French Revolution, liberty, equality and fraternity, still provides a convenient summary for much of modern political aspiration and achievement. I invoke it again here as suggesting, in ways to be elaborated, three major political themes. Although liberty, equality and fraternity properly belong together in the tradition of political analysis and practice in which they originated, they have tended to develop separately or at least with different emphasis from their beginnings, whether one dates those at the Glorious Revolution of 1688 or the American or French Revolutions a century later or with the writings of John Locke or his eighteenth-century successors. The end of absolute monarchy and the consequent freedoms of 1688 did not offer much to the Irish Catholic and little enough to the Irish Presbyterian subjects of William and Mary. The years 1776 and 1789 carried their own limitation of race or class or both. Liberty was all but not for all. The critique of 'bourgeois' liberty, most powerfully developed by Karl Marx and his associates, exposed its failure to take equality, above all economic equality, seriously. The ideological and physical struggle to which all this gave rise is still alive and well from Central America to Central Asia to Southern Africa, compounded and sometimes dominated by struggles for national independence. A hasty survey of the globe, whether in its individual regions and countries or in the round, reveals little of fraternity, 'brothers living as one' in the psalmist's words. It would not, however, be too crude an approximation to see liberty as the dominant member of the trio up to the mid-nineteenth century. By then it was joined, sometimes dominated but never replaced, by equality, often expressed in or at least related to another widely used value term: justice. In all that time, despite much hand wringing and pious talk, very little serious attention was given to fraternity. Fratricide in war upon war, international and revolutionary, was readily employed for real or pseudo-liberty and justice. It is only in the second half of the twentieth century that the possibility and necessity of worldwide fraternity or brotherhood with world peace, at least in the sense of peaceful co-existence and negotiated settlement of disputes, has come in for serious consideration. With about 160 wars since World War II involving, sometimes directly and sometimes by surrogacy, the so-called advanced countries in the first and second worlds, with at this moment a major international war between Iran and Iraq in progress for seven years, with continuous war situations of insurrection or invasion in so many places, with the flying fragments of war in terrorist attacks occurring right round the globe, it is difficult to speak of fraternity and its correlate peace as being seriously considered. It still appears very much the Cinderella of that political trio which has so influenced political consciousness and practice over the last two hundred years.

One important political development, the women's movement, has rendered the very concept of fraternity suspect at its root. One really ought to speak of brotherhood and sisterhood despite the inconvenience and the hallowed tradition. The hopes that brotherhood and sisterhood, as expressed in genuine peace, may be getting political recognition equal to that of liberty and equality/justice derive from both negative and positive developments in this century. The obvious negative one is the emergence of nuclear weapons with the potential for mutually assured destruction, indeed for the destruction of the whole planet. Such sentence of death has been concentrating some political minds anyway on alternatives to war. The fragile, frustrated and frustrating United Nations organisation and its associates provide some of the elementary structure for a fraternal world order but achievements are still painfully limited. A world consciousness born of fear of nuclear war, of instant planetary communications and of growing aspirations to a world community, provides some support and encouragement for the politics of disarmament and international peace. Another channel of peace, the vision and practice of Gandhi and of subsequent disciples like Martin Luther King, has possibilities yet to be tried at the local, national and international levels, for achieving or maintaining freedom and justice. These signs, however fragile, should encourage politicians and citizens to seek a more balanced combination of liberty, equality and fraternity/sorority in domestic and foreign affairs. Perhaps the century 1950–2050 will be the century of peace after all.

Followers of Jesus Christ have been engaged, pro and con, in all these developments of what one might call the New Politics over two hundred years. One of the early architects of the American Republic and its constitution, Thomas Jefferson, devoted some of his energies, as President and later, to developing his own Christology. His first attempt, written during his presidency in 1804, was entitled *The Philosophy of Jesus of Nazareth*. About 1820 he completed a longer work, *The Life and Morals of Jesus of Nazareth*.

The American Revolutionaries, like earlier political prophets such as John Locke, were basically sympathetic to Christianity and acceptors of Jesus Christ. Many of their eighteenth- and nineteenth-century counterparts were very antipathetic. Although the enthronement of the Goddess of Reason at Notre Dame may have been a particularly hysterical aberration, Revolution and Catholic Church (the only mediator of Christ in France) were, for the most part, bitter enemies. This infected the rest of Europe (with the notable exception of Ireland) and particularly Italy and Rome in the pontificates of Gregory XVI and Pius IX (1831–1878). Liberty, equality and fraternity, as propounded by most European politicians, sounded very threatening to papal and episcopal ears; very far from the Christological freedom and unity which St Paul had so enthusiastically proclaimed in his letter to the Galatians. Without discounting the many Catholic lay people, philosophers, theologians, priests and bishops who through the nineteenth century sought an understanding in Jesus Christ of the positive values of the revolution or the work carried on by Leo XIII and his successors in developing a much more open and concerned social doctrine for the church, it is possible, by generalising hugely, to say that the liberal revolution (with the priority of political and individual liberty) was only finally and fully accepted at Vatican II. The documents on the Religious Liberty and on the Church in the Modern World form the explicit witness to this.

Although the Council did not concern itself primarily with doctrinal issues (the *Constitution on the Church* is perhaps an exception) and above all, unlike the great councils of the early church, it did not concern itself with Christological issues, its moves in relation to society, world and the religions of the world had implications for our understanding of Jesus Christ, which have not yet been explored. The identification of the community of Jesus' disciples with the joys and hopes, struggles and anguish (*Gaudium et spes, luctus et angor*) of the modern world, reveals an understanding and image of Christ who is not the exclusive possession of Christians but really present in all people and in all human hopes and fears. Jesus Christ belongs to all and shares the needs of all and to this context offers himself to all in freedom for their freedom, liberation and salvation. The freedom of each human being to respond freely to the call of Jesus is a freedom basic to the human condition. Religious freedom to respond or no, to believe and practise religion or no, enters into basic human dignity and requires constitutional political recognition and protection. Only in such a context can the human being answer Jesus' call fully. Only so can Jesus be freely and fully himself for this human being and transform his human freedom into the freedom of the children of God.

In many ways the decade of the sixties was dominated in Catholic and wider Christian terms by freedom, as gift and task but sometimes, unfortunately, as no more than slogan or as licence to do 'your own thing'. A harsher world in Latin America and elsewhere challenged this dominantly West European and North American mood. Vatican II as it came to be applied in Peru, Brazil and the Third World generally encountered more primitive needs with mass poverty, frequently compounded or maintained by mass oppression. For sheer physical survival, economic justice within a country and in relation to the dominant economic powers of the North and West were and still are urgent priorities. Justice/equality and freedom in the most basic senses became not just political priorities but Christian, religious priorities. The church's commitment to the poor and deprived constituted its good news, its gospel of salvation. The ministry of Jesus to the poor and excluded of his own time and place became the model for his contemporary disciples. Christology quickly and radically became a Christology from below, as it is sometimes called, an understanding of Jesus Christ as the suffering servant and yet come to end suffering, setting prisoners free, healing the sick and bringing good news to the poor (Lk 4:16, 21; cf. Is 61:1-2; 58:6). Identification with the poor and deprived, service and liberation of them, these are the saving marks of Jesus which form the Christology of justice and liberation. The whole shape of the Jesus story was invoked in support of this interpretation and passages like those of the Magnificat (Lk 1:46-55) and Jesus' use of Isaiah at the beginning of his mission in Nazareth (Lk 4:16) became the equivalent of the revolutionary slogans of 'the right to life, liberty and the pursuit of happiness' (American Revolution) or of 'liberty, equality and fraternity' (French Revolution).

It is notorious in the history of Christianity that the understanding of Jesus Christ is influenced by the cultural ethos of a particular time as well as by the personal character and interests of a particular writer. It is no less true that cultural ethos and personal vision, in the West at least, have been influenced by the portraits and understanding of Jesus Christ offered in the four gospels and the other New Testament writings. This two-way interaction still operates for Christians. Cultural ethos and personal vision include politics. Politics has influenced and still influences Christology. Christology has influenced and still influences politics. Jaroslav Pellikan's recent book, *Jesus Through the Centuries: His Place in the History of Culture* (Yale, 1985) offers some telling examples of this from the Emperor Constantine to the American President Thomas Jefferson to contemporary political figures like Gandhi and Martin Luther King.

The interaction and mutual influence have been both profound and subtle. In terms of evaluation one might distinguish corruptive influences where politics or Christology or both can, at least with hindsight, be seen to have been impoverished by the interaction. The picture of Christ associated with the Crusades seems now to be of the impoverished kind, as does the picture of politics associated with the Inquisition. The interaction can be critical and corrective. Jesus' attitude to the poor and excluded has at various times exercised a corrective influence in society and politics, although in more recent times the political concern for social justice originating outside Christianity, under the influence of Marx and other analysts, has had its critical and corrective influence in a Christianity and Christology grown individualist and escapist, simply otherworldly. The critical corrective sometimes becomes genuinely creative. The emergence of limited government and human rights in the British and American political traditions were undoubtedly influenced by the Christian concept of person, founded eventually in the person and teaching of Jesus Christ.

In exploring further the interaction between politics and Christology as corruptive, corrective or creative, the democratic triad of liberty, equality and fraternity / sorority provides a convenient framework.

Liberty insists on respect for the individual person in her or his distinctiveness. The individual human being is as a person irreplaceable and inviolable. The UN Declarations on Human Rights elaborate various aspects of this. Human Rights Organisations like Amnesty International and a host of church groups seek to monitor and promote this respect for the individual and his rights.

The church interest is founded on the Christian concept of the person, mediated in the past through natural law which was also very influential in the more secular political understanding of human rights. However, today the Christian understanding may be related more directly to the person of Christ, as 'first-born of creation', original 'image of God' as Son of the Father. In Jesus Christ Christians find the ultimate basis of human dignity and of the respect due to that dignity. Respect for the humanity of Jesus himself in its differentiation from his divinity was one of the most severe challenges facing the early church. The suppression or reduction of his humanity would have had incalculable consequences for the course of Christian history. The decisions of the early church councils ensured the distinction between the human and the divine in Jesus, enshrined the church's conviction that he was truly human as well as truly divine. Respect for Jesus' humanity in face of a divinity which might have overpowered it was a great achievement of early Christology and gradually reinforces for Christians the respect due to the humanity of everyone. Christological truth can have important bearing on the liberty of the individual and human rights. The sensitivity to human dignity and distinctiveness of each human person generated by the human rights movement can influence in turn Christian sensitivity to the humanity of Jesus and to his distinctiveness as this person, this Jew, this first-century Galilean.

The Christological controversies and councils may provide further illumination in their attention to the distinctions within the Godhead between Father and Son and Holy Spirit. Respect for persons in their differentiation at this sublime level may seem remote from modern political considerations but there is some historical continuity of idea and for Christians a final absolute foundation for personal differentiation and the respect it demands.

Contemporary respect for persons involves equality of diverse kinds. Equality before the law is one political expression of this. Political discrimination on the basis of religion, sex or race is regarded as violating this equality of respect due to human beings as persons. In the Christological vision of Paul in his letter to the Galatians, the Epistle of Freedom, discrimination between Jew and Gentile, between male and female, between master and slave is excluded (Gal 3:28). The practical and political translation of that vision has taken a long time and is still in progress. The progress has often been made by politicians rather than Christian preachers. Even the preacher Paul failed to carry through on slavery, for example in the letter of Philemon.

The political liberties theoretically enjoyed by all in modern democratic states have not removed gross inequalities in distribution of the goods of the earth, in opportunities for education, employment and election to office. Inequalities of the more obvious kind based on colour or of a more pervasive kind based on sex or of the more elusive kind based on geography, climate or even accent are all too common in the lands of the free. They have often promoted and been reinforced by a distorted Christology, associated with European male power structures. A beautiful example of such unconscious reinforcement occurs in the story of the Irish bishop preaching to his flock on basic equality of all members of the people of God. 'We are all equal here,' he said, 'from me down.'

The equality he was at once affirming and denying is basic to Christianity as the radical equality of baptism whereby all are equally daughters and sons of the Father, sisters and brothers of Christ. The most theological of the documents of Vatican II, the *Constitution on the Church*, underlines this in its discussion of church as people of God prior to any discussion of structure or hierarchy. In this the Council was being true to the gospels and to Paul in ways which had been obscured by the previous emphasis on structure and authority, both of which remain essential to the church but in a different key with, one hopes, fresh expression. Christology, which takes seriously both the Jesus of the gospels and the Pauline vision of baptism as sharing in the death and resurrection of Christ (Rom 6), is unlikely to promote a church structure or practice of 'lording over people', however humble in person the particular 'lords' may be.

Authority as service, which the New Testament proposes and Vatican II strongly endorses, strengthens the vision of the church as a 'discipleship of equals'. A further stage develops with a consideration of Jesus' ministry to the poor and deprived reflecting Yahweh's bias to the poor in the history of Israel and the priorities adopted by the church. The western traditions of regard for strangers, the sick and the poor owe much to Christian vision and practice of hospitality, health care and alms giving. Its contemporary expression in the 'preferential option for the poor' by churches around the world offers a more structural and political expression of the same tradition. It is an expression undoubtedly influenced by the secular social and political developments of the last hundred years which owed so much in turn to Hebrew and Christian antecedents, with the ministry and basic understanding of Jesus Christ (Christology) as central, if sometimes implicit.

Of course, the radical equality of Christians as children of God and of all humanity as created in the image of God was not only sometimes implicit but frequently distorted. The first Catholic bishop in Zimbabwe (then Rhodesia) accepted political inequality of white and black while affirming the equality of all before God. And he was part of a long line. Authority as service and God's love of the poor were all too easily used in self-serving and self-interested ways. The challenge to contemporary Christians to follow through on this Christology is particularly acute in face of current political awareness, democratic practices and structures, means of communication and technological power. The follow-through must be by Christians in church as well as in society if it is to be true Christian witness. At present the witness to the radical equality of all is at best ambiguous in church and in society. In many areas, notably the role of women, the advantage may rest with society and its secular structures. Mutual correction and transformation in equality has however enormous scope for both church and society.

The semantic difficulty with the word 'fraternity' is not simply semantic as I already hinted. A social and political tradition which professed the freedom, equality and 'togetherness' of all carried with it in the word fraternity for 'togetherness' or 'unity' the inheritance of male superiority and female submission. The revolutionary slogan in which the earlier tradition and its Christian roots (e.g. in Galatians) had crystallised rightly discerned the interdependence of the three dimensions. The limitations of 'fraternity' were founded in the inequality of men and women and the lack of freedom for women. Political consciousness in this century has fuelled a very powerful movement for the equality and emancipation of women in society, thereby revealing the inherent difficulties of 'fraternity'. For the most part then the inspiration for such a women's movement rests with freedom and equality. On this basis the movement offers a challenge to the churches which has only been slowly and partially recognised and met. One of the stumbling blocks for the church has been a certain view of Christology in which the 'maleness' of Jesus plays a key role. The Incarnation, the 'logos' becoming 'sarx' ('The Word was made flesh and dwelt among us', Jn 1:14), has been rendered 'God became Man'. Man has in this view been interpreted not only as human but as significantly male in the sense, for example, that only male disciples may share in the work of Jesus as ordained priests or bishops. Without wishing to pursue the 'ordination' controversy here, partly because it may be premature, it must be acknowledged that the challenge to a 'male' Christology from the feminist movement runs very deep. It calls for a re-examination of one of the classical themes of the early Christological principles that whatever is not 'assumed' by or integrated with the logos is not redeemed (saved/liberated) (cf. St Gregory the Nazianzen). If the Logos made flesh is male in some *excluding* sense rather than inclusively human, there may also be difficulties about the range of redemption. The challenge of politics to Christology today is at its sharpest in the feminist debate.

However one meets the language difficulty and the feminist challenge, 'fraternity' suggests a comradeship, mutual responsibility, bonding and unity, or rather community, which freedom and equality cannot offer. One of the better current words for this, if it is not already tired, is solidarity. Freedom and equality can finally flourish only through the solidarity of free and equal members in community. Without freedom and equality solidarity is enslaving and community oppressive.

Two basic forms of solidarity require discussion here as mediating between Christology and politics. The great Pauline vision of Christians as members of one another, sharing mutual responsibility in Christ (1 Cor 12 etc.) provides a critical challenge to a society dominated by individualism where freedom and equality may be formally generated. In western society in general the legal and social forms, sometimes summarised in human rights, do not effectively overcome the social fragmentation and individualism, the personal isolation and loneliness. The sense of togetherness, of mutual belonging, common sharing and responsibility is weak, if not entirely absent. Individuals and particular groups in their hunger for wealth and power exploit the very forms of freedom or equality at the expense of the larger community with its sharing and bonding. In this area the vision and power of Christology, provided it receives adequate witness in the community of disciples, a large proviso, can help to correct and transform the fragmenting individualism of society.

On a broader worldwide canvas the fragmenting and lack of solidarity results in international hostility, exploitation and war. Fraternity/sorority demands planetary political expression in international peace and solidarity. The vision and power of the kingdom preached by Jesus, the blessed kingdom of the justice-seekers and peacemakers (the Sermon on the Mount) provides a continuous inspiration for political striving. Christians in community, in their churches and between their churches, are called to give active witness to this universal human solidarity. In the hallowed phrase emphasized at Vatican II, the church is to be the sacrament, the sign and realisation of the community of all humankind. The mutual challenge which this embodies for church, as body of Christ, and for humanity, in its political strivings for world community, is obvious. In responding to that challenge the divided churches have to take much more seriously the prayer of Jesus that they may be one that the world may believe (Jn 17) and may be one. Nowhere is this more urgent than in Ireland where the very division of the churches fuels the division of our peoples. If the coming decades are to prove further stages in developing the century of fraternity/solidarity and peace to complete the moves towards freedom and equality, Ireland will have to make its own contribution in finally resolving the murderous divisions in its own island as well as working by diplomatic peace-keeping operations and economic aid to promote peace and solidarity in the world at large. For all, the alternative to the century of peace and solidarity is apocalyptic destruction of which Jesus too was aware and against which he warned us.

Church–State Relations in an Independent Ireland

In Celebration of Garret FitzGerald at 75

In the context of a volume on religions and politics in Ireland today the title of this chapter is at once too restrictive and too extensive. It is too extensive because many of the significant elements in the discussion, such as those of health, of education and of law and morality, receive careful and detailed discussion in other chapters and will be largely overlooked here. The title is too restrictive because it suggests that there was only one church and one state or form of state involved. The four main churches, as they are called, Roman Catholic, Church of Ireland (Anglican), Presbyterian and Methodist, straddle the two jurisdictions in the island of Ireland. These two jurisdictions complicated the relations of the churches to the political authorities as well as to one another, particularly in the last forty years. In further restriction of the discussion the relations between church and state, of whichever tradition and jurisdiction, have been interpreted to refer only to the relations between church leaders and governments, between bishops (moderators) and government ministers, despite the churches' own self-definition of themselves as the entire believing (Catholic/Anglican etc.) community. It is obvious that churches and states deal with one another frequently and directly through their recognised leaders, but their regular interactions are much broader and more subtle. Recent referenda on matters of concern to both church and state, including divorce, abortion and even Europe, have shown citizens and believers to be of a different mind from their church and political leaders.

In his recent reassessment of John Whyte's classic work *Church and State in Ireland, 1921–1970*, Professor Thomas Bartlett attends briefly to some of these restrictions while acknowledging that they do not generally invalidate Whyte's account. Whyte and Bartlett write as historians and their work, and that of others such as Dermot Keogh, Patrick Murray, Louise Fuller and Tom Inglis, provide essential material for the kind of theological reflection and analysis at which this chapter aims. The further state dimension of membership of the European Union, combined with the Irish Catholic Church's membership of the European Conference of Bishops, has not received any formal attention in church–state discussion although the Irish Catholic Church has issued statements in the run-up to both referenda on the Nice Treaty, and European institutions have pronounced on previously contentious issues such as women's equality in the workplace and the legal rights of homosexuals. It is on the basis then of the narrower historical studies and of the broader and changing characters and roles of contemporary church and state, primarily within the ambit of the present Republic of Ireland, that these reflections are developed.

The Liberation of the Catholic Church and the Emergence of the Irish Free State

In what seems to many the sad or happy days of its decline, to speak of the liberation of the Catholic Church must sound an almost prehistoric note. Yet the Penal Laws of the seventeenth and eighteenth centuries, whatever the revisionist qualifications of today, have, like the Great Famine of the nineteenth century with all its contemporary qualifications, left enduring marks on the faith and politics of successive generations of Irish Catholics down to the twenty-first century. The struggle for the civil and political liberties of Catholics, for their own education system and land ownership and the more strictly political movements for the Repeal of the Act of Union and Home Rule as well as the separatist republican movements, involving armed force if necessary, were frequently intertwined and overlapping while at other times they were in opposition. Both overlapping, and opposition between the religious and political applies to the constitutional, non-violent movements like O'Connell's constitutional campaigns and their successors and to the recurrent physical force organisations from the Tone's United Irishmen of 1798 and its successors to the men of 1916 and the ensuing War of Independence. While the higher clergy, the bishops, opposed physical force and excommunicated at various times its proponents, the low-power clergy, the priests, were often more tolerant of their own local people involved in it. By the time of independence, despite the contribution by members of other churches, the Irish Free State was seen as the embodiment of Irish nationalist aspirations and that Irish nationalism was for many of its leaders and their supporters closely identified with Catholicism. Although the 1922 Constitution did not suggest anything like a Catholic state, the actual boundaries of the new state meant that it had an overwhelming Catholic majority, thereby intensifying the historical intertwining of nationalism and Catholicism, of politics and the majority religion.

It is against this background of such a Catholic majority, among legislators and citizens, and with at least the sense of final Catholic emancipation among bishops and priests, that the new state began to chart its own course independently of its former overlord. That course included much of its British inheritance in parliamentary and court procedures as well as in its administrative personnel and operations. Within its own inheritance from both the constitutional and separatist traditions, the tenets of liberal democracy and the respect for the common name of Irishmen irrespective of creed or class provided a strong counterweight to the potentially discriminatory power of an almost exclusively Catholic citizenry and legislature. The ethos of that citizenry and legislature was sufficient to abolish the right to divorce by private members' parliamentary bill in 1925 (a British inheritance) without much or perhaps any prompting from bishops. The constitutional ban on divorce in the 1937 Constitution may have simply carried forward this, although it was challenged in the Senate if not as eloquently as WB Yeats had challenged the 1925 move.

The 1925 Film Censorship Bill, the 1929 Book Censorship Bill and the 1935 Contraceptive Bill show no evidence of Episcopal interference. As Whyte and others point out, they largely reflect the conservatism of the time and not simply an Irish or Catholic conservatism. Similar provisions existed in most countries on film censorship, in many on book censorship and even in some, such as the New England states, on contraception. Yet in the immediate neighbourhood of Britain and in the minds of the many Irish Protestants who still retained strong British memories and attachments, as well as in the minds of an increasing number of disaffected writers and intellectuals of Catholic background, these moves reflected, in Tom Inglis's phrase, a growing 'moral monopoly' by the Catholic Church.

Outside the realm of morality, but more clearly and symbolically binding together Catholicism and nationalism, Catholic Church and Irish State were the two celebratory events of the centenary of Catholic Emancipation in 1929 and of the Eucharistic Congress in 1932. They also allowed the parties divided by the Civil War, Cumann na nGael under WT Cosgrave and Fianna Fáil under Éamon de Valera, to profess their own Catholic loyalties as heads and members of government. Of course there was no doubt a mutual manipulation at work here between the political and ecclesiastical leaders; symbols are not always as significant as they seem at the time. Yet there was real conviction too on both sides of the historical and contemporary connection between nation, state and Catholicism.

For most commentators, the most powerful symbol of the closeness between the new Irish state and the Catholic Church was the new Constitution of Ireland introduced by Mr de Valera in 1937. Many elements in the constitution contributed to this impression as did real and alleged discussion which de Valera had with various Catholic authorities, including his friend Fr John Charles McQuaid, the President of Blackrock College in Dublin and later Archbishop of Dublin. The preamble, not part of the constitution proper but nevertheless conveying an introductory sense of direction, begins: 'In the name of the Most Holy Trinity' and goes on to acknowledge 'our obligations to our Divine Lord Jesus Christ, who sustained our fathers through centuries of trial', an implicit recognition of the connection between the religious struggle and the political one to be made more explicit in the very next paragraph/phrase: 'Gratefully remembering their [our fathers'] heroic and unremitting struggle to regain the rightful independence of the Nation ... do hereby adopt etc. ... this Constitution.'

While this preamble remains, the more controverted elements in section I, ss2 and 3 of Article 44 were removed by referendum in 1972 without Episcopal comment as far as is known, excepting an *obiter dictum* by Cardinal Conway that he would not shed a tear at its removal. Its presence and its removal were alike witness to its rather empty symbolic value.

In conversation with the author in the 1960s, Mr de Valera, while he was still President of Ireland, recounted some of the genesis of these subsections. He knew that there was a theory that a state with a dominantly Catholic population should recognise that church as the one true church, in other words make it the established church of the state as the Church of Ireland was up to 1869 and the Church of England still was/is in England. He did not, however, wish to consult Archbishop Edward Byrne with whom he had differences over the Civil War so he went instead to the Papal Nuncio, Archbishop Pascal Robinson. The Nuncio said he could not interfere and that he (de Valera) would have to consult the leader of the Irish hierarchy, Cardinal MacRory, Archbishop of Armagh. The Cardinal insisted that the Constitution should recognise the Catholic Church as the one true church. Mr de Valera felt he could not do that as it would be offensive to other Christians, south and north of the Irish border.

As the formula he had devised to meet these difficulties, the formula which subsequently appeared in Article 44, I, 2, was not acceptable to the leader of the Irish church, and he knew he would have difficulty in getting the whole constitution passed by the Irish electorate due to the strength of the political opposition, he decided to have recourse to Rome. His emissary, Mr Joseph Walsh of what is now the Department of Foreign Affairs, saw the then Secretary of State at the Vatican, Cardinal Pacelli, later Pope Pius XII. According to Mr de Valera, the cardinal was sympathetic and said that he would consult the pope, Pius XI. The pope turned it down, seeking a similar recognition to that asked for by Cardinal MacRory and not uncommon in Catholic countries even then. Mr de Valera persisted. Joe Walsh was despatched to Rome yet again to go through the same motions with Cardinal Pacelli, only to be told eventually that the pope would remain silent on the matter and neither approve or disapprove. So the referendum went ahead and the constitution was adopted by the people by a fairly small majority. Any overt opposition from the church might well have seen it defeated as Mr de Valera feared.

In his Christmas message of that year, Cardinal MacRory offered his congratulations to the Irish people on their adoption of the new (Christian) constitution. In 1958 on the occasion of the constitution's twenty-first anniversary, Mr de Valera went to Rome to present a specially bound copy of the constitution to Pope Pius XII (Pacelli) and to receive the pope's congratulations and special blessing. Mr de Valera's constitutional ingenuity in word and action had received approval at the highest level in the Catholic Church.

In the intervening period, a lay group of right-wing Catholics, with the name Maria Duce, supported if not inspired by the writings of a Holy Ghost priest, Denis Fahey, had been agitating for, among other things, the revision of the constitution to have formal recognition of the Catholic Church enshrined in it. As their activities became more extreme, they were banned by Archbishop McQuaid, formerly a member of the Holy Ghost Order, although in traditional Irish style they regrouped and continued their activities under another name. There were always groups of Catholics, whether they were conventionally described as right and left or as liberal and conservative, for whom the bishops did not speak. This was most obvious in earlier times on the issues of the use of armed force but it extended to a wide range of other issues such as the legislation on contraception, homosexuality, divorce and abortion on which Catholics on the liberal or left wing of the church disagreed with Episcopal views. Catholics on the right wing disagreed with the views of the bishops and the Conference of Religious of Ireland on issues like social welfare, development aid, the eradication of poverty and the treatment of immigrants, refugees and asylum seekers. A proposal by the Irish Bishops' Commission for Justice and Peace, drawn up primarily by its lay staff to include certain social as well as personal rights in the constitution, was ignored by all the political parties except the Labour Party.

The Catholic Church in its fullness could never be reduced to the bishops and their views as leaders were not always accepted by loyal

Catholics as the last word on a particular religious or moral issue. This was most sharply tested on an issue which in retrospect seems marginal to the church's previous moral concerns. The dispute over the Mother and Child Bill in 1951, which was declared by the bishops to be contrary to Catholic social teaching, brought down the inter-party government of the time after the most explicit, even obsequious acknowledgement by members of that government of the authority of the bishops in moral matters. It was in many ways a last hurrah for such authority. A simple symbol of the changing atmosphere occurred later in the decade at the time of the Fethard-on-Sea boycott of Protestant businesses by local Catholics because of their alleged involvement with the 'abduction' of the child of an inter-church marriage. The Catholic action seemed to have the support of the local bishop as well as of the parish priest. However, in reply to a question in the Dáil, the Taoiseach, Éamon de Valera, spoke out against it and it subsequently fizzled out. This was in marked contrast to the reaction in 1931 of both W.T. Cosgrave, then head of government, and de Valera, leader of the opposition, on the refusal to appoint a Protestant as librarian in Castlebar. Catholic politicians and citizens were no longer so behoven to Catholic bishops or clergy in public matters even when they seemed to involve religion and morality. And they were becoming more conscious of their need to rise above the religious divisions which had plagued the country for so long.

New Contexts, New Relationships

The sixties were notoriously years of change, rapid and radical, for good and for ill, in church and state, in Ireland as well as in the wider world. Still some of the old sparring between politicians and bishops continued. Even Seán Lemass, who as Taoiseach was rightly regarded as the first architect of modern Ireland, seemed to have yielded to Archbishop McQuaid's objections to extending the National Library into the grounds of Trinity College, which Catholics were still forbidden to attend without the archbishop's express permission. However, Lemass's implementation of the First and Second Programmes of Economic Development led to the first real economic prosperity in the history of the state, which was to provide a significant change in context both for church and state. This coincided with the media explosion which saw the establishment of Ireland's first television station, the participation by Ireland in UN peace-keeping missions and the opening of North–South dialogue in Ireland between Lemass and Northern Ireland's Prime Minister, Terence O'Neill. This opening of a hitherto isolated Ireland culminated in its admission in

1973 to membership of the European Economic Community, as it was then called. All these political and social changes offered Irish people a vision and a confidence which older, complacent and even arrogant church leaders would ignore at their peril.

By what seemed at the time a stroke of providence, the recently elected 'transitional' Pope John XXIII summoned the Second Vatican Council in 1959 and its first session opened in autumn 1962. The Irish Catholic Church played no significant role at episcopal, theological or other level in its deliberation or conclusions. However, it was followed avidly at home due to the outstanding journalistic work of Seán MacRéamoinn for RTÉ, Louis McRedmond for the *Irish Independent* and John Horgan for *The Irish Times*. With further enlightened commentary in such journals as *The Furrow* and *Doctrine and Life*, many priests and people at home seemed more informed and were certainly more enthusiastic about the council debates and decrees than the bishops who attended. The major *Constitution on the Church* itself made clear the church's primary character as a people, 'the people of God', after which came the hierarchical and clerical structures of servant–leaders. In conciliar terms it was entirely wrong to reduce the church to the bishops (and clergy) even in speaking of church–state relations. As pointed out earlier in this essay this was the traditional definition of the Catholic Church which was conveniently ignored by supporters and critics of the bishops.

The Church in the Modern World document (*Gaudium et spes*) revealed a context and method of church activity in national and global society which moved way beyond the arthritic provisions of previous church–state theory as laid out, for example, in Manuals of Public Ecclesiastical Law and which had underpinned episcopal and papal objections to de Valera's refusal to recognise the Catholic Church as the one true church. The two 'perfect societies', as they had hitherto been called and which were expected to have formal relations of a *concordat* style, were now overtaken by a world church and its local embodiments seeking to fulfil its mission in a society which could not be identified with the state. Meantime the state, the Irish state in particular, was being integrated into wider continental and global structures.

The Council's *Decree on Ecumenism* made any talk of a privilege state position for one church vulnerable to serious criticism. This was reinforced by one of the clearest and most powerful documents of Vatican II, *The Declaration on Religious Liberty*. The restrictions on religious freedom of belief and practice which affected minorities in dominantly Catholic or Protestant countries for so long after the Reformation divisions, according to the principle *cujus regio, ejus religio* (only the religion of the king or prince may be practised), was finally and radically set aside by the highest authority in the Catholic Church, the pope and council. To complete the liberating moves, the decree *Nostra aetate* (In Our Time) recognised the value of other non-Christian religions, pre-eminently that of the Jews, and opened the possibility and necessity of dialogue with them. Archbishop McQuaid's comment on his return from the council that nothing had happened to disturb the faith of the Irish faithful may have been true in a way he never intended for the many who had followed the council's proceedings so eagerly. Disappointment and disillusionment at the bishops' and indeed Rome's later foot-dragging and even reversal of the council's intentions in some areas inevitably followed. Yet the great sea change had happened. For the relationships between the Catholic Church and political authorities there was no real returning.

Yet in that very decade, two significant events occurred which ever since have dogged relationships within the Catholic Church, between the Irish churches themselves and between the Irish churches and the political authorities north and south of the Irish border. The first of these, the issuing by Pope Paul VI in July 1968 of the encyclical *Humanae vitae*, banning all forms of contraception, was primarily a matter for relations within the church as bishops, theologians and lay people disagreed, sometimes fiercely, on the truth and binding force of its teaching. For many committed Catholics in Ireland and around the world, it weakened the teaching authority of pope and bishops in moral matters. But it was not exclusively an internal concern. In the incipient dialogue between the churches, moral discussion particularly in the sexual area tended to be off limits, giving at times a certain unreality to the whole ecumenical enterprise. Division within the Catholic Church and between the churches on an issue of such practical import to all citizens presented difficulties to Irish politicians faced with demands for legislation on precisely this issue, the availability of contraceptives. As this issue has received so much attention over the years from theologians, including myself, I leave it aside here.

The second event or series of events began later that year in October with an attack on the Civil Rights march in Derry protesting at discrimination against Catholics and nationalists in Northern Ireland. At least this occurrence could be seen as the symbolic start of the 'Troubles' that resulted in so much death and destruction. Divisions between the churches were naturally exacerbated. The Catholic Church in bishops, priests and laity was mainly in sympathy with the nationalist cause, if frequently and explicitly condemnatory of the violent methods of the IRA. The Protestant churches at every level were mainly in sympathy with their own unionist people if also condemnatory of the violence from the unionist/loyalist side. All this affected British and Irish governments as well as politicians, North and South, in their search for a peaceful resolution of the conflict as in their dealings with the churches and their leaders. It is noted here as one of the major changes in context in which churches and the state had to operate throughout this period.

Two minor episodes over the next decade or so illustrate how the 'thinking' church and the 'thinking' politician were reviewing the church–state relations in the aftermath of Vatican II and in the context of the violent divisions in Northern Ireland. On 17–18 December 1971 the Irish Theological Association (ITA), whose membership was inter-church if Catholic in majority, organised a conference on Christian Reconciliation at Ballymascanlon Hotel outside Dundalk and close to the border. It was attended by a wide range of theologians and clergy from all the churches, North and South. After some very intense and moving debates, among the conclusions it was agreed that genuine reconciliation could not be achieved where the law appeared to be discriminatory or divisive on religious grounds. The assembly therefore requested the executive committee of the Association to establish a working party in the republic and to make recommendations on this issue. At the AGM of the ITA in January 1972, the proposal was approved and the executive asked to nominate the members who were drawn from the different churches and from different disciplines. In June 1972 the working party presented its report at a general meeting of the Association and it was published (*The Furrow*, June 1972).

Maintaining that the constitution should be simply the basic law of the state (its *Grundgesetz*), the committee proposed and presented a new secular preamble free of the religious and nationalist content of the present one. It recommended in the same spirit the removal of ss2 and 3 from S1 of article 44, the subsections which recognised the special position of the Catholic Church and recognised the other churches named. It also recommended removing the ban on divorce from Article 41 and the amendment of the law 'to remove the restrictions on the freedom of choice in methods of family planning'. While the report sparked off a serious debate within the Theological Association and attracted a fair amount of publicity, its recommendations were only taken up and to some extent implemented long after the report itself had been forgotten.

Despite the position and reputation of its author, a somewhat similar fate seemed to befall the second initiative of relevance here. In the midst of the hunger strike crisis in August 1981, the Taoiseach, Dr Garret FitzGerald, declared in the course of an interview on RTÉ that the Irish State 'as it had evolved over the decades was not the non-sectarian state that the national movement for independence had sought to establish, one in which Catholic, Protestant and Dissenter would feel equally at home; it had rather become a state imbued with the ethos of the majority in our part of the island'. This he could not accept. 'I want to lead a crusade,' he said, 'a republican crusade to make this a genuine republic.' If he could do that, he believed,

> we would have a basis on which many Protestants in the North would be willing to consider a relationship with us. If I were a Northern Protestant today, I cannot see how I could be attracted to getting involved with a state that is itself sectarian – not in the acutely sectarian way that Northern Ireland was ... (but) the fact is our laws and our constitution, our practices, our attitudes reflect those of a majority ethos and are not acceptable to Protestants in Northern Ireland. (*All in a Life*, FitzGerald,1991)

While this interview resonated with the more sober terms of the ITA report and echoes what Dr FitzGerald had voiced in diverse ways and contexts before, it attracted some very sharp criticism even within his own party. His position as Taoiseach, the continuing pressure of the hunger strike, above all the use of the word 'sectarian', however justified and qualified, incensed his critics and disturbed some of his supporters. A speech in the Senate ten days later presented a more rounded account of his views. His proposal to establish a committee to review the constitution had not been implemented by the time his government fell in January 1982. By the time he returned as Taoiseach in late 1982 he had decided to give priority to the establishment of the New Ireland Forum in preparation for negotiations with the British and in which all constitutional parties in the island were invited to participate.

Of course the reference to the special position of the Catholic Church had been removed in late 1972 along the lines recommended by the ITA report. The debates on contraception, divorce and abortion lay ahead and are dealt with elsewhere. The preamble remains untouched and the proposal for a whole new constitution, which Dr FitzGerald among others has sometimes suggested, is at present at least parked.

From Church and State to Law and Morality: The Liberal Agenda

From the mid-seventies church–state debates became almost exclusively debates about law and morality. What became known as the liberal agenda, moves to liberalise the laws on contraception, divorce, abortion and homosexuality, dominated discussion and prevailed with various qualifications. With the exception of the laws on homosexuality, these changes have been charted adequately elsewhere. The change in the law on homosexuality, a law dating back to 1861, took a familiar form, a challenge to its constitutionality in the Irish courts, appeal to the European Court of Human Rights, victory there and a new Bill passed by the Oireachtas (1993), providing, it was claimed at the time, the most liberal provisions in Europe. A distinctive feature of this move was the lack of Dáil debate or indeed public controversy. The ethical and legal problems occasioned by biological developments such as *in vitro* fertilisation have yet to be resolved despite the long-established practices of some of these activities.

The liberal agenda, as understood here, dealt with personal freedoms or individual rights, particularly in the areas of sexuality and human reproduction. The disputants usually blamed the other side for being over-preoccupied with such matters. In truth 'liberals', 'conservatives' and media in the debate reflected a natural if sometimes unhealthy interest in the sexual doings of our citizens; natural because sexual activity and human reproduction are critical to the survival and thriving of a society; unhealthy because so many other matters critical to the survival and thriving of society, such as domestic, criminal and 'political' violence, could be overlooked or marginalized by the concentration on sexual issues. Whether, now that the liberal agenda in such matters is more or less complete, other neglected matters will come to the fore is uncertain. The continuing disclosure of child sexual abuse, particularly by clergy, seems certain to overshadow the corruptions of wealth and the degradations of poverty among other critical social concerns.

Women's Rights

One of the major issues involving church and state in the second half of the twentieth century was that of the status of women. While women in Ireland enjoyed the vote from the 1918 election on the same terms as men (unlike their situation in some European countries), and they actively participated in the struggle for independence, their representation in public life and in the workplace was limited by the ethos of the time and discrimination in regard to pay.

Article 41 of the 1937 Constitution on the family reflected what women critics at the time regarded as an oppressive or at least restrictive ethos in regard to women. Section 2 has two subsections which read as follows:

1 In particular, the state recognises that by her life within the home, woman gives to the state a support without which the common good cannot be achieved.

2 The state shall, therefore, endeavour to ensure that mothers shall not be obliged by economic necessity to engage in labour to the neglect of their duties in the home.

Apart from the removal of the ban on divorce, this article remains in place although the status of women within and without the home has moved on quite a bit. The government's establishment of the Council for the Status for Women in the late fifties began a change which only really took flight with the various forms of the Women's Liberation Movement/Feminism from the late sixties. Despite the participation of committed Catholic lay women and religious sisters, the church as a whole or in its official pronouncements did not play a significant role. Indeed it was regarded as at least a silent opponent of women's rights with its official position still very close to that of Article 41. This emerged particularly in the debates leading up to the referenda on divorce, where the primacy of the family and the potential damage to the good of society (the common good) were frequently stressed by official spokespeople for the church, although not only by these. It was assumed by many supporters and critics that Article 41 reflected Catholic social teaching and may have been directly influenced by the drafters' clerical advisors. Given the general situation in the twenties and thirties and Mr de Valera's views as expressed in the Dáil debate on this article, clerical advice was hardly necessary. It remained true, however, that little support was forthcoming from bishops and clergy as the rights of women continued to be asserted and achieved. In fact, in response to the pressure from women's groups, the Irish courts and European institutions rather than the Irish legislature were the chief promoters of women's rights. The symbolic climax to the development of women's rights in Ireland came with the election in November 1990 of the first woman as President of Ireland, Mary Robinson, who had herself as politician and lawyer been engaged in the struggle for greater equality for women. The change over the decades was reinforced at that same symbolic level with Mary Robinson's successor, the current president, Mary McAleese.

The Catholic Church at any level could not be untouched by all this. Catholic lay and religious activists ensured that voices of women were more effective in changing attitudes and activities and even structures in minor ways like the introduction of women as eucharistic ministers and more belatedly (for trivial reasons) as girl altar servers. More serious moves saw women achieve limited responsibility in church commissions like that of Justice and Peace or agencies such as Trócaire. The appointment of Judge Gillian Hussey to head the independent Audit Committee to report on how far dioceses and religious orders have implemented the official guidelines on clerical sexual abuse is perhaps the most striking of all. (This committee, overtaken by events, has since been stood down.) Naturally perhaps the Conference of Religious of Ireland (CORI) have had women taking major responsibility in every area of its work. While much of the official church recognition of women has been born of necessity, it would hardly have happened at all if Irish society and then the Irish State had not led the way. For both state and church changes in the wider society usually provide the lead and, in this socio-moral matter at least, the state responded more quickly.

The most serious challenge by women to the present structures of the church is the movement for women's ordination. While this movement gathers momentum worldwide it has a strong following in Ireland, operating under the name BASIC (Brothers and Sisters in Christ). In July 2001 BASIC organised the first international Catholic conference on women's ordination in Dublin. Some years earlier it held its own national conference at which the keynote speaker was the Professor of Law at Queen's University, Belfast, and later President of Ireland, Mary McAleese. The interaction between the socio-political and the ecclesial through the activities of lay Catholics still operates as frequently now in the 'liberal' as in the 'conservative' direction.

The Social Agenda
While political leaders over recent decades have been promoting with varying degrees of commitment the liberal agenda as described above, and church leaders have often been resistant to it, what might be called the social agenda of fairness on society through redistribution of resources, combating poverty, improving the conditions of the deprived and excluded such as travellers, those with disability, immigrants and asylum seekers, has been promoted largely by voluntary organisations including church organisation like the CORI Justice Desk, the Justice and Peace Commission and the St Vincent de Paul Society. Similarly the pressure for a fairer world by assistance to the developing world has come mainly from voluntary and church organisations like Trócaire, Concern and Goal. Of course

politicians and government agencies have played an increasingly important role but much of the inspiration, information and implementation has come from these civic and church bodies. Why the church and its agents might feel happier with social rather than liberal issues requires further analysis.

In the law and morality debate in which political and church leaders have been frequently engaged in recent decades, some changes of emphasis and terminology have been significant. While the constitution speaks of 'personal rights' and these have been expanded judicially to include rights implicit in the constitution such as the right to privacy, today the usual term is human rights. And while the wider Catholic Church of the nineteenth century was sharply critical of the concept and term 'human rights' as destructive of all authority including divine authority, in the late twentieth century, at least from Pope John XXIII's encyclical *Pacem in terris* of 1963, the whole Catholic Church including the Irish Church has been a staunch promoter of human rights and in some critical regions of the world one of their most effective defenders. This does not mean that there are not sharp differences about what constitutes a human right in specific instances, as in the foetus's right to life versus the mother's right to choose. And there is a very broad debate spanning secular and religious circles about the status of social and economic rights as listed in the UN Declaration of Human Rights. Church leaders and spokespeople tend to support the equal status and justiceability of social and economic rights with those of civil and political rights, while politicians and civil lawyers tend to deny this, with the notable exception among others of Mary Robinson, UN High Commissioner for Human Rights 1997–2002.

At the socio-moral level of analysis, the divide turns on the more individualist attitude to society of those who would deny the full legal impact of social and economic rights, as against the more unified and interrelated concept of society of the advocates of social and economic rights. 'Solidarity in unity' is another current expression used by mainly religious commentators to overcome a rampant individualism. It was on this basis that the Irish Episcopal Commission for Justice and Peace proposed including four social and economic rights in the constitution (*Re-righting the Constitution*, Dublin, 1998). The present Article 45 on such matters is specifically denied the possibility of vindication in the courts. In a different idiom, the traditional concept of government and law was directed to the good of the whole community or 'common good', the term used in age-old definitions of law and in the preamble to the Irish constitution, but now in retreat before an aggressive individualism coupled in Ireland with a certain antipathy to terms thought to be peculiarly Catholic in provenance. The term 'natural law', which had been thought to transcend religious affiliations and to embrace the whole range of human morality and rights, has suffered a similar eclipse partly due in Ireland to the Catholic Church's claim to be the official interpreter of natural law. As the recent church–state antagonisms diminish, these terms and concepts, or related ones, will recover their real value and usefulness.

A couple of further issues should be mentioned even if it is impossible to deal with them adequately here. Socio-moral issues and their legal implications must now, it is widely recognised, cover environmental protection. A certain amount has been achieved legally in Ireland although much of this has been under pressure from Europe. Apart from members of the Green Party, few politicians have taken this issue beyond their own backyard. The church, clerical and lay, has been equally negligent in recognising the moral and indeed deeper Christian significance of respect for the earth. Priests like Sean McDonagh have given an important lead without attracting much support from mainstream Catholics at any level.

The last point in this hasty coverage of issues in law and morality concerns the current debate arising out of the clerical sex abuse scandals on the relation between Canon Law and Civil Law. Unless arrogance and stupidity prevail on either side, this is a pseudo-problem. Of course the church has the right constitutionally and legally to manage its own affairs and discipline its own personnel. Where, however, these personnel are accused of civil crimes and there is no suggestion that such criminal laws are contrary to the moral law and human rights, then the church authorities have a moral obligation to cooperate fully with the civil authorities in the investigation of these alleged offences. Canon 1395 par 2, which deals with such offences by clerics as child sexual abuse, creates no difficulties itself for this cooperation, whatever particular interpretations might suggest. And natural justice, a term shared by church and state, would demand protection as far as possible of the reputation of the accused as presumed innocent until found guilty, while at the same time, in accordance with the church's own guidelines, protecting children against the danger of possible further abuse by removing the priest from pastoral, chaplain or other hazardous duties. The solution to these practical problems demands good faith and willingness on the part of church and state but should not be all that difficult. Recent dilatoriness on both sides, but particularly on the church side, has aggravated the dangers to children, increased difficulties for the accused, damaged the credibility and leadership of the church and created unnecessary tensions between church and state.

Re-envisioning the Church and its Mission in Society

Much of the cooperation and the tension between church and state derived from an earlier vision of church and state as two powers, the spiritual power or church and the temporal power or state. This vision had originated with emancipation of the church by the Roman Emperor Constantine in the fourth century and its establishment as the church of the Empire by the Emperor Theodosius later that century. What came to be known as Christendom, the union of throne and altar, of the powers spiritual and temporal with, in church eyes, the priority of the spiritual, continued through the centuries. Through the East–West divisions of church and empire, the divisions of the Reformation and the Counter-Reformation in the sixteenth century and the rise of the nation states, the vision of the two powers and the actuality of the cooperation or antagonism persisted. Even after the American and French Revolutions and through the rise of democracy, there lingered in many European countries this vision of two powers. However, their relationship might be reversed with the civil power now the dominant one. In the new independent Ireland, despite its massive Catholic majority which had before independence known the reality of an established church, that option of establishment was not taken. However, the vision of spiritual and temporal powers as characterising church and state was unconsciously and, as we saw, sometime consciously at work. There was in the first fifty years of the new states, South and North, an informal establishment of the Catholic and Protestant churches. Christendom lingered on.

It still does, at least in the attitudes and practices of many church leaders. What Tom Inglis has charted in his book *Moral Monopoly*, with the subtitle *The Rise and Fall of the Catholic Church in Modern Ireland* (1998), treats the Irish church and more particularly its episcopal leaders as a social (quasi-political) power, as reliving the vision of Christendom. In that sense the church was bound to fall as politicians became more independent and self-confident and politics itself more secular.

Vatican II provided at least partly for a church which could carry out its evangelical mission without depending on or restricting state activity. It was genuinely seeking a way out of the Christendom inheritance, which had become such a burden to the universal church over almost two centuries both in countries supportive of it and countries hostile to it. The documents already listed, particularly *The Church in the Modern World* and the *Declaration on Religious Liberty*, show that the church was catching up with the democratic revolution in politics and with other aspects of the modern world. Some contemporary critics of Vatican II see it as having gone too far and as having sold out to 'modernity' just when 'postmodernity' was replacing modernity's belief in scientific rationality and inevitable human progress. Vatican II's supporters respond that, as Chesterton said of Christianity that it hadn't failed because it had never really been tried, Vatican II had never really been tried because of official resistance to it, particularly in Rome. That is a debate for another occasion. The present task is to sketch some vision of church which will free it to fulfil its gospel mission in a society which is at once heavily secularised in its structures, attitudes and practices and yet with many of its members explicitly or implicitly in search of one or all of the following: some ultimate meaning for life, a foundation for morality and some kind of transcendent or spiritual experience.

A possible framework for the sketch of church in society required here might involve three of the major characteristics of biblical literature, of the biblical peoples, Israel and the Christian community, and of the major biblical figures, for Christians their founder and continuing head Jesus Christ. These characteristics of the literature, the peoples and the leaders may be termed the priestly, the prophetic and the kingly or, in the equally authentic term relevant to us, the wise. New Testament literature and Christian commentators have frequently spoken of Jesus as priest, prophet and king while remembering the injunction attributed to him in the gospel of John as he stood before Pilate that his kingdom was not of this world. A primary quality of the good king in the Hebrew scriptures was wisdom and much of what was spoken of as 'wisdom literature' was given kingly authorship, as with David and the psalms, while the wisdom of Solomon was legendary. In Jesus, in his person and teaching, divine and human wisdom recurred without any pretensions to the kind of earthly kingship which some of his contemporaries and even some of his close disciples expected up to the very end: 'Wilt thou at this time restore the kingdom of Israel?' There was never at any time a hint of the kind of kingdom which many in Israel expected and desired and which Christians subsequently promoted in various versions of Christendom.

The followers of Christ as constituting a priestly people, with its New Testament origins, was restored to its primacy in Vatican II's *Constitution on the Church*. This people embodies the mystery of God's presence to the world at large. And it is the whole people which embodies the presence of God, not the religious officials of whom Jesus was very critical in his day and who were deferred to a later chapter for consideration in Vatican II's treatment of the church. Immediate challenges arise for the church as to how it is to be made visible and effective as primarily a community of the believing and baptised, and not be perceived as an episcopal or clerical body. In some reactions to the (partial) democratisation, declericalisation and demystification set in train by Vatican II, a restorationist spirit has been at work. Episcopal and clerical primacy, prestige and power have once again been stressed and so has a return to older forms of liturgy and of clerical and religious dress. Often the reason advanced for these moves is the restoration of the sense of mystery, of the transcendent and divine in life and liturgy.

It would be foolish to deny that the sense of mystery and of the transcendent is weakening in church life and liturgy and that the council as implemented so far has done little to renew that sense. But the weakening was already at work, at least partly because the pre-Vatican II church had not confronted the positives as well as the negatives in the changing and secularising world. That church had preferred to stay with forms which spoke increasingly of mystification rather than mystery and consciously or unconsciously betokened human power rather than divine grace. In a renewed vision and structure of church, the sense of transcendence and mystery which people need and which so many despair of finding through the present power structures, the liturgy and activities of the Christian community, must help keep the whole society open to a liberating transcendent and refuse the temptations of the parallel social powers characteristic of Christendom.

The temptations of the priestly dimensions of the church to seek power and the associated prestige and property in society should be offset by the prophetic voices in that community. Prophets in the Hebrew scriptures were particularly critical of the neglect by the religious leaders and their associates of the poor and excluded in their power-seeking and wealth accumulation. One of the most cherished names for Jesus has been that of prophet. His refusal of the trappings of wealth and power gave substance to his prophetic teaching. Indeed his self-emptying even to death on the cross, as described in St Paul's Letter to the Philippians (chapter 2), provides a permanent prophetic critique of the worldly aspirations of religious leaders, with their seeking of the first places in synagogues, church or civil forum. At the more obviously moral level, the traditional prophetic class for justice and peace provide a final basis in the divine Creator, the ultimate and absolutely Other, for the equal respect due to human creatures in their dignity as images and children of God, and for the respect due by them to all creation in its rich diversity. Such a prophetic community, in deed as well as in word, will bear witness within society to the highest aspirations and attainments of human beings and offer a necessary and continuing critique to the individualist self-seeking of the strong at the expense of the weak. Only where the prophetic voice is effective can the priestly people authentically worship and witness to the transcendent and incarnate God of Jesus Christ.

Prophets have their own temptations. Power and prestige also beckon for them if in more subtle forms than that of conventional fame and fortune. Their summons to the others to change and be converted may well disguise from themselves their own self-seeking and their own need for conversion. In themselves or certainly in the community they serve, these temptations may be overcome by wisdom, personal and communal, human and divine. The wisdom literature of Israel borrowed heavily from surrounding cultures while integrating that wisdom into its own faith in Yahweh, the one true God of Israel. The Israelite, Jesus of Nazareth, inheritor of that wisdom tradition, enlarged and deepened it in his parables and proverbial sayings, while ultimately subjecting it, in Paul's vision, to the divine wisdom which despite their protestations led him to lay down his life for his friends. In the end divine wisdom may sometimes look like human folly. Yet as a protection against self-indulgent or simply irrational prophetic pretensions, human as well as divine wisdom may be needed. Living in this world but not finally of this world demands that disciples of Jesus be wise as serpents and not just simple as doves, in a typical 'wisdom' saying of Jesus himself.

In its attempt to cope with the modern world, the church must wisely evaluate and accommodate. In a fresher vision of church and world, the ambiguity of each becomes clearer. The sense of mystery, divine and human, in creation and creator evokes the priestly response not just of Christians but of people belonging to every religion and none. It is the Christian responsibility to engage in wisdom with these other traditions in order to expand the awareness and understanding of the mystery of God's presence in the world among themselves and among their partners in dialogue. Wisdom provides protection against the mystificatory conservative temptation of the priestly, and against the self-indulgent radical temptation of the prophetic. It has its own temptations of course to yield to worldly accommodation and ease in face of the authentic demands of true worship and inclusive justice. Wisdom's resistance to these temptations requires the challenge and support of the priestly and prophetic in the church.

The vision of the church as a priestly, prophetic and wisdom community, in the senses described, helps to locate it in the broader society without immediately prescribing reforms in structure. Assuming the priority of the believing people after the teaching of Vatican II, and adhering to the basic service structures which originated in New Testament times and have developed in response to inspirations and needs with inevitable accommodations and compromises, wisdom suggests that a clean break with the Christendom mentality is necessary. That really means an end to clericalism, to the caste system of bishops, priests and religious with their power and privileges. They will be integrated as servants into the believing community they are to serve while confirmed in the unity of the whole church by local bishops and by the church's traditional symbol of universal unity, the Bishop of Rome. There need be no formal relations with the political powers. The church's mission in society, of promoting a meaningful and moral life, will be effected through all its members with their priestly, prophetic and pastoral wisdom gifts, who enter wholeheartedly into the familial, social, cultural and political life of the society. Catholic Christian citizens, drawing on the inspiration of their faith community, should be full and free citizens in promoting the human rights and the common weal of all members, more immediately of their own civil society but ultimately of the whole globalising world. Their distinctive civic attribute might well be their concern for the excluded and discriminated. Their ecclesial leaders will no longer have any civic role beyond the role of citizen and the freedom to preach the gospel and serve their people.

The Emerging Paradigm: Religion and Society

To some extent any new vision of church in society is continually being overtaken by events. Vatican II has been criticised by radicals in Latin America and by conservatives in Europe for accommodating itself too much to the liberal and largely unbelieving European middle class. Trying to fit the universal church into such a context could only distort it according to these two sets of critics, otherwise utterly different in their analysis of the past, and in their prescription for the future church. The analysis and prescription of Vatican II had, in the *Declaration on Religious Freedom* and in its less substantial document on ecumenism and inter-faith dialogue, prepared the way to some extent for the situation which has developed since. The obvious vitality of the major religions in the world has given, as mentioned earlier, many sociological scholars cause to rethink their belief that secularisation, European-style, was unstoppable around the globe. The fundamentalist nature of some of these religious groups is obviously a cause for great political as well as religious concern.

Of more relevance to this discussion is the sheer plurality and variety of religious communities in most countries, including Ireland. In some recent debates in Ireland it was almost assumed that the pluralist society to be desired would be simply a secular society with religion a purely private and personal reality in so far as it existed at all. Of course many religious and non-religious commentators saw the inherent contradiction in equating pluralist and secular in this context. It will be more difficult to make the equation from now on with the growth in the Muslim and other religious communities. In fact, to speak of a secular society may soon be as outdated as speaking of a Catholic or Christian society. Part of the difficulty here has been the tendency in the nation-state to identify society and state. In face of a much more diverse society at home, with so many more connections abroad and in face of a growing sense of the necessity and power of voluntary organisations and interest groups, the state will have to be distinguished much more sharply from the society it serves in its legislative, judicial and administrative roles. In that situation, the Catholic Church will have more Christian freedom and less social power. For the sake of religion and morality it will have to foster effective dialogue with other churches (ecumenism) and with other faiths (interfaith dialogue) and indeed with those of no religious faith but with a sense of the need for human meaning and civic morality. By then the debates of the twentieth century may seem as obsolete as those of the fourth, the century of Constantine.

The Risk of Peace and the Risk of God

In Memory of Monsignor Edward Farrell

In the call to Christian leaders and theologians for 'the Abolition of War', which Professor Stanley Hauerwas of Duke University and myself presented in 2002 at the University of Notre Dame and elsewhere, we naturally emphasized the radical Christian basis of this appeal. Founded in the non-violent, liberating and peace-making teaching, ministry and death of Jesus, the appeal seemed particularly appropriate at the beginning of a new millennium and at the close of the century which had experienced the most destructive wars in history. All the more inhuman and scandalous, these wars were initiated and conducted by states with powerful Christian and humanist traditions, and which flattered themselves as being the most culturally civilized and scientifically advanced in the world. Even in the few intervening years since, the urgency of that appeal has intensified and the generous timescale suggested then, 'abolishing war in the twenty-first century', has already begun to shrink.

Without repeating the arguments of that appeal or of later separate and joint publications by us, I wish to honour this occasion by reflecting on the risky human enterprise of making peace and making it universal, and on the risks already taken by the Creator and Saviour God in the pursuit of Shalom. Shalom, the messianic peace promised by the prophets, hymned by angels at Jesus' birth and used as Kingdom greeting by Jesus himself.

1. Abolishing War or Abolishing Humanity

In the Cold War period there seemed at times a real risk of a nuclear conflagration which could completely destroy this planet and its inhabitants. The MAD policy of 'mutually assured destruction' was indeed the lunatic prescription for ensuring a peace of the dead, human, animal and vegetable. The moral ambiguities of threat, of retaliation, while rejecting the first strike option, the incomplete or unrealistic treaties to limit the spread and reduce the actual arsenals of nuclear weapons combined with surrogate wars between the nuclear powers across the globe could hardly be described as genuine peace. However, the feared nuclear catastrophe was avoided, and with the collapse of the USSR new hopes for real peace were once again raised. How far they have been dashed by inter-state, intra-state and less definable wars needs little emphasis here. The number of wars, of the collective use of armed force by or against government or peoples, or however one describes such violent conflicts, which have characterised the years even since the fall of the Soviet Union, is large and growing. And with the increased availability of nuclear weaponry their non-use, even by established powers, can no longer be taken for granted. The Apocalypse still looms, although not in the providential way some of our fundamentalist fellow Christians may sometimes imagine.

It is not primarily in such terms that I wish to discuss the theme of this section of the paper, 'Abolishing War or Abolishing Humanity', real and frightening as such terms may be. All war and not just nuclear war abolishes humanity at least in part, and not just the humanity of the obvious losers on both sides, of the killed and bereaved, of the disabled, displaced and disgraced. The survivors, nay the triumphant, are diminished, dehumanised by their experiences of the horrors on the frontline or by their lack of such experiences in their comfortable military or political offices. Sending people to fight and kill and die by remote control and for reasons scarcely intelligible to those fighting, killing and dying, is already to anaesthetise a significant section of one's human feeling and insight. Even the mere observers, listeners and readers of television, radio and newspapers are at risk of having their sensibilities dulled and their tolerance of human horrors enlarged. In a world of global communications nobody is untouched or unsullied by war. As the war propaganda heats up and the home forces become heroes beyond all reasonable criticism while the enemy forces (and people) are reduced to barbarians, another 'mutually assured destruction' of the humanity of both sides is at work.

All this does not happen through a single war. All wars have long overtures, often other and recent wars between the nations and peoples in conflict. More significantly the seemingly endless history of human warfare has made war respectable, even glorious, while rendering the human imagination insensible to possible alternatives either in self-defence or in resolution of others forms of conflict. Without the vision to anticipate or resolve hostile differences peaceably the human skills of peacemaking have atrophied to the point where it appears necessary and acceptable, all the while preparing the way for further war. War as addiction for those involved from soldiers to politicians to journalists is powerfully illustrated in Chris Hedges' fine book, *War is a Force that Gives us Meaning* (2002). Yet for humanity as a whole it is a chronic disease which could yet prove terminal and is always seriously disabling.

The psychological disablement is already evident in the immediate preparations for a particular war. Politicians and other propagandists bear the deeper responsibility for this but almost everybody on a particular side, even those opposed to the war, carry some responsibility and some mark of the disablement. Those most seriously disabled, even before a shot is fired or a bomb dropped, are the military themselves. At ground level their training is geared to making them effective killers, partly by its dehumanising influence on officers and men. Maintaining morale, so-called, is almost always at the cost of morality. The recent revelations about torture of prisoners-of-war in Iraq and the attempts to cover them up echo back over the centuries. In passing it might be asked why clergy of all denominations and religions accept the status of army and naval officers when they could and should have a properly pastoral role and status in caring for all involved in a war. The dehumanising of the fighting forces is not relieved by pastors becoming members of the forces themselves. The risk of eliminating people's humanity in the midst of war should not include the risk of eliminating their Christianity as well.

2. Of Arguments and Armaments

In the western, including the Christian, tradition the arguments justifying as well as restraining war are ancient in origin and have not substantially changed over the millennia. The developments in weaponry from spears to bows and arrows to guns, bombs and missiles and in social organisation from tribes to empires and states have altered the forms of war in initiation, conduct and conclusion but not the substantial arguments invoked to justify it. The concepts of just cause, primarily self-defence, and right intention in undertaking war, of respect for non-combatants in pursuing it and of a just settlement in ending it are still honoured in theory, if with varying interpretations, by both theoreticians and practitioners. The distinctions in theory between just-war defenders and political realists of varying hues suggest they belong to the same family with the inevitable family quarrels about detail. In the actual practice of war however and again as it spans the centuries, theory has usually proved a very inadequate guide. It would be difficult to identify a single actual war which satisfied all the criteria its wagers claim to respect as part of their political and moral traditions.

Such recurrent violations need not make the theoreticians or war leaders invoking them in a particular war situation sheer hypocrites or the theories themselves inapplicable. To adapt GK Chesterton's phrase about Christianity, theories of just war may not have failed; they may simply never have been tried. It might also be argued in their favour that they have frequently had some restraining influence in delaying the start of war and in its conduct even if that influence proved eventually to be totally inadequate.

In seeking alternatives to war and its proposed justifications it is important to recognise their strengths at least as they still appear and appeal to so many citizens and Christians, political and religious leaders. However, there is such an extensive literature dealing with all this that only a brief if honest recognition is necessary in this context.

Among the various factors which may readily undermine regard for just-war criteria and in particular the just cause of self-defence is the combination of economic and military power. 'The military-industrial complex', which President Eisenhower warned against in 1959, has taken on a whole new potential in the era of a single military superpower belonging to the world's strongest economic power. This situation poses grave temptations for the superpower, to impose its will economically and militarily around the world but also temptations for the less powerful, particularly those who see themselves as victims of the superpower, to resort to armed response where economic and other responses seem futile. And inherent in the close connection of the economy and arms development is the arms trade, which fuels so many conflicts within and between the poorer countries.

Domestically the major arms manufacturers exploit the security fears of their nation and the power complex of political and military leaders by designating certain arms programmes obsolescent and seeking larger government grants both for research and development and the production of new programmes. It is very difficult to be sure of the effectiveness of programmes old or new without the trials of actual war. And so the vicious, but for some financially profitable, circle continues.

3. Vocation and Temptation: Christian Dilemmas on Peace and War
Ambiguities of Christian History

As Jesus was a child of Jewish parents and born into and educated in the Jewish tradition, so Christianity is a child of Judaism in issues of peace and war as in so much else. Of course children do not simply replicate the beliefs and ways of their parents and Christianity represented a serious breach with Judaism despite their original relationship. In matters of peace and war Judaism offered a clear double inheritance in its succession of wars both against oppression and in pursuit of conquest. Israel's warriors, sometimes as they saw it, inspired and even led by God, contrasted with Israel's prophets of peace inspired as they saw it by the same God. The resolution of this contest and contrast was to be achieved in the messianic time of peace, of Shalom, not perhaps without its final devastating war.

In Jesus, as in his prophetic anticipators such as Isaiah, the promise of peace predominated. It was voiced in his post-Resurrection greeting to his disciples. Earlier and more powerfully it was pronounced in his call to forgiveness of enemies in the Sermon on the Mount, in the prayer he taught his disciples and in his appeal on the Cross to the Father to forgive these his enemies. His renunciation of protection by the sword in Gethsemene indicated how forgiveness and non-violence were integrated into his person and mission without being in any significant way qualified by his expulsion of the traffickers from the Temple.

All this is well known and repeated here to underline the later ambiguities which successive communities of Jesus' disciples fell victim to. The earlier communities remained faithful to Jesus' word and example in face of severe if intermittent cruel persecution and martyrdom at the hands of the Roman imperial authorities. However, with the 'emancipation' of Christians by the Emperor Constantine and the gradual ascent of Christians to positions of authority in the imperial service new problems and temptations presented themselves. For Christian leaders, bishops and theologians such as Ambrose and Augustine in the fourth and fifth centuries, the defence of innocent Romans against the attacks of the invading 'barbarians' demanded a new strategy which in their view and that of other Christians required the use of force, a violent repelling of the 'murderous' enemy and even follow-up punishment on their territory, property and even people. There were important Christian restrictions on violent, defensive retaliation at this stage. The motive should be effective love of neighbour, the innocent neighbour subject to unjust aggression. Despite the acceptance of punitive follow-up the response should be limited to just defence and just punishment for the crime. Those innocent of any involvement in the attack should be spared punishment. A striking example of this restrictive attitude emerged in Ambrose's condemnation and excommunication of Emperor Theodosius for his massacre of six thousand rebels at Thessalonika in 390 CE. For all his acceptance of just war or just killing in certain circumstances, Augustine in the City of God and elsewhere upheld peace as a primary characteristic of Christian living in accord with the Reign of God.

The ambiguities in theory and practice of what eventually became known as 'Just War Theory' continued down in to the twentieth and even the twenty-first centuries. In its earlier stages of development rather strict if sometimes arbitrary restrictions were put in place such as not fighting on Sundays or Holy Days or during Advent and Lent. This in theory offered the prospect of truce leading to peaceful negotiation and clearly reflected some of the non-violent legacy of Jesus and the early church. The prohibition on clergy engaged in violent conflict reflected some of that legacy also as did perhaps the exclusion of women and children from being perpetrators or victims of aggression. In further violation of the earlier legacy came wars and violent persecutions undertaken for religious reasons. The Donatists of North Africa in the fifth century were perhaps the first notable victims of this but as the centuries wound on other religious groups suffered similar fates at the hands of Catholic rulers working closely with religious leaders from Popes down. Indeed as the conditions for a just war were gradually refined Christian violence against heretics, Jews and Muslims became more common and destructive. The Medieval Crusades to the Holy Lands of Jews and Muslims as well as Christians, one of them preached by the 'mystic' St Bernard, one known as the Childrens' Crusade and all blessed by various Popes and bishops, showed how far the teaching and practice of Jesus and the early church had been distorted and at times abandoned.

Christian political practice was not however entirely dominated by war. Serious efforts to restrict war-making and promote peace-making were made by clerical and lay leaders for Christian as well as pragmatic reasons in the first half of the second millennium. The rise of the nation states, the competition for control of the newly discovered worlds and their resources, and above all from the Christian perspective, the dissolution of the united western church by reformation and counter-reformation resulted in at least a century and a half of war, partly if not dominantly inspired by Christian divisions. The Peace of Westphalia in 1648, concluding thirty years of 'Religious Wars', did not of course conclude the persecution of Christians in states ruled by prince or king of a different church. Violence in the names of both Christ and Caesar continued. To confirm the ambiguities outstanding Catholic scholars like Erasmus developed an anti-war stance and the 'Peace Churches', as they were called, emerged from the chaos of the Reformation.

The Enlightenment, which was in many respects reacting to religious authoritarianism and religious warfare, sought to promote tolerance between peoples and religions and in the work of Immanuel Kant offered a serious contribution to thinking about peace. However, revolution and war from the late eighteenth century and through the nineteenth, culminating in the two world wars of the twentieth, indicated how little influence the role of reason as opposed to or even combined with religious faith had in controlling inter- and intra-state violence. Indeed the twentieth century exceeded in the horror and extent of its global wars all previous centuries. The twenty-first has begun as if prepared to exceed even the war exploits of the twentieth. And the early signs suggest a deeper and more bitter entwining of religion with the waging of war than has been known for centuries.

Strands of Christian Witness and the Reign of God

In both the Hebrew and Christian scriptures and traditions there persisted a vision of the Messianic future or Kingdom/Reign of God with three discernible strands, connected for Israel to both its history and its future, and for Christians to Jesus the Christ and the Kingdom which he proclaimed and inaugurated. These are frequently described as the priestly, prophetic and kingly or wisdom strands. In this context Jesus came to be described as prophet, priest and king, although his kingdom, he insisted, was not of this world. In seeking further insight into the ambiguities of the Christian Churches, and in particular of my own Catholic Church, in relation to issues of peace and war it may be helpful to examine how these strands of the tradition interacted with one another in church and individual Christian and with the political powers of their day.

In the priestly strand, associated naturally with the priestly role, the emphasis is on the recognition and worship of the one true God. In the early days of the Christian Church this was a supportive reason for refusing military service as that involved worship of the Emperor. With the conversion of Constantine and the gradual establishment of Christianity that reason disappeared. However, the example of Jesus as renouncing violence might have found priestly support in reverence for the human being as created in the image of God, reinforced by the belief in God become human in Jesus Christ and in other human beings, the human as incorporated into the Body of Christ. As the church became assimilated to the Empire and its power, Christian priesthood became heavily involved in service and preservation of the Empire, its power and wealth. As the prophet Amos had proclaimed in the eighth century BCE, the seduction of the priesthood by the powerful and the wealthy had undermined its worship of the one true God. Such temptation and seduction has affected the Christian priesthood frequently in the course of its history to the point of abandoning its peacemaking role and even endorsing wars which by its own criteria were far from just.

The critique by Amos and other Hebrew prophets of the priestly betrayal of the powerless and the stranger by their option for the powerful was radicalised by Jesus in his teaching and practice. His option for the poor and excluded, his preaching of love of enemies, his refusal of earthly kingship and his practice and preaching of non-violence manifested his role of prophet, of shalom, the peace of the messianic era and of the Reign of God. The priestly people which formed the community of disciples, the church, was in this as in other respects to be a prophetic people. Prophecy like priesthood has its own temptations. The voice crying in the wilderness may not always be the voice of God. False prophets, as Jesus warned us, are always a risk. And within the givens of human ambiguity even true prophets may themselves yield to the temptations of self-centredness and power-seeking. Discernment of prophetic truth, the work of the Spirit in human history, can be a slow and painful task for the Christian community. Both the priestly and wisdom dimensions of the community share in that task.

The wisdom strand in the Hebrew and Christian scriptures develops in dialogue with other traditions, both religious and non-religious. Many of the teachings and parables of Jesus, such as his Sermon on the Mount, pick up on this Hebrew tradition in combining the prophetic with the wisdom. That Jewish–Christian development still continues as the dialogue partners of Christianity change and develop. It might be argued that emergence of Just War Theory as one example and of the church's current position on human rights as another were the result of such dialogues, and so integrated into the prevailing Christian wisdom. However the prevailing wisdom will always need the corrective of the priestly and particularly of the prophetic tradition. The abolition of slavery and the struggles against racism are obvious examples where both the ecclesial and the political power and wisdom require the challenge of the prophetic. In the contemporary situation, given the horrors of wars, the potential alternatives and the rediscovery of Jesus' prophetic teaching on non-violence by prophetic voices of our own time from Gandhi and Mandela of the quite different continents of Asia and Africa, the heroic sons and daughters of the American continent such as Martin Luther King and the first recipient of the Cardinal Dearden award, the late Rosa Parks, to Thomas Merton and Dorothy Day, the wisdom tradition itself, both religious and secular, may finally endorse the abolition of war.

4. The Risks of Peace and the Risks of God

Like any other truly human achievement, peace is not without its risks in the making or in the keeping. That much the assassinated freedom-, justice- and peace-leaders Gandhi and King already understood. Despite their religious and cultural differences, they derived insight and inspiration from the message and example of Jesus. The insight and inspiration have, as Christians believe, both human and divine bases. At the human level the strangeness and otherness of the other, individual or people, can appear and be realised as either potentially enriching or potentially destroying, as gift or threat. Too often the potential threat dominates the potential gift leading to mutual hostility in understanding and action, and sometimes violent action. In individual terms the threat may be to one's person or property, and personal security is a basic need of everyone which in properly policed countries under the rule of law is the responsibility of the state authorities and not of the individual himself. Gift and threat between persons go much deeper than anything involving law or law-enforcement can reach. In ordinary daily contact respect for the other involves a courtesy, honesty and even trust which law usually cannot command. Mutual trust, involving some self-entrusting to the other(s), is the key to stable personal relationships and fruitful social harmony. And in that trust, essential to peaceful relations between persons and peoples, lie the risks of peace and reconciliation. Where the true peace of Shalom, flourishing together in community and not just the absence of war, does not prevail, negotiation and reconciliation as the means of true peace demand the building of trust. Realistically this will take time and move through various stages. The first and minimal stage lies in the mutual recognition by the estranged others through non-violent coexistence, a stage still to be reached in many current estrangements. On this basis of coexistence, mutual collaboration on negative dividing factors (the threat) and positive possibilities (the potential enrichment) may begin. Beyond the process of collaboration lies the prospect of community and of flourishing together in that community. This messianic Shalom of the Hebrew prophets was announced and inaugurated by Jesus at a new level and at a new cost, that of laying down his life. The risks of peacemaking may be as drastic as that for others, as Gandhi and King exemplified.

It may be appropriate at this stage to turn briefly to the more enigmatic phrase in my title, 'the Risk of God'. It has a double significance in that it refers first of all to the risks which people take in taking God seriously, in being serious Christians in our context. Many Christians can more easily accept the comforting and consoling aspects of Christianity: 'Come to me all you who labour and are burdened and I will refresh you.' There are more demanding requirements, of forgiveness of enemies, of going first to be reconciled with your brother before you bring your gift to the altar, and above all of the renunciation, even of life itself, in certain if rare circumstances: 'Unless the seed fall into the ground ...' All these risks which Christians incur in varying degrees as they seek to incarnate love of God in love of neighbour, particularly the strange and estranged neighbour, also open the way to a deeper relationship with God. 'I was hungry and you gave me to eat ... As long as you did it to one of these least ones ...' And this applies more widely to the whole human family in love of neighbour as part of their human condition. Starting from such neighbour response means taking the other human being as irreducibly other and never as a simple extension, tool or still less possession of the self. The self in turn is also irreducible other to all other human beings. Encounters between humans as irreducible others involves encountering mystery, the irreducible as finally unknowable and unpossessable. In Hebrew–Christian scriptures the ultimate mystery, the ultimate and absolute Other, is Yahweh, the God of Jesus Christ. To accept the neighbour as truly other is to risk encountering the God who is in the New Testament terms Love, with all the enrichment and surrender of self which that involves. It is to enter the domain of peace with all of God's family with all the attendant risks to personal, national and international security.

An even more mysterious relationship between the risks of peace and the risks of God may be discerned in the whole creation–salvation initiative of the Creator–Saviour. In creating human beings in the image of Godself with powers of recognising and responding freely to the others and the Other in love, God risked refusal, which duly and frequently occurred. The further pursuit of divine love for humanity moved through the fidelities and infidelities of the covenanted Israel to finally sending his own Son, who 'emptied himself, taking on human form, unto rejection and death'. The affirmation of this mission in Resurrection and the renewal of the gospel of life and love is only partially recognised and accepted in the subsequent human community. The Kingdom/Reign of God as Jesus described it and of which Shalom is a key characteristic will only be completed in the eschaton, beyond history. Yet the historical responsibility of Christians in particular is to promote the coming of the Kingdom, including its central feature. In this they will be serving as well as seeking to engage the whole human community, the whole family of God. In this century at least we should accomplish the minimum conditions of Shalom, the abolition of war and devising of alternative methods of personal, national and international security. If all that could be accomplished within so many nation states so quickly we should have the courage and creativity to establish the same internationally in the century which lies before us.

Love and Justice: In God and Church;
In Sexuality and Society

For Martin Pendergast at 60

Neil Astley's second major anthology of modern poetry, *Being Alive* (2004), sequel to *Staying Alive* (2002), opens with a poem by Elma Mitchell simply entitled 'This Poem' and it reads:

> This poem is dangerous; it should not be left
> Within the reach of children, or even of adults
> Who might swallow it whole, with possibly
> Undesirable side-effects. If you come across
> An unattended, unidentified poem
> In a public place, do not attempt to tackle it
> Yourself. Send it (preferably, in a sealed container)
> To the nearest centre of learning, where it will be rendered
> Harmless, by experts. Even the simplest poem
> May destroy your immunity to human emotions.
> All poems must carry a Government warning. Words
> Can seriously affect your heart.

The friend who gave me this volume as a present suggested that 'theology' might well be substituted for 'poem' as 'dangerous' to children or to adults if 'swallowed whole'. The simplest theology 'May destroy your immunity to human emotions' and 'seriously affect your heart'. Of course it too may be 'rendered harmless by experts' at 'the nearest centre of learning'.

If all this seems an over-elaborate introduction to a theological essay on 'Love and Justice' in honour of a friend, at least it helps underline the dangers any theologian faces as would-be poet or would-be expert in reflecting on the divine and human mysteries of Christian faith. The poem, the poet and the friend offer not only timely warning but loving support in facing these dangers. Too much theology lacks the human warmth of friendship, human friendship modelled on that of Jesus and his human friends, and on the love of God and neighbour, the primary characteristic of Christian life and thought. And the blessed justice seekers of Jesus' Sermon on the Mount (a truly dangerous poem) might learn something of the searching demands of justice from the poet's search for the *mot juste*, the word that 'can seriously affect your heart'. All this applies more sharply to a moral theologian particularly in his efforts to relate love and justice across the spectrum of God, church, sexuality and society.

Liberating Moral Theology

The manuals of moral theology which dominated Catholic moral teaching from about 1600 to 1960 had very limited, legal perspectives on justice and sexuality and completely ignored love/friendship. With their scholastic background they might have been more mindful of their ultimate ancestor Aristotle and his discussion of friendship in the Ethics and of their primary Christian teacher Aquinas and his much broader virtue approach to morality and in particular his insight that charity/love was the form of all the virtues. Intended as handbooks for training confessors in the wake of the reforms of the Council of Trent, they concentrated on sins as violations of a legally formulated code of morality and gave sexual morality a very negative bias, while restricting justice issues almost entirely to issues of exchange between individuals. From 1960 and particularly after Vatican II a much broader and richer view of moral theology as a theology of Christian and human life began to address these limitations with at least some success. However, the task of such a moral theology is far from complete and given the historical and eschatological character of Christian and human life it never will be.

In many ways moral theology has made its most significant recent progress in areas of justice. This may be most effectively illustrated by comparing church attitudes to human rights in the late nineteenth century when it firmly rejected them to the current enthusiasm for them at the highest level. Indeed the Catholic Church and the late Pope John Paul II count among human rights' strongest defenders on a global scale. This does not mean that church authorities or moral theologians agree among themselves or still less with the wider world about particular public claims as human rights. The bitter divisions over abortion are proof enough of this and there are many other examples, some of which will surface later. More problematic and controversial still is the 'western' tendency to translate all moral issues into 'rights language', offering a new version perhaps of the legal codes of the old manuals and with many of their reductionist consequences. While human rights are an integral part of justice discourse and so have a role in developing a morality of love/friendship, justice and sexuality, they should not exclude other approaches to a fuller moral understanding of these and other issues.

Justice and Love

While justice and sex may have been restricted and distorted in the manuals of moral theology, love or charity, like its companion friendship, was completely ignored except for a strange and brief treatment of 'the sins against', such as scandal or cooperation in the sins of another. This undoubtedly related to the manuals' role as guides for confessors and confession of sins, but was more deeply based on the split between moral theology and the rest of theology, particularly the study of scripture. Vatican II's recall of moral theology to its scriptural base, which had already been initiated by various scholars, restored charity/love to the primacy that was its by New Testament right and which it had enjoyed in the seminal writings of theologians such as Augustine and Aquinas. Gerard Gilleman's *The Primacy of Charity in Moral Theology*, published in the late fifties, provided a crucial anticipation of the Council's ambition. At the same time inside and outside the Council, debates and documents such as John XXIII's *Pacem in terris*, Paul VI's *Populorum progressio* and the Council's *Gaudium et spes* expanded and deepened the understanding of justice in its personal and social senses. Although it did not become a primary concern of Catholic moral theologians then or later, the relation between justice and love is critical to any authentic theology of Christian living or moral theology.

Love and Justice in God

In many spheres of discourse, religious and secular, academic and popular, love and justice have been sharply opposed. At the extremes of theological discourse the God of the Old Testament, Yahweh, was contrasted with the God of the New, Abba, as a God of Justice opposed to a God of Love. More careful biblical scholarship and more sophisticated theological analysis revealed the critical love dimension of Yahweh, God of Israel, and the critical justice dimension of Abba, God of Jesus Christ and of Israel.

Distinguishing but not separating or opposing justice (sedeqah/mispat, Hebrew Bible) and love (hesed/ahab,HB; agape, NT) is the true message of the Hebrew and Christian scriptures. Jesus' exchange on the greatest commandment of the Law (mispat), clearly referring to the inherited Law, asks 'How do you read'. His interlocutor's reply, 'Thou shalt love [agape] the Lord your God with your whole heart and your whole soul and your neighbour as yourself', offers, as Jesus confirms, a true life-summary for the justice seekers who are listed in the charter of discipleship, the Beatitudes of the Sermon on the Mount.

The unity of love and justice in the Godhead and in the divine creative and re-creative activity recorded in the Old and New Testaments reflects the mysterious unity and simplicity of Godself. How this unity and simplicity are combined with three distinct persons has taxed the intellectual endeavours of the greatest theological minds in the tradition from Augustine and Aquinas to the Barths and Rahners of the twentieth century. Yet the divine diversity in unity and simplicity can illuminate the meaning of both love and justice between Creator and Creation and within creation itself, as well as the interrelation of love and justice internal to the divine and human spheres. Indeed it is in and through the interactions of God with human beings, history and society in the life, death and resurrection of Jesus Christ, that the tri-unity in God becomes known. These interactions in turn, from the overshadowing of Mary by the Holy Spirit at pregnancy through the distinctive roles of Father, Son and Holy Spirit at Jesus' Baptism to the integral drama of Jesus' death into the hands of the Father, his resurrection and sending of the Spirit at Pentecost bear the indelible marks of divine Love and Justice in face of human sinfulness and lovableness. The God, who so loved the world as to send his only Son to give his life a redemption for many, was in him reconciling the world with Godself. And God completed that work of justification, restoring just relations in love- reconciliation, Paul's words, by sending God's Spirit of reconciliation to call and enable Christ's disciples to be ambassadors of reconciliation in turn.

The Trinity as Unity of Love and Justice

The Mystery of the Triune God surpasses all human understanding. Yet as it creates and nourishes all human existence, personal and social, it challenges that understanding to trace God's image and likeness in human person and community. The *vestigia Dei Creantis et Trinitatis* in cosmos and humanity have fascinated theologians and contemplatives for millennia. In recent times theologians such as Jürgen Moltmann have concentrated on the Trinitarian shape of human community. A sharper, if less ambitious, analogy might seek to relate love and justice as analysed in human experience to the life of the trinity as indicated in scripture and described by some mystics.

The differentiation of Father and Son, of the First and Second Persons of the Triune God, is by name and by the analogy of creation reflected in the relationship of human father and son, the relationship of two human beings. (The gender language may be laid aside for the time being.) At the divine and human levels such differentiation involves recognition and respect. ('This is my beloved Son in whom I am well pleased'; 'Into thy hands Father I commend my Spirit'.) Such recognition of identity and otherness is the basis for justice in relationship, what the moral tradition following Aquinas called *debitum ad alterum*, what is due to the other. And it is only on the basis of such difference, recognition and respect that love and true communion or unity are possible. It is that love between divine Father and Son which constitutes the third mysterious person of the Trinity and in its distinctiveness receives the recognition and respect in justice/equality of the first two persons as it completes their unity in love. Human differentiation involving recognition and respect in justice as basis for (comm)unity in love is ultimately rooted in the tri-personal life of God, however crudely it reflects it.

In the Community of Disciples: The Church

Love and justice in the community of disciples operate at a number of levels. At the level of the Body of Christ, the theological and mystical substance of the community, love and justice come together as distinct, yet unified, as in the Godhead itself. As we have just seen, the love which unites Father and Son and issues in the Holy Spirit respects the otherness of each divine person in the ideal of justice. So with the church as founded in that divine reality through the mediation of Christ, each member is to hold every other in the bonds of love and the differentiation of justice.

That is the gift and call of membership of Christ's Body, of the graced sharing in the Trinitarian divine life in its unity in difference, of the baptismal insertion into the communion of saints. History, however, makes clear that the communion of saints is also a communion of sinners. Love and justice are engaged in a struggle with each other and with a range of other incomplete virtues in the individual and ecclesial life of Christians. It is in this incomplete historical era that the church seeks, in hope rather than certainty, for the fuller expression of the love and justice for which it was founded, both within its own life and structures and in the wider society. Only in the eschatological fulfilment of the reign of God will love and justice coincide and prevail. Such fulfilment is the final stage of the human, indeed cosmic, embodiment of divine justice and love.

In the aftermath of the death of Pope John Paul II and the impact of his funeral it is clear that he contributed powerfully to love and justice in the world. His striking message on developing a 'civilization of love' and his range of encyclicals on justice in the world, as well as his travels, particularly to the poorer regions around the globe, gave eloquent testimony of this. Internally to the church many Catholics were less enthusiastic about his exercise of justice in different areas, from theology to the role of women to the treatment of gay and lesbian people. In most of this John Paul was carrying on the tradition of his immediate predecessors so it would be unfair to single out his papacy as the only or even the primary culprit. The internal structures, attitudes and activities of the institutions of church have failed for centuries to match, in varying degrees, the love and justice which ought always to characterise the church as people of God and body of Christ.

These failures have been failures in theology, in the understanding of faith–hope–love as much as in the practice of kingdom values such as justice. How the first apostolic community, the company of Jesus' friends and followers, assumed over the centuries the present, centralised juridical structures is too long and complex a story to recount here. Much of this may have been justified in particular contexts as the Christian community sought survival or faced unusual challenges of growth or decline. And the efforts at evangelical reform from time to time did not always meet with widespread acceptance. Here it is necessary to concentrate on love and justice and their understanding and practice within the church.

The Trinitarian insight of the distinction and equality of persons remains primary. Only the recognition and respect for others as equals in their otherness enables them at once to be given their due in justice and to be bonded in love and communion. The radical equality of Christians in communion rests on their baptism into Christ, which then becomes through the gift of the Spirit their call and capacity to love one another as Christ has loved them. Only equality in difference permits true community and the love and justice which it embodies. The call to particular ministry in that community to guard and guide it must be fashioned after the particular model of the serving Christ and not the model of the lording gentiles. In this context baptism maintains its primacy over ordination and the people of God over its clerical and episcopal ministers, as Vatican II tried to express. The neglect of these insights have resulted in unloving and unjust treatment, even exclusion of various individuals and groups within the church. And it has prevented many from making the contribution to faith-understanding and practice. Theology and other faith initiatives have suffered over the centuries from the absence of lay experience, skills and energy, perhaps particularly those of women, because of male clerical dominance and distrust. This has frequently been manifest in poor Christian understanding of the 'secular' worlds of civil society and sexual community/relationships.

Love and Justice in Sexual Relationships

In the liberation of moral theology referred to earlier, the theology of marriage was moved out of constraints of a contract in canon law to the more humane and Christian category of a community of love open to life. This allowed for a much more personal view of marriage and of sexual relationships as primarily loving rather than as primarily reproductive. This development has presented its own difficulties but it has been a powerful liberation in Catholic moral discourse just the same. No longer are sexuality and sexual relationships to be treated as either exclusively directed to reproduction or otherwise demeaning, even dirty, but as vehicles in the right circumstances of the highest Christian value, that of love. Of course the right circumstances are very important and sometimes highly disputable. In resolving the potential disputes the justice dimension of love will be a key element.

Pope John Paul II's understanding and promotion of 'a civilization of love', including sexual love, had all the hard qualities of justice, which always involves a certain equality. That equality in sexual relations operates first of all in consent, in the equal capacity to consent so that paedophilia is excluded, for example. But the equality required also excludes the kind of power play and exploitation in which one party intimidates or blackmails the other. The violence of rape is not only opposed to justice but to love also. Equal or just consent is not simply a matter of the freedom of both parties but also of their maturity and commitment to each other. In biological, social as well as phenomenological terms the intimacy of bodily union betokens a mutual and continuing acceptance which one-night stands or deliberately short-term relationships do not express. Exclusivity and fidelity are part of just sexual loving.

Sexual differentiation and openness to procreation are a traditional and crucial part of sexual relationships. It has, however, been accepted in many traditions, including the Christian, that an infertile or childless relationship can be a moral and real marriage. The recognition of the woman's infertile period as a way of regulating procreation for Catholics from the time of Pope Pius XII has, despite the encyclical *Humanae vitae* of Paul VI, persuaded many theologians and married couples that other means of birth regulation are acceptable and in a further step that sexual loving may not be irrevocably confined to just heterosexual relationships. However, such other relationships between people of the same sex would have to satisfy the same just requirements as those between people of different sexes. Equality in capacity to consent, in commitment and so in fidelity and exclusivity would be clear demands of homosexual as of heterosexual loving. In sexual relations, heterosexual or homosexual, as already emphasized for members of Chirst's body, each partner is to hold the other in the bonds of love and the differentiation of justice.

A Christian blessing of such love and justice, without involving the sacramental character of Christian marriage, could be appropriate to faithful disciples, if not generally accepted as yet. More urgent may be legal protection of gay citizens and partnerships from various kinds of discrimination, although also belonging to the following and final section on love and justice in civil society and culture.

In the long journey of humanity and Christianity to a fuller understanding and living of love and justice in sexual relations as in other areas of life, the concept and reality of friendship with God and one another will bear much revisiting. In such prayerful and reflective revisiting the love and justice inherent in God and manifest in Jesus will enrich our understanding and correct some of our inevitable mistakes.

Love and Justice in Civil Society and Culture

John Paul II's call for 'a civilization of love' might be regarded as sentimental tosh, if he had not shown the world in deed, word and symbol his commitment to freedom, justice and peace, crucial characteristics of love. A brief digression on the Pope's achievements in the world might confirm the power of his words. His contribution to the liberation of Poland and other countries under the tyranny of the USSR witness his regard for political freedom as does his later promotion of human rights. In the later part of his pontificate, his encyclicals *Laborem exercens*, *Sollicitudo rei socialis* and *Centesimus annus*, celebrating the centenary of the first social encyclical, included criticism of free market capitalism as well as Marxism. Together with his visits to the poorer countries and his pleas for debt cancellation for the poorest and for fair trading regulations, the Pope proved one of the major advocates of the global anti-war campaign. In his final years his anti-war stance became more pronounced as evident in his persistent opposition to the war in Iraq.

However, love and justice in society and culture belong to a much older and broader tradition, Christian and secular, than that represented by the era of John Paul II. And we must not forget his overlooking some of the achievements of the enlightenment and democracy, particularly in the western world. The relations between religion, morality and law are indeed more complex in the present mixed democracies than the Pope seemed to realise. And the witness of the church to the truth, as it sees it, may not be simply imposed by the church on the democratic state, where other visions of the truth have a claim on voters and legislators. The interplay of love and justice, of the preaching and promotion of the reign of God and its values, tasks for the church, do not readily translate into political choices and civil legislation. Recent documents and regulations on the responsibilities of Catholic legislators, in the United States of America for example, failed to recognise the dangers, to the church itself as well as to the state, of attempting to restrict unduly the freedom of voters and legislators, and to turn complex political programmes into one or two issue agendas, with heavy emphasis on gender and sexual matters. The exclusion of some Catholic politicians from the Eucharist on the basis of their distinguishing between their private moral conviction on abortion and their acceptance of the law of the land at this point, did not really exemplify either love or justice. Such ecclesial behaviour was further undermined by particular church authorities ignoring the positions of other candidates on the legitimacy of capital punishment or of the war in Iraq, equally condemned by the highest authority in the church.

In response to the deprived and exploited, to the poor and the sick, many church leaders and agencies gave both powerful witness and effective help in a striking combination of love and justice. That too has a long Christian history. In recent decades, as the poor of the world became more visible and audible through mission and media, the mutual inhabitation of love and justice exercised a significantly transformative effect on ecclesial and indeed political aid programmes. It is in this area that the Christian insight, that love without justice is ineffectual and justice without love inhuman, is so important.

Among the many spheres in which such insight might be pursued, a neglected one is that of artistic achievement, the realm of what is sometimes grandly described as 'high culture'. Without the space, the technical (pictorial) equipment or the competence to pursue this at any great length or depth, one might reflect on love and justice in the form and matter of a single poem. As hinted in the introduction, ethics, moral theology and theology in general have been diminished by their distance from artistic creativity and aesthetic analysis. This applies in particular to ethical dimensions of love and justice in all human relationships and communities.

The poem selected here is by an Irish and Cork poet, Seán Dunne, who died prematurely in the 1990s before he was forty. In its free yet disciplined form, it reveals even in the abbreviated version quoted here what Yeats described as poetry 'truth seen with passion', in word, image and rhythm. Its combination of practical love and sense of injustice needs no prosaic commentary.

Refugees at Cobh

We were sick of seeing the liners leave
With our own day in, day out, so when
When the boats edged with refugees to Cobh
It was worth the fare to travel

From Cork to glimpse on railed decks.

They hadn't a word of English but we gave
What we could: sheets and rationed tea,
Sweets, blankets, bread, bottles of stout.
The night they sang for hours

And then moonlight fell on silence.

So strange to see emigrants to Ireland

It was our Ellis Island: hunched
Lines of foreigners with bundles

In time we turned them away. Most stood
As still as cattle when the ship drew out
And the pilot boats trailed after it.

Still we turn them away, we Irish who depended for so long on not being turned away. The love which gave what it could in Cobh is still active in Ireland as elsewhere but it lacks the sustenance and substance of justice in dealing with the new refugees, asylum seekers and immigrants. Poets and artists often see further and deeper than politicians and church leaders, would-be guardians respectively of justice and love in the world. Love and justice with their associates, human rights, freedom and peace, belong together in a truly human society, its politics and economics, but have to be worked out in detail in their structures and practices.

Such talk, like 'This Poem', is dangerous. And the danger reaches back to the biblical poem of Genesis 1-3 and the first creative act of God. The risks taken in that divine initiative involved deeper risks still as finally God sent his own Son. His execution did not stay the divine hand and the sending of the Spirit inaugurated the New Creation, the reign of God preached by Jesus. That reign or kingdom is still in the making, in its dangerous making. A theology which would serve it cannot avoid the danger and the risk and yet it must attempt in its ham-fisted way to reflect and promote the love and justice intrinsic to the Triune God. Above all the words of that God, the poem that is that God can and should seriously affect your heart.

Moral Theology and Transformative Justice

In Honour of Sean O'Riordan

The original title for this contribution to the conference in honour at once of two remarkable Redemptorist theologians, St Alphonsus Liguori and Fr Sean O'Riordan, was: 'Does Moral Theology Exist?' Clearly in the context of such a distinguished gathering of moral theologians for a great moral theological occasion, it was intended to be sharply provocative. But not only so. Since I was first appointed to teach moral theology almost thirty years ago, I have been haunted by a theological version of Pritchard's question in 1904, 'Does Moral Philosophy Rest on a Mistake?' Not for quite the same reasons of course. And the astonishing changes in the method and matter of moral theology since my appointment at Maynooth in 1958 might be fairly urged in support of a strongly affirmative answer to my own question. And no doubt it could be very persuasively urged by other contributors to this conference, including such outstanding pioneers as Bernard Häring and Josef Fuchs, who have done so much to develop these changes. Three of their achievements are relevant to my further concerns here: the restoration of the theological dimension of moral theology, particularly by return to its biblical roots; the exposing of the historical dimension of morality both in its theoretical understanding and in its practical expression; the emphasis on the personal subject rather than the individual action. These three achievements at least have enabled moral theology to transcend its manual exposition which dominated the Catholic theological world from about 1600 to 1960. And such basic developments are by no means at an end.

Moral Theology: Achievements and Reservations

My reservations, however provocatively expressed, relate directly to these three positive achievements. Moving in the reverse order, I find in the extraordinary richness of the development of person as subject an almost inevitable tendency to overshadow the community dimension of morality and moral theology. Of course, one might respond by recognising that the person is always perceived in relationship with other persons and in community. Still, the location, perception and expression of morality is discussed primarily, if not exclusively, in personal terms. Personal awareness, personal understanding, personal decision and personal activity: these are stuff of moral analysis for philosophers as well as theologians. Community awareness and understanding, decision and activity are not analysed in similar ways. For all the genuine community concerns of moral theologians, community remains extra and extrinsic to their primary analysis.

A possible central reaction to this would be parallel to the current moral theologian's reaction to the manualist's preoccupation with individual actions rather than with person-in-act. It is intrinsically incomplete and so unreal. Preoccupation with the person as distinct from the person-in-community and as, more obviously, not placed in balance with community-of-person is intrinsically incomplete and so unreal. I have dealt with morality/moral theology as based on both persons-in-community and community-of-persons elsewhere in more general terms. In this paper I will be concentrating on a particular aspect of it under the rubric of justice.

The second important achievement instanced earlier was the discovery or recovery of the historical dimension of morality in theory and practice. In terms of moral theology itself this has been an important advance. Natural Law, which has been fundamental to moral theory in the Catholic tradition at least since Aquinas, has been seen more recently to incorporate the historical dimension of humanity, human culture and human morality. This has in parallel, if not in an always directly related fashion, influenced moral theology's understanding of the person as developing and historical. It may be too much to say, given, for example, the theological stress on conversion (Häring et al.) and the philosophical stress on fundamental option (Fuchs et al.), that continuity has been stressed at the expense of discontinuity. Yet much moral theological discussion of person and community seems to take the evolutionary, gradually developing sense of history more immediately into account than the eschatological, transformative sense of history. Creation, as in the debate about the specifically Christian ethic, is more directly and clearly at issue than new creation. Incarnation is more significant than redemption or resurrection. This I take to be more clearly applicable to *social* morality and its theology than to *personal*, where certainly for Häring, Curran and others conversion and discontinuity have played an important role. Indeed the fuller dimensions of continuity and discontinuity between Creation and New Creation involve person, community and cosmos.

All of which argument moves towards the final question and first assertion about the 'new' moral theology. How biblical and theological has it become? Is it more directly derived from or at least more substantially influenced by the Judaeo-Christian tradition than its manualist predecessors? Is the biblical-theological language and reference in the end no more than a veneer on the naturalistic, legal ethics rather narrowly expressed in the manuals? Or is there a genuine sense of the gospel at work in the shaping of moral theology and in its more particular discussions whether of special areas of Christian living such as sexuality or of concrete decisions such as the use of *in vitro* fertilisation?

Answers to these questions and to the earlier ones raised on person, community and cosmos, as well as on history and eschatology demand more lengthy and delicate re-evaluation of the meaning and task of moral theology than is possible in this paper. However, the originating question, 'Does moral theology exist?' will continue to disturb.

A Theology of Justice and its Morality

The strategy adopted here, not primarily as evasion of the deeper and more comprehensive question, is to examine the role of justice in current theology and its discussion of morality. The phraseology is, for the moment, quite deliberate as justice, like other moral concepts such as truth, freedom and peace, has much wider theological ramifications today than even contemporary moral theological writing might suggest. And theology's discussion of morality leaves open for the moment the difficulties alluded to about the phrase 'moral theology'.

The return of justice to a central place in theology in the seventies and eighties has been no doubt for a number of different reasons. Dominant among these may be the emergence of various 'liberation theologies'. Hitherto justice had been the exclusive concern of manual moral theology or, more marginally in its social implications, of Catholic social teaching. Even with the gradual theologising of papal social encyclicals and other Christian social documents in the sixties and seventies, the heart of western systematic theology remained untouched. It is seldom remarked how seriously the doctrinal tradition in theology has suffered from the impoverished theological condition of moral theology, manual and renewed. Central doctrines of God, Christ, Holy Spirit, salvation, grace, church and sacraments have suffered from aridity and distortion by their distance and lack of challenge from the living concerns characteristic of moral theology.

A theology of meaning, however related to the cultural, philosophical movements of its time, risks unreality unless it is closely integrated with a theology of living. The one theological ideal of the great scholastics, if no longer capable of such systematic unity in elaboration and expression, must for the sake of the doctrinal as well as the moral theologians, operate as stimulus to dialogue, critique, correction and conversion among the many specialised theologians. A doctrine of the trinity which has not confronted theological thinking about marriage and society and a moral theology of truth which ignores the great Christian doctrine of revelation and saving truth are both reduced and distorted.

Justice, as I have been suggesting, offers a singularly important and illuminating example of this disjunction and impoverishment. Its manual and even scholastic history were not illuminatingly theological and Christian. The influence of Aristotle as opposed to that of Amos, as opposed to the biblical–theological tradition, ensured a clear analysis of justice as dealing with claims between individuals, as exchange/commutative or restorative justice with the important extension of distributive justice on regulating claims of individual citizens against the *polis* or state. All this was considered in the context of a general virtue of justice which might be interpreted as the most generally virtuous condition of the good person. It provided for Aquinas et al. as cardinal virtue a principle of organisation for a whole range of subordinate virtues, including that regulating the relation of human beings to God, religion.

There was a clarity here in one-to-one relationships, in giving the other his due, which remains essential to the maintenance of ethical human relationships and the survival of society. It was balanced by an acceptance of distributive justice within society and qualified by important exceptive situations such as urgent need (*evidens, et urgens necessitas*, Aquinas, *S Th*, II.II. 66.6). There was, then, an openness to larger considerations and possibilities of development which were, however, largely overshadowed by the dominantly individualist concerns and the focus on the possession, dispossession and restitution of property. Manuals of moral theology, in 350 years' reign, could scarcely escape from this. The gradual growth of Catholic social teaching, initiated by Pope Leo XIII, at once retrieving an older patristic tradition and developing a contemporary one, were not regarded as hard-nosed moral analysis of the kind on offer in Noldin-Schmitt or Aertnys-Damen. And neither manual, down to 1960, was particularly interested in the central truths of theology.

The integration of individualist and social morality and the emergence of some theological concern (cf. Synod of Bishops 1971) have at least made important connections. It would be too much to say that these developments have in ethical terms truly integrated personal and social justice, made it a unified virtue affecting the relations of person, communities and cosmos. It would be even more misleading to see these moves as exposing the deeper doctrinal/theological meaning of justice, as revelatory of God and of God's saving work in Jesus Christ.

Renewing the Justice Tradition

A quite different line of theological development, that of liberation theologies, has, as I mentioned and despite its title, taken 'justice in society' as a central theological theme. The connections between justice and liberation have obvious historical, social and political dimensions. The emergence of human rights as criterion of justice in society clearly provides a bridge-concept between right as basis of justice (Aquinas) and right as freedom (Locke to UN Declaration). Theologically, liberation is the equivalent of salvation, redemption and justification, in that genuinely theological sense of the justice of God transforming unjust human beings into *the just*. (The Reformation debates as to the meaning of justification and its distinction from sanctification, for example, are, I believe, no longer relevant here.)

The Aristotle–Aquinas tradition, which dominated justice discussion for so long and, in an attenuated form, shaped the manuals of moral theology, was rich and subtle. This was evident in Aristotle's reflection on how the just human being behaves as critical and in their shared division of justice and distributive justice. The definition as the constant inclination to give every person his/her due with right (jus) as the object of justice was all the more developed in Aquinas but on the basis of Aristotle. Pride of place in this tradition went to exchange justice between individual human beings involving 'exact' equality. Distributive justice as between state/society and the individual did not seem quite so significant although it provided a basis in the later manuals for a rather weak presentation of taxation and welfare laws. The purely penal law attitude to taxation laws, so prevalent in moral theology until recently, fitted into this weaker sense of distributive justice. Real justice, for moralist and confessor, involved an obligation of restitution on violation. Only violations of exchange, or commutative justice involved such obligations.

The potential of this tradition was of course much more than fully realised later. Catholic social teaching did extend many of its central ideas into the idea of just wages and conditions for workers, an extension of exchange/contract justice and special care for the weak and deprived, an extension of distributive justice. Meantime a secularised version of the tradition, which held that right was the object of justice (Aquinas), moved into natural rights, rights of man and human rights. These in turn found their natural place in late Catholic social teaching (*Pacem in terris* etc.)

Between Aristotle and Amos

Yet recent theological concerns have exposed some of the limitations of this tradition. For Christian theology, human dignity, based on creation in the image of God and new creation as daughter/son of God, has given respect for and response to persons and their human rights a depth and urgency which purely secular theories finally lack. More significantly the recovery of the biblical tradition of justice has thrown much revealing light on this historic phenomenon.

For the biblical as opposed to the 'philosophical' tradition, justice (sedaqah) is primarily a characteristic of God in his/her dealings with the covenant people of Israel. Yahweh/God is at once the origin and standard of sedaqah, rendered in the Septuagint as dikaiosune. This justice of God is not so sharply differentiated in Hebrew as in Greek and later western vocabulary. It overlaps with fidelity, loving–kindness and mercy. Hebrew monotheism clearly plays a role in Hebrew understanding of the unity and overlapping at this transcendent level of the qualities manifested by Yahweh in his dealings with his people Israel. An isolated justice which might become simply vindictive as in 'an eye for an eye' hardly seems faithful to the God whose justice and mercy were so deeply intertwined. In his clarification and development of mercy and forgiveness in the Sermon on the Mount and elsewhere, Jesus was being true to the deepest thrust of his own Hebrew tradition.

The transcendent origin of sedaqah and its role as standard for Yahweh's people involve also, of course, their gracious God in providing a divine enablement. If they were to be just, as God was just, they must enjoy the presence in power of that God. The biblical tradition knows of human weakness in justice as in other areas in ways which the philosophical tradition can only touch on post-factum. Enablement from God and for Israel is included in the challenge of covenant justice. The awesomeness of justice as transcendent in origin is balanced by the intimacy of justice enablement as immanent to the people.

Neighbourly relations within the people of Israel have individual aspects analogous to the great philosophical traditions. This is evident in the Decalogue, for example. Yet the great prophetic tradition stemming from the eighth century BCE exposes the essentially social character of covenant justice in ways that are scarcely developed or even discernible in philosophers before Marx. Amos seems in this respect to stand in great contrast to Aristotle. It is the injustice of the society as a whole which is the object of his denunciations. This is specified by his attacks on society's officials, the judges, for their acceptance of bribery to render false judgements, in the extravagant behaviour of wealthy women, and generally in the neglect and exploitation by the wealthy and powerful of these by now traditional categories of the oppressed in Israel, the poor, the widows, the orphans and the strangers. (He has his own version of class description, if not yet class analysis.) For this the religious assemblies of Israel are unacceptable. For this their society, like neighbouring unjust societies, will be destroyed.

These features of injustice in society as a whole, the unjust behaviour by wealthy, officials and powerful, the exploitations of particular weaker groups, recur in the other great prophets. It was this tradition which Jesus inherited and developed in his teaching and ministry, in his denunciations of the rich and powerful and in his fellowship with the weak and excluded.

The biblical tradition then offers a much stronger sense of justice in society than simply justice between single individuals. It takes as a final criterion the treatment of the poor and the weak, the sick and people with handicap, isolated women and strangers or immigrants. But it does not leave it at that. Amos, in some ways the angriest prophet, urged by the priestly leader to go back to his village and his shepherding, has a vision too of a new society and a new justice. The promise, which undergirds the whole history of Israel, of justice and peace flourishing in a society and cosmos transformed, keeps open the hope of Israel in God's power to bring about a new kingdom. It is that trust in the transformative power of God, in the transformative justice of God, which sustains the people until the Messiah should appear, the time be fulfilled and the kingdom come.

The Jesus Way

Jesus' paradoxical way of meeting these promises left many in Israel perplexed. Yet the time was at hand and the kingdom had come. The new Israel and new creation in Paul's phrase ensured the justification of all. The transformative justice of God was at hand and at work. The end time had begun. Justice and peace should reign. The gift of God's justice and mercy was available in the gift of the Spirit through the risen Christ. History must still continue its ambiguous way, but the final, eschatological breakthrough of God in justice had occurred. The human task was to let that justice take root in person and community, in relationship and structure. What Amos had foreseen was to be realised, if still partially and fitfully, but effectively as the transformation of human beings and human society.

The vision of such a just society, the gift of it on offer and the power of the grace to achieve it which summarises the Judaeo-Christian tradition of justice seems rather remote from the more careful and calculated analysis of an Aristotle or even an Aquinas. It may have been Karl Marx, undoubtedly drawing on his Jewish prophetic roots but unable to accept their essential connection with a transcendent God of justice, who restored to the philosophical tradition of justice something of the vision and fire-power of transformative justice. In this the liberation theologians are following and going beyond his work to its truly biblical and transcendent roots.

From Managerial to Transformative Justice

Of course the Aristotle–Aquinas tradition has never been simply individualist and never been closed to developments in the social area. These developments have been for the most part incremental, adapting to various changes in society rather than inspiring or generating them. This would be true of various contractual theories also, many of which – including such sophisticated and fair ones as that of Rawls – do offer ways of at least improving society in justice terms.

I believe that these forms of justice are therefore essential to the management of society. They constitute, to invoke a much-used analogy in moral and theological discussion, the grammar of personal and social relations. Without them our everyday and much longer-term dealings could not operate fairly and, in the true human sense, fruitfully. The sustaining of social life like the sustaining of conversation depends on observing the rules of grammar embodied in the regulations of what I might call managerial justice.

It is, I think, a useful phrase as long as it is not used in a pejorative or dismissive sense, and as long as it is not understood as simply static or paralysing of the status quo. It has its own openness to gradual change like all rules of grammar.

However, much of the injustice confronting the modern world requires a more visionary kind of justice, because the people concerned, races, impoverished countries and classes, women, people with handicap and so on have rights to an entirely new quality of life, relationship and structure. Visionary, because slow, incremental improvements based on present structures will simply not prove effective or timely. That kind of vision to meet that kind of need requires transformative justice, a justice that sees such transformation in a particular way as the right as well as the need of the particularly deprived.

The Example of International Debt

There are a number of areas where one could illustrate the importance of both managerial and transformative justice. A particularly acute current set of problems is that of international debt. Within the accepted range of managerial justice much of this debt of third world countries could be recognised as already paid or as to be written off or as to be drastically rescheduled by western countries and financial institutions in ways that are fair and indeed of mutual benefit. The Economic Summit in Toronto in July 1988 seemed to be making moves along these lines. They are to be welcomed by all anxious to redress the fundamental injustice underlying first world–third world economic relations and the particular injustices to third world countries involved in many of these loans. (First-world institutions were handing out money irresponsibly in the seventies, often to national leaders who had no popular mandate and had clearly no interest in anything but their own enrichment.)

However, such welcome expressions of managerial justice do not attack the underlying structures. A new economic order has been proposed frequently enough in the last fifteen or twenty years. The requirements of justice, transformative justice, include such a transformation of the world economic order. It is no longer to be treated as a utopian dream or neglected in favour of occasional exercises of overdue managerial justice as at Toronto.

Other examples, such as women in society or race relations or the place of particular groups in particular societies, travellers, people with handicap, unemployed, enable one to see the value and limitations of a progressive managerial justice and the final necessity of transformative justice.

Transformative justice, with its origins in God's self-giving in covenant and finally in Jesus, with its divine summons and divine grace or enablement, transcends but does not displace the managerial justice which has been the main preoccupation of the philosophical tradition. This may be a paradigm for the relationship between Christian faith with its implicit morality and what is sometimes described as human or secular morality. It could, therefore, offer a way into a genuinely theological moral theology. And en route it could allow a further exploration of the God who is justice and the God who is love as a way of establishing a more satisfactory relationship between justice and love than hitherto available even in renewed moral theology.

Faith and the Cure of Poetry: A Response to the Crisis in the Catholic Church in Ireland

For Gabriel Daly

In seeking a theme appropriate to Gabriel Daly's major contributions to Irish church, academy and society, it seemed right to connect his two great interests of faith and culture to confront the continuing crisis in the Irish church. My own interest in the poetry dimension of Irish culture helped specify the theme more exactly.

The title of this paper is not entirely original, taken in part from a book by an American literary critic, Mary Kinzie, called *The Cure of Poetry in an Age of Prose* (1993). But having reflected on the crisis in the church in Ireland – and it is still a crisis – very many of what might be called the *conventional* responses do not connect with where the *real* problem is. So this is, in a sense, an experiment in how we might approach some of these difficulties. Let me briefly indicate some elements in the crisis.

The crisis hit centre stage in the early nineties and front page and headline news with the resignation of Bishop Casey. There followed a series of clerical sexual abuse cases, one of which actually brought down the government in very bizarre circumstances. While that itself was shattering for many people, it was to some extent more a symptom than a cause. It was more the coming to expression of a long-standing and developing crisis than a simple explosion, because we had been in crisis in the Irish church, I believe, at least since 1968. Some people in my generation think the world ended in 1968. But we can take 1968 as a handy, kind of 'after the Council' date – the revolutionary year in Europe and elsewhere, and, internally to the Catholic Church, the year of *Humanae vitae*. All of that was feeding into a modernisation that was taking place in Ireland anyway, for which my church was ill prepared and with which it did not begin to deal for a long time. Curiously, the visit of the Pope in 1979, a striking public success, if it did not intensify the crisis, certainly obscured it. People lapsed back into thinking that all was well with traditional Catholicism in Ireland.

Through the eighties this was clearly not so, and the two bitter referenda fought on abortion and divorce left a bad taste, and left many people worried about where we were going as a society, and what kind of leadership the Irish church could offer in a rapidly changing society. But the rapidity of change increased greatly again in the 1990s. This was partly political, partly compounded still by the troubles in Northern Ireland, partly economic in that we had been through a certain number of upswings and some serious downswings. And then the upswing started to take over. Can the church thrive in a prosperous society? Can the Irish Catholic Church handle a prosperous country in which there would be people of much more independent mind? Could it recover from the scandals? These were important questions but I believe that there was a deeper underlying difficulty which was certainly about the church and its mediation of the gospel of good news. This was an underlying difficulty about God, about faith, a difficulty that was not being recognised by bishops, clergy or even by some theologians. And maybe that was because we might not be able to face it in ourselves. Because the faith question was too searching, we stayed with the church question. The God question, and what might be called the risk of God, was too difficult for people who were trying to keep the show on the road, keep people going to church and Catholic schools full. We did not notice a kind of darkness growing inside ourselves, a kind of opacity to the presence of God and the light of the gospel.

Of course, there were many counter signals. There were many people doing remarkable things both in the Irish church and out of the Irish church, particularly remarkable in regard to poverty at home and development abroad. These things were still moving on, catching and attracting young people of considerable talent. Yet in some ways over that period there was a closing down and a closing in. The church was busy at some level, whether it was in catechetics or in justice work or in parish councils or in liturgy development, or whatever it might be, which did not reach where the closure was occurring. We were moving into a dark, opaque stage as far as our minds and hearts were concerned in relation to God, and we did not recognise it. This of course was not only revealed in what we might call the numbers game. There was still in 1990 about 85 per cent weekly Mass attendance, although that had dropped by 1998 to something like 61 per cent. There was an extraordinary drop in vocations, by about 90 per cent between the early 1970s and the mid-1990s. That was part of what I mean, but in those of us who put ourselves forward as church, there was a lack of openness to the spirit of God, a kind of darkness into which we were being drawn, and maybe we needed the darkness. Maybe now we have to live with it and in it and take it fully seriously. Part of the swings and roundabouts of the last ten or fifteen years has been like the aftermath of the papal visit: you get a great upswing when something good happens, and then you get a great downswing when some other scandal emerges. But it is not here that we should be concentrating our attention or our energy.

There is in our culture and in ourselves an increasing darkness in terms of the true meaning of our humanity, and the ultimate meaning of it that we call God. And that darkness we cannot banish by any particular tricks, even any particular eloquence or any particular pastoral strategies. And it is not peculiar to Ireland and not peculiar to the Catholic Church. It is something that is shared much more widely, if not always remarked upon or it is remarked upon in a kind of fundamentalist, apocalyptic away, that actually misunderstands the darkness and misunderstands above all that it could be a generative darkness for us. I chose for my topic 'Faith and the Cure of Poetry' because I thought that the poets and the artists among us might have some experience of that darkness, some experience of its creativity and generativity, and that they might indeed be stumbling on some things that we need, in terms of the graciousness of reality, of its liberating quality and richness. I also selected it because there has been an enormous resurgence in the arts in Ireland in tandem and roughly contemporaneous with the decline of the church.

Just as the decline of the church is not something homogeneous or simple, but complex, with developments as well as declines, so the resurgence of the arts is not all masterpiece. There is bound to be a lot of dross in the amount of activity that is going on in Ireland, in music, painting, sculpture and writing. But it is less important that there is a lot of dross than that there is a great deal of creative effort, and a considerable amount of creative achievement with which the church needs to make contact. Traditionally, we have thought of the great Catholic Church as being a patron of the arts. Related to that characteristic of the Catholic Church is what we call its sacramentality, that is, its embodiedness. When you think about it, faith is above all a body language. It is the body language of the members of the body of Christ. It is the body language of people who entrust themselves to one another in love, which is the great faith act of our lives. It is the body language of God and his chosen people – in the incarnation, in the whole of creation – described by Sallie McFague as the body of God (as taken from *The Body of God: An Ecological Theology*, 1993). And that body language seemed to me important because if we are stumbling around in the dark, if we are taking our darkness seriously, we have to listen more carefully to our own bodies, we have to listen more carefully for other bodies; we have to be tactile; we have to feel our way. And that language, all language, is body language. It resonates out of our bodies, it comes through in a way beautifully described by Micheal Ó Siadhail, an Irish poet, in a remarkable article, 'Spirituality and Art' (as taken from *The Furrow*, 48, 1997). The resonance of speech as it comes through the body is so important. And this again is the embodiedness of the body language of our faith, characteristic of us as Christians and, particularly, dramatically true of Catholics.

We have, however, distorted and suppressed much of that body language. We have only to look at the drab line of people going up to communion to see how lacking the body language is for this great bodily occasion – receiving the body of Christ, as members of that body of Christ. It seemed to me that we would find something of help from those artists who, out of their bodies, offer us encounters with reality, encounters with truth, whether in word or painting or music. I was drawn further to that, partly by our own tradition, partly by listening to the artists themselves, like the wonderful Irish painter, Tony O'Malley, who died recently, who used to say that the paintings happened to him. The graciousness of it, the gift of it, is received before it is achieved. That is the remarkable theme of the novel *Gracenotes* (1997) by Bernard McLaverty, a Northern Irish writer. One of the astonishing elements of that book is that it is a man writing about a woman composer – and women critics say that he gets it right. But what is remarkable is its account of how the notes come and how the composition begins and how she agonises through it, all pieced in with her own agonising, the birth of her child, the abandonment by her partner and her own painful origins back in Northern Ireland. But again it is that graciousness embodied in us which prevails, and that we have to rediscover.

In reading Mary Kinzie's *The Cure of Poetry* and a number of other critics, including Richard Kearney's *The Wake of Imagination* (1994), we see not so much that kind of attention to the resonance and the resource and the cave, as Heaney says, where these images begin, but attention to what Kearney distinguishes as the ethics and the poetics of imagination. And in his ethics of the imagination, he is concentrating on the embodied, or the facial, presence of the other, taking his cue I have no doubt from Emmanuel Lévinas among others. But it is that presence that is the call to use, and it is the inventiveness, the poetic imagination as he calls it, which allows us to devise a response appropriate to that presence, recognise it and respond to it; whether it is in writing or painting or music. And it is that kind of alertness, that attention to the other, which Kearney talks about, that instils in us, as it were, the disciplines necessary for creative responses, so that the disciples and the creativity come together. This is also very much a theme of Mary Kinzie's book, as she analyses a whole range of poets, and sees poetry as a calling; and a calling must eventually be rooted in reality, in the reality of human others, in the larger reality and the responses to it. The articulation of it is a matter of receiving the grace and answering the call, but also of developing the skills, the voices, the words, and so on. But it will always be an embodied response, a body language.

In pursuing that just a little further, we can see that Eavan Boland, in her book *Object Lessons* (1995), is talking also about the ethics, that call and gift, internal to poetry itself, internal to language, but then rooted in the political – as she sees it in the place of women in society and in the role of woman as poet. All this is pushing the project of faith and poetry on, but it has to be tackled more concretely. As we stumble around in the dark, as we try to find, to recognise, to articulate, as we learn from the artist, as we develop both the ethical imagination and the poetic imagination, of which Kearney and Kinzie both write, we may begin to see where the cure element comes in. This is addressed and named directly by Seamus Heaney in his Oxford lectures, *The Redress of Poetry* (1995), as somehow setting things right in a particular way. He is thinking about it in literary and political terms, in European and Irish terms, but also in personal terms. It is not yet what you might call redemption; it is not explicitly Christian in that way, but he is into that mood which is beyond ethics and invention, and is about setting right, redressing. And as we move in that direction, we could pick up on Ó Siadhail's article, where he sees in the making of a poem the bringing together of reality, that there is a reconciling act at work. And that is taking another step, in another way.

In George Steiner's *Real Presences* (1989), the poem or the painting is a way of mediating presence – human presence – but also ultimate presence; Steiner is working again out of a tradition that is not simply his own. And the best example of all, of books of recent vintage, is a reprint of a book by Elizabeth Jennings entitled *Every Changing Shape* (1996) – a study of what she calls mysticism and the making of poetry. And it is at that stage with Jennings that we come to understand something of the cure of poetry. But you cannot rush these stages. I have named them, but not worked through them. I have not yet found the cure. I think I know the line along which it might lie. Some examples are needed that would help us to understand that line, and enable us to take the darkness seriously, and so begin to move towards the light. To that end I have chosen a number of poems by contemporary Irish writers.

I do not wish to press the poems into a false context, but what Heaney and so many other critics say is that the good poem, taken in its own meaning and on its own merits, has a transformative value. After wrestling with these good poems for some time, I think that their transformative capacity has enabled me to see something that – perhaps – the poets did not have in mind, but which I hope will not involve a travesty of their poems. The first of these is by Derek Mahon, in some ways the most underrated poet of his generation in Ireland, and in some ways the most powerful and the most European. This poem is called 'A Disused Shed in Co. Wexford'. In a startling opening stanza, Mahon introduces us to the prison hours of the lost spirits of the world: 'Peruvian mines, worked out and abandoned/... Indian compounds where the wind dances/... And ... a disused shed in Co. Wexford', which he comes upon with friends and camera and where:

> Deep in the grounds of a burnt-out hotel,
> Among the bathtubs and the washbasins
> A thousand mushrooms crowd to a keyhole ...
>
> They have been waiting for us in a foetor
> Of vegetable sweat since civil war days ...
>
> Those nearest the door grow strong –
> 'Elbow room! Elbow room!'

These 'Powdery prisoners of the old regime' recall the dark dungeons of so many human prisoners, past and present. They conjure the darkness which the many inhabit and which inhabits the many. Mahon's final stanza re-echoes those screams, the cries for salvation we need to hear from others and to release in ourselves, and, I would add, in our church.

> They are begging us, you see, in their wordless way,
> To do something, to speak on their behalf
> Or at least not to close the door again.
> Lost people of Treblinka and Pompeii!
> 'Save us, save us,' they seem to say,
> 'Let the god not abandon us
> Who have come so far in darkness and in pain.
> We too had our lives to live.
> You with your light meter and relaxed itinerary,
> Let not our naive labours have been in vain!'

The next poem at least hears the cry for help and is troubled by it. It helps us to pick up too what we suppressed in our own tradition and what might have saved us from some of this darkness if we had been alert and listening. It is a poem by Eavan Boland, entitled 'The Oral Tradition'. After a public reading the poet is getting ready to face the winter journey home. As she puts on her coat she hears two women talking in the shadows, capturing her attention with words like 'summer', 'birth', 'great-grandmother'.

> 'She could feel it coming' –
> one of them was saying –
> 'all of the way there,
> across the field at evening
> and no one there, God help her …
>
> … it was nearly night …'
>
> '… when she lay down
> and gave birth to him
> in an open meadow.
> What a child that was
> to be born without a blemish!'

The poet recalls how she had become drawn into the experience in all its sensuous vivid significance, conjoined with these women in a living oral tradition.

> One moment I was standing
> not seeing out,
> only half-listening
>
> staring at the night; the next
> without warning
> I was caught by it:
> the bruised summer light …
>
> where she lay down
> in vetch and linen
> and lifted up her son
> to the archive they would shelter in:
>
> the oral song
> avid as superstition,
> layered like an amber in
> the wreck of language
> and the remnants of a nation.

It is commonplace to say that the Catholic Church, and the Irish Catholic Church, have neglected the oral tradition of its women, have neglected their dignity and their need, have neglected the hints and innuendos that lie underneath the surface, and so have lost that sense, a sense 'suddenly of truth, its resonance'. It is the overhearing in the half-light that may help us through the darkness, but it will be an ambiguous darkness, ambiguous light. Going still deeper into the structure and poetic skills of the poem would be still more revealing of the healing effect of the poem.

To come back to my earlier figure, that of body language with its own enormous ambiguities, it remains central to us in the great mysteries of human loving, and in that symbol of divine human loving we call the Eucharist. The centrality, the ambiguity and the possibility of healing are wonderfully expressed in Nuala Ní Dhomhnaill's poem, based on an old Irish tale. It is called 'An Féar Suaithinseach' or 'Marvellous Grass'. I use Michael Hartnett's translation. She begins by addressing her priest-lover:

> *Nuair a bhís id do shagart naofa*
> When you were a holy priest

She then relates how this priest dropped 'the blessed host' when he saw her approaching him for communion. She was ashamed, became seriously ill and nearly died. To her in bed came all the usual experts, medical and religious, but no cure. Let men go out to 'cut the bushes, clear the rubble … the misery / that grows on my tragic grassland'. There they will find 'a patch of marvellous grass' from which the priest will bring the host lost to her; on her tongue 'it will melt and I will sit up in the bed / as healthy as I was when I was young.'

This poem was, of course, written long before we knew of the recent clerical scandals, but it does convey something that many of Ní Dhomhnaill's poems convey: the relationships between the marvellous, the 'marvellous grass'; the body, the sexual body; the body of the Eucharist, the mystical body; how we cannot, as it were, evade these. And while again, one has to respect the poem as it is – and it is not easy to understand the different levels – it does strike me as pushing us back again to taking seriously our physical bodies and our body language, and our body as a community.

I should like to continue this discussion not with a poem but with another image of body and its resonances. In our present situation we in our western world are seen very much as consumers. And when we look at the people in disused sheds in Uganda, or Burma or wherever it may be, we pass by, or put our few pence in the box. We forget the screams, half-silent screams, because we are too busy consuming; a bit like the mushrooms, those at the front, crying, 'Elbow room' in Mahon's poem. But we are consumers because we are bodily beings. It is part of our glorious and gracious condition that we consume. We could not live without consuming, and our universe is in some extraordinary way a self-consuming universe. But as we are consumers we are communers. Communion is as important to us as consumption; they can be at odds. Because we consume so much, we are not in communion with very many of our fellow human beings around the world, who are deprived. In the story, the story of the good news, beginning even in Genesis and the marvellous communion between God and humanity, and Adam and Eve, there is the breach in that communion by the sin of consumption, the particular sin of consumption as the myth and the great poem of Genesis tells us.

This breach became so characteristic of the history of humanity that though given the fruits of the earth to enjoy that we might commune with one another, we tried to seize them, to get more than our share at the expense of others. That is the history of our relationship with God, the breach in communion because of our push to consumption, so that God had to become consumer and took flesh. And he was a consuming foetus within his mother's body and consumed at her breast and grew up knowing the difficulties of and the need of consumption – and how it had to be in the context of communion. To make that clear, he established a tradition of meals. Whether they were meals of miracle or simply meals of companionship, it was the new kind of meal that established the new communion, the new *koinonia*.

All that was too much for the powers that were, and they conspired – as they often do – to have him eliminated. As they did that, it seemed that even God's last, best throw of overcoming this enmity between consumption and communion had failed. In the story of Good Friday, as we used to read it in the old liturgy and the Vulgate, are Jesus' famous final words: *consummatum est* – it is consummated; it is finally consumed. And Jesus is finally consumed by his enemies, by death, by the earth in which he is buried, and that might seem the end of the effort to overcome the enmity between communion and consumption. But a couple of women on Sunday recognised him; and a couple of people on the way to Emmaus were joined by a stranger and persuaded him to stay to break bread, and in the breaking of bread they recognised him. They knew the meaning, because on the night before he died, he took bread and he blessed and broke and gave to them and said, 'Take and eat, this is my body' – bodies again – 'Take and drink, this is my blood. Do this in memory of me.' It is by consuming the body and blood, the bread and wine, that Holy Communion is established. The breakthrough, whereby the body language of communion would be ultimately and irreparably the body language of consumption, and *vice versa*, had been established; established in Jesus, established for humanity, but yet to be realised in history.

It is that body language that we have to pick up again. It is in this darkness that the disciples felt when they left the supper room, or at Calvary, that we can begin to get the sense that consuming together is communing together, and that it is a divine call for the whole world. And that the ambiguities in all our communing and consuming mean there is still a patch of 'marvellous grass' – and we will be as well as we were when we were young. And this is what we look to, hope for, attend to.

It may be that from these and other poems, from the poems of people's own lives, from the poems that are scripture, from the poetry and drama of the Eucharist, we will begin to recover a sense of the marvellous, begin again to move out of the darkness. But we have to be prepared to start at the beginning. We have to relearn the fumbling body language. We have to trust the first encounters we make, strange and demanding as they may be. It is too much to hope that poetry will cure our ills, where all the doctors and friars and priests summoned to the bed did not. But we will at least, from these and other artists, learn to read again the body language of our world, and of our own scriptures and our own sacraments, and in that we begin to respond to the crisis that is surely ours, but which could be grace and not destruction. Perhaps the community of faith could yet be what it was meant to be, 'a patch of marvellous grass'.

Give Beauty Back: Art, Morality and Mission

For Vincent MacNamara

Vincent MacNamara's artistic interests were always evident to his friends. Music in particular was the great love of his life. His work and person have always conveyed a sense of the beauty at the heart of things. It is not surprising that in his writing, his sensitivity to language and his range of literary reference, explicit and implicit, made him the most readable of moral theologians. And he had a theology to match the style. His theology was not self-consciously or deliberately aesthetic, but in its grace and subtlety of analysis it rendered Christian ethics a matter of aesthetics also. Ever conscious of his missionary background he thought and wrote for a globalising church and world and moved easily between Kiltegan/Kimmage and Nairobi. This small contribution to celebrating his life and work wishes to explore some connections between art, morality and mission under a title borrowed from that most elegant and powerful of poets, Gerald Manley Hopkins, 'Give Beauty Back'. Poetry is Vincent's second artistic love and Hopkins he has used in his ethical and theological writing to significant effect.

Creator, Creation and Creativity

From the theologian's perspective art and morality have their roots in creation and creativity, the creation and creativity of God and of humanity. In the sharp debate about the relation between Christian faith and ethics and how far ethics was autonomous, a debate to which Vincent MacNamara made a notable contribution, some confusion occurred among Christian moral theologians whose terms of debate centred either on revelation versus reason, or on revealed morality versus natural (law) morality. A more radical resetting of revelation, reason, morality and natural law within the context of the Christian doctrine of creation would have illuminated some of the difficulties. The particular difficulties of Christians in dialogue with those of other religious and moral traditions or those of a purely secular moral tradition would then need further investigation, but should not prevent Christian theologians from clarifying their own starting points now or even from entering into effective conversation with these others.

For the Christian theologian the Creator of the universe and the Lord of history is the God of the Old Testament and the New. Creation is

Yahweh/God's first testament or covenant both in the sense of God's original commitment to his world and in the sense of his original script or scripture, in which his intent and achievement might be finally deciphered. With the creation of human beings, God had partners to his creating covenant and decipherers of his creation script, 'In the image of God he created them. Male and female he created them.' Creation had become personal and relational, establishing community, however fragile, between Creator and creatures and between creatures themselves. How fragile it was and is needs further attention later. For now it is important to dwell on the divine originator and creator, on the action or better the process of creation, not only in its week-long fable of Genesis but also in its incalculably long cosmic evolution and in its millennia of human history, and finally on the product of creation, unfinished as it may be, the world we experience, celebrate and lament.

'Creator' (and its associates) appears in a theological context to be a properly divine term. Only God can create in the full and proper sense. The Bible itself begins with the announcement that God created the world: *barah elohim*. Later theological speculation favoured the interpretation that this was creation *ex nihilo*, creation out of nothingness. A favourite theological apologetic poses the question: how can there be something rather than nothing? Converging questions and insights would suggest that creation, creating and creativity should be used strictly as attributes of God. Yet these terms are human terms and in whatever language they are used of God, they must be originally human terms, applied, as technical theology might say, in an analogical way to God, that is, in a way similar to regular human usage and yet one as profoundly different as the profoundly different and transcendent God requires. As with so many other crucial words like person, love, community, law, only a continuing dialogue between the Christian biblical/theological traditions and particular cultural traditions with their philosophical, political, moral and artistic usages can provide the deeper discernment needed in moving between divine and human creation.

The divine image characteristic of human creatures, according to Genesis, was symbolised and realised primarily in their covenant–partnership with God and one another (their communicating, relating-loving and life-giving capacities) and their responsibility for and therefore ability to decipher the world entrusted to them (intellectual and imaginative capacities). From their life-giving, deciphering and communication endowment the entirely new continued to emerge; in another human being, in a fresh understanding and depiction of the world, communicated to one another by newly minted sentences, stories, songs, by primitive paintings or sculptures, in new and fruitful ways of encountering that world, ensuring survival and developing human communities. Human creativity was at work from the beginning not only in interaction with other humans and the world about them, but also in interaction with their God in ritual, song and story.

Theologically speaking, human creativity is a derived creativity, deriving ultimately from the originating creativity of the Creator–God, however mediated in biological–genetic and historical–cultural terms. In range human creativity is as wide as the world of human encounter and its potential reaches as deep as Godself, as mystics and religious geniuses bear witness. In form it is primarily responsive but no less free and innovative for that. Human encounter with the environment, cosmic and human, elicits a free and multi-form response in farming and engineering, in desiring, loving and hating, in speaking and writing, painting and praying, in all the moral, skilled, artistic and religious activities which characterise human living. In that larger context morality and art belong together to humanity's responsive and creative capacity. In that larger context also, humanity's reach and response is always on the move, seeking to transcend current boundaries, imbued with a fresh mission. The mission statements of today's commercial enterprises, for all their pretentiousness, signal something of that human urge to go forth and go forward in terms which they may have immediately borrowed from a religious context but which also belong to the human enterprise and vocabulary as a whole. The more exact connections between art, morality and religious mission will be explored later against this background.

Creating and Differentiating

If God be truly God how can there be anything else, different, other? A recurring intellectual difficulty for believers. Christian scripture and tradition, building on their Jewish inheritance, wrestle and live with the paradox without finally resolving it. Resolution would undoubtedly deny one or other term of the Creator–God and finite creation duo or at least dissolve the difference between them. And the difference is essential to the identity of both and to the whole value of the cosmic and human enterprise. Creation as differentiation at the originating, divine level, differentiation between Creator and creation and differentiation in a necessarily different sense within creation provide the structure for all human creativity, including the aesthetic, the ethical and the religious. The emergence of the different, of the other, enables creative dialogue between Creator and the creative creatures we know as human beings as well as between human beings themselves.

At the divine level and in Christian belief it is clear that creating results is something totally other than the Creator. Yet the otherness of creation in relation to God does not exclude communication between Creator and creation. On God's side this includes the continuing and one may say creative care of the whole universe, even to the sparrow that falls to the ground. Divine providence has always been seen by both Jews and Christians as part of God's commitment, as part of the fidelity and self-giving involved in the very act of creating. So divine creating might be better described as a process of divine activity without which creation would lapse into nothingness. The clock-maker God of deist thinking, whereby God set the universe ticking and then abandoned it to its own resources and devices, could never be reconciled with the God of Abraham and of Jesus Christ. Not that the understanding of God as continually caring and creative does not present its own serious difficulties, some of which will have to be considered later, but fidelity to the biblical tradition allows for no other understanding.

On the creation side communication with God belongs to humanity, at least as far as our current knowledge goes. Divine–human dialogue permeates the history of Israel and Christianity and indeed of the whole of humanity in different ways. Even the atheistic surge in recent centuries in the western world may be no more than a historical phase as some sociologists, previously defenders of the inevitable secularising of the world, now seem prepared to admit. In any event secularising comes in many forms, not all of them necessarily atheistic. And some forms of atheism may be healthy rejections of a distorted God in a search for the final truth, in Christian terms a search for and so a response to the ultimate other or God, however implicit or nameless that search and response may be.

Without impugning the integrity of those who declare themselves atheists, if they belong with the searchers they belong in that sense with the most sensitive Christian believers, whose journey of faith lies between darkness and light. It is a journey in hope, always incomplete, often uncertain about its next step and supported only by trust in the frequently elusive guidance of the Spirit. In the image of dialogue with their God rather than of journey towards that God, humans stammer and stutter; ill-chosen words and unfinished sentences are too often the best that the believer, individually or in community, can offer. Creative responses in prayer to God despite or perhaps because of a long sophisticated tradition from the psalmist to the mystic, are seldom adequate for the occasion. For this inadequacy there are usually aesthetic and ethical reasons, although the deeper reason remains that of the sheer difference, the infinite otherness of God in relation to humanity. That otherness was expressed for the Hebrews in the word *qadosh*, translated later as *hagios*, *sanctus*, holy. 'Holy, holy, holy is the Lord God of Israel.'

The pattern of divine creating issuing in others, human and cosmic, is reflected in a limited way at human level, both in human participation in the introduction of human others to the world in procreation and in parenting, in the useful development of the resources of the cosmos and in the artistic creation of beautiful objects for their own sake and for the illumination and joy of human observers. Such human creating, dependent as it is on the givens of divine creation, requires a God-like respect for the humanly created others. This applies in a unique and irreducible way to the human others, unique and irreducible as they are in their imaging of God, and in Christian terms 'other Christs', manifestations of the Incarnate God. For Christians this is the ultimate foundation of morality between people, whether it be expressed in values and virtues, in rights and responsibilities, in law, natural or divine. The human face of the other, in Levinas' figure, calls for unconditional regard. In more rounded, Christian terms each human other is gift (grace) and (moral) call in his or her human otherness. Using the other as means simply and not as end to be respected in herself violates that condition of uniqueness and irreducibility, her status as (ultimately divine) gift and call.

The details of such respect and implied response in all the dimensions of human relating and living are for another occasion. It might however be emphasized that this recognition and respect for human otherness is not an individualist ethic as some readers of Levinas and of other personalist philosophers might assume. Respecting difference as a way of building community is the lesson of the Scriptures, Hebrew and Christian. Beyond these intra-human concerns God's celebration of the pre-human creation in Genesis, Job and elsewhere and the divine entrusting of the earth to human care as well as use, provide a basis for treating our cosmic environment as gift and call. If its otherness is not so sacrosanct as that of human beings who may and should use it, they must all respect and cherish it and not simply exploit it.

The relationship between divine creating and human moral responsibility could seem self-enclosing or at most open to religious activity and responsibility. Yet human creativity is an immediate reflection of the divine and human morality itself has always had close, if sometimes contentious, ties with morality. The contention usually turned on the content of the artist's work which appeared to some to be pornographic, humanly degrading, politically seditious, even blasphemous. Such controversies may never be disregarded as trivial or irrelevant but in Christian perspective they need to be subordinated to the sheer wonder of humanity's creative and artistic capacity. Although involving many of the crafts and skills which humans are continually developing in the reach for a better life or sometimes just survival, artistic creations are not primarily useful. They enrich human living as ends in themselves, not as means to something else. To use them primarily for prestige or profit, as many collectors or dealers may, is to miss the point and the experience. The experience may be multifaceted and varies with the particular art form, be it music or painting or poetry. One recurring facet is that of joy in the sounds, the colours and the words. 'And God looked at it and saw that it was good,' indeed beautiful so that Solomon in all his glory could not compare with the lilies of the field. The artist looks and listens and feels the world about her and looks and listens and feels her experience into notes and brush-strokes and word-rhythms. Not of course in any simple or direct translation. The way of the artist is often indirect, whether by recollection in tranquillity or forgetfulness in clamour as mind and hand, ear and eye draw out of the foul rag-and-bone shop of the heart the images which she expresses and discovers in sound and colour and word and which have the power to challenge the listener or viewer or reader.

The creation of the real artist invites our recognition of it as truthful in its account of her interaction with the world and solicits our appreciation of it as beautiful in its form of expression. For the artist and the viewer the completed artistic creation as an end in itself forms in some sense an independent world. It is a new other open to fresh encounter with the artist as well as the viewer. And of course it may elicit quite different reactions from artist and viewers and be subject to varying interpretations. Yet as an independent and, in an important sense, an original expression of truth and beauty it enables and calls for recognition of its particular truth and joy in its particular beauty. Such recognition and joy affect its audience more or less deeply, in proportion to the power of the creation and the receptivity of the audience. With a really powerful created object and a really receptive audience illumination and elation may be apt descriptions of some of the effects. As the music of Bach or Beethoven resounds through a sympathetic and attentive listener or she surrenders to a beautiful poem or painting, the sense of new creation and creativity, and of new dimensions of the world and of the self may be experienced. Artistic creation as source of illumination is revelatory of the deeper mystery of humanity. While in its finitude it remains opaque to the fullness of that mystery, it may alert the recipient to the further and fuller possibilities of what may be called the transcendent. Such spiritual effects of the true and beautiful as incarnate in music or word are part of the religious tradition of Christianity certainly. In a more secular era artistic experiences may be the primary spiritual experiences for many people, but however secular in content they may still provide gateways to the religious transcendent for believers and openings for a spiritual if less specific transcendent for the others. At their limit artistic experiences with their potential for self-transcending are akin to prayer and sometimes important preliminaries or companions to it, even if they may never be simply identified with it.

Creation, Differentiation and Reconciliation

The created as an expression of the creator and yet differentiated from and other than it causes a certain tension, even estrangement or alienation between creator, divine or human, and created. Parents and children begin their lives together as strangers, as aliens. Over time this differentiation may prove the foundation for a loving community or for yet another dysfunctional family. The drawing together of family members as distinct others into a genuine community respecting, indeed encouraging and rejoicing in that otherness, is a life task, the life task of reconciling diversity in unity. It is now increasingly a global human task if the compression in time and space of so many different peoples, cultures, religions and interests is not to cause the human family as a whole to self-destruct. Such reconciliation might well be considered the primary moral task of humanity at present. A great deal of moral imagination and creativity will be required for its fulfilment. In Christian theological terms the task of global reconciliation could be interpreted as crucial to the promotion of the Reign of God as announced and inaugurated by Jesus Christ, the task of Christian mission. To this we must return.

At the micro-level of the individual artist's work the differentiation of creator and created demands a different kind of reconciliation. The artist has at some stage to accept the work as his own best self-expression at least for the present and he has to let go of it into the wider world. In all this he is both trusting himself and entrusting himself to what may prove a critical and even hurtful audience. The differentiation achieved in his artistic creation may also become a source of hostile estrangement for himself and from his critics. Creation and reconciliation should belong together in the artistic as well as in the moral life.

If human creativity and creation are rooted in the divine so is reconciliation. The otherness of the Creator–God and the divine creation already discussed have at least the potential of hostile estrangement. The

Hebrew scriptures wrestled with the actuality of such estrangement in the very first accounts of creation, in the story of the Fall which is at once accompanied by the promise of salvation and reconciliation. The subsequent stories deal with divine attempts to reconcile humanity with its creator, with itself and with the wider creation. The climax reached in the life, death and resurrection of Jesus Christ as Son of God made man is described by St Paul in the same passage (II Cor 5:16 ff), as both 'new creation' and God's presence in Christ 'reconciling the world with himself'. This divine creating–reconciling mission will be led by the Spirit until Christ comes again. Humanity is finally re-created or reconciled in hope, beyond history, but the first fruits of that hope are already at work in history. The Reign of God has already begun.

The Cost of Creating

In letting others be, bringing them into existence, the creator, divine and human, may and frequently will enjoy the process and the product. In the Genesis story the divine Creator rejoiced in his handiwork, he looked on it at various stages in the process and saw that it was good or very good. The beauty of his world had made him glad. But it came at a price even for the infinite and infinitely loving creator. It was different and demanded that it be respected in its difference. Creation imposed what the Scottish theologian Donald MacKinnon among others has called a self-limitation on God. And in a much cruder image one could say God was stuck with creation. Of course a God of infinite power could undo his creation but what would this say of a God of infinite wisdom and love? This self-surrender of God both in the act of creating and in the living reflection which the divine product manifested was only the beginning of the price which God had to pay.

As creation in its climactic achievement, humanity, turned sour, as the difference became hostile estrangement, God became more deeply, more lovingly and more painfully involved. The inadequacies of human language invoked here should not obscure the painful trajectory of God's increasing engagement with human and cosmic history. Last of all he sent his own Son. The reconciliation and the new creation issued by divine choice in the self-emptying of God, the complete surrender to the human, created condition in all its vulnerability and mortality (cf. Phil 2). Not grasping at equality with God which was his by right, Jesus Christ went to his death as a criminal on the cross, the ultimate testimony to God's creation–commitment and the source of his new creation initiative in finally reconciling the original creation with Godself. The costly beauty of divine creation, process and product was transfigured and transformed by the mission of Jesus Christ. In his life, death and resurrection was revealed the real extent of the divine creative loving and of the painful surrenders which it involved. It is in this context of the painfully wrought beauty of new creation that Hopkins speaks of Christ as the touchstone of all human artistic achievement.

Hopkins, like so many other human artists, was intensely conscious of the pain of human creation, with one of his later sonnets, as he put it in a letter to Robert Bridges, 'written in blood'. His reaching after God, which on his first entry into the Jesuits seemed to him to preclude him from writing any more poetry, later became embodied in his poetry, adding to the joy of creating in poems such as 'The Windhover' and 'God's Grandeur' and to the 'crucifixion' of it in the 'desperate sonnets'.

The pain and the joy, the agony and the ecstasy have always been closely associated with human creation and procreation. Yet the judgements of Yahweh in Genesis, 'In pain you shall bring forth children', 'in the sweat of your face you shall eat bread,' yield to the consoling words of Jesus in the gospels of the mother's labour pains turning to joy as her child is born into the world. For Hopkins as for Jesus the joy beyond all further pain and suffering only comes with the fullness of new creation, in final resurrection. Divine and human creativity can in history only reach towards that fulfilment.

A much more secular worldly version of the joy and the pain is reflected in the work of another favourite poet of Vincent MacNamara, WB Yeats. In a poem, significantly entitled 'Adam's Curse', he has much to say on the labour pains of the birthing of the beautiful:

> We sat together at one summer's end,
> That beautiful mild woman, your close friend,
> And you and I talked of poetry.
> I said, 'A line will take us hours maybe,
> Yet if it does not seem a moment's thought,
> Our stitching and unstitching has been naught,
> Better go down on your marrow bones
> And scrub a kitchen pavement, or break stones
> Like an old pauper in all kinds of weather;
> For to articulate sweet sounds together
> Is to work harder than all these, and yet
> Be thought an idler by the noisy set
> Of bankers, schoolmasters and clergymen
> The martyrs call the world.'
> And thereupon

That beautiful mild woman for whose sake
There's many a one will find out all heartache
On finding that her voice is sweet and low
Replied, 'To be born woman is to know –
Although they do not talk of it at school –
That we must labour to be beautiful.'

I said, 'It's certain there is no fine thing
Since Adam's fall but needs much labouring'. ...

The painful self-giving of the poet, as a line may take him hours, at its best issues in the birth of the beautiful. But the process and product have a further regenerative and healing effect on the language itself and on the community which uses it. Without the redemptive effects of literature the banal, the cliché and the crude would have a more seriously corrupting effect on the language and its community. In labouring for the beautiful, artists are serving the community in ways of which most of the community that 'the martyrs call the world' may be entirely unaware. This is not true just of literary artists but of all artists. The great painters enable one to see more clearly and deeply, the great composers to hear more deeply – provided of course people are willing and able to respond to them. This will require effort and pain on respondents' part also; the effort and pain of loving surrender to the otherness of the artists' words, sights and sounds, of their different, healing and enriching worlds.

The Ethics of Creation

The ethics internal to artist and art audience is kin to other ethics, personal or professional. As one expects doctors or lawyers or bus drivers to undertake their training and carry out their operations responsibly, one may expect of artists, art critics and audiences that they also adhere to the internal ethical demands of their operations. In all these areas of ethics, personal, professional and artistic, there are important differences which may be easily ignored by some outsider ignorant of the particular gifts and obligations of this professional or that artist. Of course, the professional and the artist are primarily human beings and the ethics particular to their avocation may never properly include destruction or degradation of their own humanity or that of others. Scientists may not use other human beings as fodder for experimentation, although how far experimental drugs or surgery may be used in certain circumstances may be a matter for legitimate moral debate. Similarly artists will need to retain a certain basic respect for human dignity.

In the notorious example of erotic literature versus pornography, Professor Peter Connolly of Maynooth explored in a groundbreaking article in the *Theological Quarterly* in the 1960s how differently the novelist William Faulkner and the 'pornographer' Harold Robbins treated apparently similar rape scenes. While Robbins increasingly focused the reader on genitalia and genital activity, Faulkner opened the reader up to the larger humanity and larger world of both the rapist and the victim. In the Robbins example the writer was clearly reducing the protagonists to genital agents and so exploiting sexual preoccupations of the reader to the exclusion of any larger human sensitivity. For Faulkner these remained two human beings as the language, imagery and dynamics of the story of the episode revealed. By using literary criteria internal to the works themselves Connolly was able to show how the one was art and the other not. Not every example will be as clear-cut as that and not every literary critic, let alone reader, enjoys Connolly's literary acumen. However, the main point is clear: it is by criteria internal to the artistic work and its genre that the work must be first evaluated. That evaluation has larger ethical significance for artist and audience as human beings.

As the would-be producers of works of truth and beauty, artists must, as Yeats once instructed Irish poets, learn their trade. The relation between talent or genius, learned skill and dedicated application varies from artist to artist and from work to work. Yet it is the honesty and integrity of the artist which is at stake in achieving the right relationship of the three in any particular work. Lack of talent is not blameworthy unless the untalented unfairly seek to lure their audiences into false estimates of their work. In the commercial art-market of the day such deception of the self and others is inevitable and frequent. From the talented or the genius there is a justified expectation of developing skills and persistent dedication. They remain, however, free to create or not to create, to create in this way or that independently of the audience's expectation. It is to their expectations of themselves that they may feel most bound as they sit in front of the blank screen or empty canvas. As screen or canvas begins to fill up their commitment to truth and beauty, their honesty and integrity as artists come into play with all the pain they may entail. It need hardly be said the destructiveness and destruction of human beings is a suitable, indeed often a necessary, subject for the artist. Depiction of such ugly scenes does not obscure deeper truth and beauty as Picasso's *Guernica* or any of the powerful paintings of the Crucifixion demonstrate.

Art, Morality and Mission

The ethics internal to art forms a distinctive part of the ethics internal to human community and its life in the cosmos. Personal, social and environmental ethics are illuminated and enriched by the less easily defined or described ethics of the artist in relation to his gifts, his training, his application of his materials and skills, his respect for his audience. An artist like Marc Chagall would push this artistic ethic further towards the ethical summit of love when he says: 'If the theoretical and scientific sources of art of which I have spoken could be subordinated to love, their results might become more valid and more just. In connection with Art I have often spoken of the colour which is Love.'

For the good artist as for the good (moral) person there is a desire to promote the beauty and goodness which is appropriate to their talents and situation. Desire becomes commitment as they seek seriously and urgently to enable others to share their vision and practice of beauty and goodness. These are the missionaries of beauty and of goodness, often in some particular form like freedom or justice. They frequently enjoy the sense of calling and of being sent which have been traditionally associated with religious missionaries. WB Yeats and his companions were missionary in this sense, as were so many artists and artistic movements over the centuries. In more obviously ethical terms the world is teeming with missionaries as freedom movements, justice seekers and peace makers and a host of other governmental, inter-governmental and non-governmental bodies labour for a better world. Beyond the strictly ethical missionary movements, if one may call them that, there are very large and energetic religious missionary movements of which the most newsworthy at present is Islam. How far Islam offers a single missionary movement and how far that movement is the menace it is often represented to be, are at least disputable. In the context of this essay priority must be given to Christian Mission.

Renewing Christian Mission

When Vincent MacNamara began his theological studies at St Patrick's College, Kiltegan, locus of the headquarters and seminary of the Missionary Society of St Patrick (the Kiltegan Fathers), the twentieth-century Irish missionary movement was at its height. There has been a famous decline in numbers since, right through the Irish clerical and religious church, missionary and domestic. More important may be the decline in morale undoubtedly intensified by the spate of clerical and religious scandals. Yet even previous to that, the Irish Church's sense of mission had been weakened, despite the obvious success of development agencies such as

Trócaire, which attracted many lay workers who in previous decades might have joined missionary societies like Kiltegan. For the sake of the local church itself as well as for the sake of the churches around the world with which Ireland still has very close ties and in service to the emerging global Reign of God preached by Jesus, the Catholic Church in Ireland badly needs to renew its sense of mission.

The artistic and moral missions discussed earlier can and should feed into this renewal. They can do so first of all by Christians recognising that the promotion of beauty and truth, goodness and justice are clearly aspects of the in-breaking reign of God, although art and morality may not be simply colonised for religious purposes. Christians and their leaders must rather seek dialogue and partnership with the artists and justice seekers who may well wish to steer clear of any explicit religious involvement. Further lessons may be learned for the integrity and commitment of these people in their search for the beautiful and the good and from certain artists' humility in offering their work to be freely accepted or rejected by critics and public. The hurt which rejection often entails and how it is borne may have its own lessons for preachers of the gospel, for Christian missionaries. Writing to his son in 1944, JRR Tolkien suggested art, virtue and insight as the primary requirement of the good Christian sermon. It might well be applied to Christian missionary work as a whole. The Christian insight and knowledge which the missionary brings to the work must be accompanied by some of the insight and skills of the artist as well as by the moral insight and practice of the good person. Beauty and justice are both a reflection of presence of God in the world and a summons to uncover that presence as Christian presence within and without the believing community. To the uncovering of that affirming and empowering presence Christians are called, and called to be missionaries.

Jesus and the Reign of God in a Multi-Faith World

In the aftermath of Vatican II with its (limited) openness to other churches and faiths and to the modern world in general, some of the older concepts of Christian mission were in need of revision. Despite changes in the intervening decades older concepts hang on, slow down the rethinking and retooling which would renew the understanding and practice of Christian mission. One of the crucial difficulties is how one combines belief in the uniqueness of Jesus Christ and his mission as Incarnate Son of God with the acceptance of salvific truth in other religions. The Vatican II document *Nostra aetate* did not and could not resolve that difficulty. Neither did the more recent Roman document *Dominus Jesus*. And it is not likely to be resolved satisfactorily in the near future.

Such a difficulty need not be paralysing as it has sometimes tended to be. Following the paths of artistic and ethical dialogue in a multicultural world may provide some guidance for multi-faith dialogue. The plurality of artistic traditions and achievements does not preclude some mutual appreciation, cooperation and indeed integration between them. Gauguin would be one obvious example but there are endless others between cultures and generations. The inter-ethical dialogue may appear more difficult but it carries on fruitfully despite being weakened by the economic, political and military power of dominant western partners. These are not simply examples which Christian missionaries might follow. They are in themselves testimony to the divine presence in beauty and goodness throughout the world, a testimony, if implicit, to that universal Reign of God which Jesus preached and which his disciples are called to preach and promote.

If the God of Creation (and New Creation) is discernible in artistic and moral traditions and achievements of the diverse cultures in which religions very different from Christianity predominate, it is to be expected that these religions themselves reveal something of that one God. In its strictly religious mission Christianity will engage with these religions as partners in search of a fuller understanding of this God of Creation. The particular religious insights of non-Christian religions will at once challenge and enrich Christianity's understanding of itself and its founder, Jesus Christ. Continuing and constructive dialogue is the way to reconciliation in diversity as already emphasized. Such dialogue will serve all religions in their distinctiveness and serve all humanity in its need to be kept open to the immanent and transcendent mystery of the world, its Creator–God. The renewed Christian mission will embrace artistic and ethical dialogue and cooperation while making its own original contribution in the promotion of inter-faith dialogue and cooperation.

Justice, Beauty and God

In many ways the virtue and practice of justice has become the cutting edge of moral discourse in the contemporary world. One has only to look closely at any human situation to realise how many people are not being treated fairly, not being given their due in accordance with their dignity and basic equality as human beings. Rampant injustice makes for rampant ugliness in exploitative human relationships, in deprived and scarred human bodies and minds, in disfigured landscapes and polluted atmosphere. The mission for justice and beauty go together in restoring and revealing the inner and outer beauty of people and places, the beauty that is finally God.

In one of Hopkins' most accessible but untitled poems the missionary unity of beauty, morality and faith is brought together for poet and reader in the person of Christ.

> As kingfishers catch fire, dragonflies draw flame;
> As tumbled over rims in roundy wells
> Stones ring; like each tucked string tells, each hung bell's
> Bow swung finds tongue to fling out broad its name;
> Each mortal thing does one thing and the same;
> Deals out that being within each one dwells;
> Selves-goes itself; myself it speaks and spells,
> Crying What I do is me; for that I came.
>
> I say more; the just man justices;
> Keeps grace; that keeps all his goings graces;
> Acts in God's eye what in God's eye he is –
> Christ – for Christ plays in ten thousand places,
> Lovely in limbs, and lovely in eyes not his
> To the Father through the features of men's faces.

It is in that spirit that the theological and missionary vocation of Vincent MacNamara with his artistic interests and ethical concerns may be summarised in Hopkins' plangent call:

> Give beauty back, beauty, beauty, beauty, back to God, beauty's
> Self and beauty's giver.

Theatre, Tragedy and Theology

For Sean Freyne

Sean Freyne and I come from a famine county, the 'snipe-grass' country of Irish writer and journalist, John Healy. Born and nurtured within a few miles of each other we followed much the same educational trajectory: local national school, St Jarlath's College, Tuam, and Maynooth with various postgraduate outings in Rome and Germany. Despite our subsequent worldly wanderings we have maintained an affection for and commitment to our native county and villages, even if that has not yielded very much in practical benefit for them. As a remarkable athlete and footballer as well as an outstanding academic Sean Freyne has kept the pride of Mayo alive and well from Tooreen to Jerusalem and Athens and from Trinity College, Dublin to Sydney, Australia and all parts in between. His transformation of theology in TCD and the consequent influence on theology in Ireland is saluted by peers and students alike, although that cannot be the focus of this essay. The bonds of Mayo origins and of lifelong friendship, as they affected our shared engagement with theology, have found many and diverse expressions over the decades. In continuity with some of these this effort will seek to connect his early classical and theological education, his biblical/theological concerns in all their prophetic, poetic and dramatic interpretations of Yahweh/God's interaction with humanity and the cosmos, with current dramatic and poetic interpretation of our present world and particularly of our Irish world. The remarkable literary achievements of the biblical writers so familiar to the biblical scholar Freyne could throw fresh light on the recent achievements of Irish dramatists also remarkable in their very different ways.

A little further historical and biographical background may help set the scene for this perhaps curious conjunction of biblical/theological and Irish secular drama. In the impoverished Mayo of our overlapping youth, apart from directly church activities, the two notable sources of cultural involvement were the local GAA club and the local drama group. Not that the GAA club was without its drama and really high drama in Croke Park, in which Sean himself figured, while the drama club quickly extended its repertoire from John Murphy's Charlestown to Arthur Miller's Salem, Massachusetts. For the future seminarians and would-be priests this was no bad preparation. The interclass football and hurling dramas on High Field, Maynooth, were frequently exhilarating and the main theatre productions in Maynooth at November, Shrove Tuesday and St Patrick's Day, under the direction of Abbey actors including former Maynooth student/seminarian Ray McAnally, proved a rich cultural experience for participants and audience which often bore fruit in their parish assignments, as promoters and sometimes directors of dramatic and musical productions. It must be admitted that no real connection was made in these student days between biblical studies and theatrical productions. Given this year after the Abbey Theatre centenary and the extraordinary dramatic richness apparent among recent as well as more established Irish dramatists during decades that have seen such a decline in Irish religious participation, attempting to explore a couple of major Irish plays, in this instance of tragic mode, might be illuminating for as well as illuminated by biblical and Christian tradition without impugning the integrity of either dramatic or faith traditions.

The focus on plays of tragic mode (a less definitive term than tragedy) has personal and social as well as dramatic reasons. Many of the best Irish plays of what might be called the Abbey century are dominantly tragic in character. From Synge's *Riders to the Sea*, which premiered on the Abbey's opening night in 1904 through plays by Yeats, O'Casey, Beckett, Molloy, Murphy, Friel, Kilroy, Keane, McGuinness, Parker, Barry, Carr, Jones, McPherson and McDonagh, (the list could go on and on), playwright, director and cast have exposed audiences to the specific sufferings of a range of characters and situations that have been all too true to the human condition but seldom resolved in human peace or happiness. Not that many of these plays were lacking in moments of rich comedy but the laughter only reinforced the overall tone of revealing lamentation.

In personal terms it proved impossible to escape from the shadow of a countryside devastated by emigration and neglected by successive British and Irish governments. Mayo was no country for young men. Poet John F. Deane's Achill 'egg-woman' and mother knew that world; 'Sons, to boys, to men; she cried/each time they left to build/Birmingham and Liverpool, they , too, /obedient to the laws of the world's orbit. Kyrie/eleison'. Sean Freyne had the further personal pain of losing his father when he himself was just five years of age.

How far increasing exposure to poverty and now the plague of HIV and AIDS in the developing world has influenced this author's preoccupation with tragedy on stage is not easily assessed and one can never rule out the influence of individual temperament based on nurture or nature in such preferences, even when such influences are no longer accessible to the conscious mind. All one can say is that tragedy on stage is one of the great transforming experiences available.

In the recent, if rather superficial, debate about the end of history, there seemed to be at least a suggestion for people in the West of an end of tragedy as well. Such a delusion was only effectively eliminated for these people by the horrors of September 11, 2001. The people in deprived worlds, personal and social, have lived with tragedy for so long that they may also become immune to it. To compound the problems the privileged who saw themselves as protected from tragedy and even death are now tempted in their fresh terror to see the deprived as all terrorists. Today one may well adapt Seamus Heaney's famous line to 'history and tragedy rhyme' once again as he himself hints in his own recent Abbey play adapted from *Iphigenia, The Graves at Thebes*. To return to Sean Freyne, sportsman and classical scholar as well as theologian, one might reflect on a recent comment by classical scholar, Simon Goldhill:

> Theatre and the gladiatorial games, these archetypal entertainments of Greece and Rome, are very much still inside us, either through the artistic tradition or in the popular imagination. Partly because of this, they turn out to be a particularly valuable route in reflecting critically on what we do. They give us a necessary vantage point to see ourselves. If you want to know what you think you are doing, the theatre and the games are a good place to do that thinking from.

Athens and Jerusalem Once More

The western tradition of theatre and tragedy has its classical source in the Athens of the fifth century BCE. More particularly in the Dionysian festival, at which dramatists competed with one another, presenting a trio of tragedies each over a number of days. Out of these competitions emerged the great dramatists, Aeschylus, Sophocles and Euripides with such powerful and still influential works as *Oedipus Rex, Antigone* and *Medea*. How the gods, fate, human blindness and self-destructiveness combined to inflict such futile human suffering and dying may vary from play to play. They all revealed to their male citizen audiences the inner tensions and weaknesses of god, city and citizen, particularly of leading or royal citizens including women like Medea. Women were not citizens or among the actors or audience. The complex and, in that religious and cultural context, plausible plot, the characters, language and verse offered, what Aristotle in his Poetics described as catharsis, an intellectual and emotional resolution which entered into the soul of the audience member to the point of personal transformation. At least such experiences are available to the modern audience member at a contemporary production such as that of Fiona Shaw's Medea in a relatively recent production at the Abbey Theatre, Dublin.

The setting of the religious festival of Dionysius with its surprising emphasis on tragedy, the intervention of the gods and the confrontation of some of humanity's deepest needs and frustrations put Greek tragedy firmly in the context of religion. Even at this secular time authentic productions and adaptations carry that context with them, however implicitly or disguisedly. A review of western theatre and tragedy in the post-medieval period, something well beyond the scope of this essay and the competence of the essayist, would probably find that the religious context had receded if not disappeared, certainly in the case of somebody like Shakespeare. This may be partly due to the cultural presence of Jerusalem through the medieval period and its increasing absence thereafter. For many believers, artists and critics the events of Jerusalem excluded the possibility of real tragedy. Hope had replaced despair; the life of the risen Christ the prospect of futile killing and death. The supreme literary artist of the period had his classic work entitled, 'The Divine Comedy'.

Such a simplistic and crude review of the recurrence of great tragedy could not possibly do justice to the interaction of Athens and Jerusalem over two millennia. Yet in the modern and even postmodern times a very different approach may be necessary for the Christian believer or theologian who finds modern drama and particularly its tragedies so disturbing and enriching in human but also in faith terms. To track that disturbance and enrichment while respecting the integrity of a particular play and the particular Christian faith of the theologian is the difficult, perhaps the impossible, task of this essay.

The two Irish plays chosen for this study were selected primarily on the basis of their disturbing and enriching impact on this theologian–playgoer, although they have both received much critical acclaim as significant modern tragedies. In the modern Irish theatrical canon John Millington Synge and Brian Friel are two of the great names. Synge's *Riders to the Sea*, first produced at the official opening of the Abbey Theatre in December 1904, has long entered the canon of world theatre as one of the great modern tragedies. Friel's *Faith Healer*, although first produced on Broadway, New York in 1979 with James Mason in the lead, may not have attained that status as yet but in this author's opinion must eventually do so. As some commentators have noted Synge was one of the first tragedians to attend to the tragic lot of lower-class, working people as opposed to gods and heroes, warriors, kings and queens. Of course this has become commonplace in the twentieth century from Miller's *Death of a Salesman* to a range of works by such compatriots of Synge and Friel as O'Casey, Murphy, McGuinness, Barry, Carr et multi alii. Despite Chesterton's quip, not all Irish songs are sad, but many of their best theatrical works certainly are, as the two examined here will illustrate, except that 'sad' is much too feeble a word for their achievement and impact.

Riders to the Sea

The two major protagonists in *Riders to the Sea* are Maurya and the sea; the Atlantic Ocean and the frail old island woman, presumed to be of Aran, who has lost her five sons, their father and his father to that insatiable sea. As the curtain rises her two daughters are examining some clothes that may belong to Michael, the latest son to go missing and whose body has not been recovered. Maurya is resting off-stage, exhausted by her grieving for Michael. The only surviving son, Bartley, is about to set out for the horse fair in Galway although his mother begs him not to go. When he persists she follows him to give him some newly baked bread and her blessing. She returns completely inconsolable because of the 'fearfullest thing' she has just seen: Bartley on his horse leading his pony and on the pony the last lost son Michael rides, 'with fine clothes on him, and new shoes on his feet.' The girls explain it can't be Michael as they have meantime identified the clothes found in the far north as his. Maurya's lament and its search for closure is interrupted by the entry of the keening women and the return of Bartley's body wrapped in a wet sail like that of an earlier drowned brother. 'The gray pony knocked him into the sea, and he was washed out where there is a great surf on the white rocks', one of the women reports. Maurya's closing lamentation has echoes of both Athens and Jerusalem and indeed of many traditions of grieving but it is a magnificent personal and poetic cry in the face of natural and inevitable catastrophe. Such crude summary is utterly inadequate to the living play as presented on stage around the world. It also misses completely the high poetry of the language itself and of its shaping by playwright to the pain and dignity of one of theatre's finest final facing of mortality.

In this essay one must be satisfied to let the language, particularly that spoken by Maurya, echo around the mind and on to the page. Without simply repeating the whole text, which is a sore temptation when one is talking about this play, it is very difficult to convey power of persona, word and action. Quoting from some of Maurya's more poignant passages seems the only way forward.

As her daughter Cathleen tells her that Michael's 'body is after being found in the far north, and he's got a clean burial by the grace of God', the death of Bartley is almost taken for granted and Cathleen begins to keen. Nora, the second daughter, tries to console them: 'Didn't the young priest say the

Almighty God wouldn't leave her destitute with no son living.' Maurya (in a low voice, but clearly):

> It's little the like of him knows of the sea, ... Bartley will be lost now, and let you call in Eamon and make me a good coffin out of the white boards, for I won't live after them. I've had a husband, and a husband's father, and six sons in this house – six fine men, though it was a hard birth I had with every one of them and they coming to the world – and some of them were found and some of them were not found, but they're gone now the lot of them ... There were Stephen and Shawn were lost in the great wind, and found after in the Bay of Gregory of the Golden Mouth, and carried up the two of them on the one plank, and in by that door.

> *(The girls notice some commotion off stage but Mauya continues:)*

> There was Sheamus and his father and his father again were lost in a dark night and not a stick or sign was seen of them when the sun went up. There was Patch after was drowned out of a curragh that turned over. I was sitting here with Bartley, and he a baby, lying on my two knees, and I seen two women, and three women and four women coming in, and they crossing themselves, and not saying a word. I looked out then, and there were men coming after them, and they holding a thing in the half of a red sail and water dripping out of it – it was a dry day Nora – and leaving a track to the door.

As the women begin to come in again and men carry in the body of Bartley with a bit of sail over it and lay it on the table, Maurya (raising her head and speaking as if she did not see the people around her):

> They're all gone now, and there isn't anything more the sea can do to me ... I'll have no call now to be up crying and praying when the wind breaks from the south, and you can hear the surf is in the east, and the surf is in the west, making a great stir with the two noises, and they hitting one on the other. I'll have no call now to be going down and getting Holy Water in the dark nights after Samhain, and I won't care what way the sea is when the other women will be keening. ... Give me the Holy Water, Nora, there's a small sup still on the dresser ...

After dropping Michael's clothes over Bartley's she sprinkles the Holy Water over him, and then:

> It isn't that I haven't prayed for you, Bartley, to the Almighty God. It isn't that I haven't said prayers in the dark night till you wouldn't know what I'd be saying; but it's a great rest I'll have now, and it's time surely. It's great rest I'll have now, and great sleeping in the long nights after Samhain, if it's only a bit of wet flour we do have to eat, and maybe a fish that would be stinking.

After arrangements for making the coffin are made by the daughters and neighbours, Maurya sprinkles the last of the Holy Water on Michael's clothes. She lays her hands on Bartley's feet and says:

> They're all together this time and the end is come. May the Almighty God have mercy on Bartley's soul and on Michael's soul, and on the souls of Sheamus and Patch, and Stephen and Shawn; and may He have mercy on my soul, Nora, and on the soul of everyone is left living in the world.

> *(Pause as keening of women rises and drops again when she continues:)*

> Michael has a clean burial in the far north, by the grace of the Almighty God. Bartley will have a fine coffin out of the white boards, and a deep grave surely. What more can we want than that? No man at all can be living for ever, and we must be satisfied.

> *(She kneels down again and the curtain falls slowly.)*

The special language of Synge's plays and his musical deployment of it were based on his own study of the Irish Gaelic language but above all on his acute listening to the language of the local people who became his friends and neighbours in Aran, Mayo, Kerry and Wicklow. Adopting or translating as the occasion required he forged a new language of the theatre which enabled him, for example, to express the keening thoughts and feelings of Maurya in the mastering cadences of her speeches throughout the play. But Synge was no simple language master. The dramatics of the play which can only exist on stage are finely wrought. And behind and beyond all that are the human depth and tragic glory of Maurya, her family and her story.

At the time of writing Synge had abandoned the rather rigid Protestant Christianity of his mother. This may be why some critics are inclined to dismiss the overt piety of Maurya or reinterpret it as part of an ancient pagan inheritance in the references to Samhain or as influenced by the Greek tragic tradition with Maurya becoming Moira, the Greek word for fate. There is no doubt something to both these suggestions. Irish Christianity always maintained a certain connection with its pagan and Celtic antecedents and Synge was schooled in the great Greek tragedies. The action in his play as in the Athenian works take place off stage, his keeners are reminiscent of the Greek chorus and the unrelenting force of the sea is indeed akin to the force of fate, of moira, even if it is force of nature rather than of the gods, closer to tsunami than to Dionysius.

Synge's fidelity to his Aran islanders and other local peoples led him to respect their piety as well as their language. And at least in the play Maurya's religious beliefs and practices are given their due. Her very name, despite its unusual spelling, almost certainly derives from Mary, the Mother of Jesus, as the Almighty God she invokes is in her mind the God and Father of Jesus Christ. At the back of her praying and keening lies such New Teastament stories and image as Rachel bewailing her children after the slaughter of the innocents by Herod; Simeon's words to Mary on the presentation of her Son in the temple; Mary at the foot of the Cross and the endless images of the Pieta. Synge would not, perhaps could not, be consciously aware of all this but faithful to the grieving mother he created he would not exclude it either, at least not for Maurya's co-religionists as they responded to her prayerful lament in ways different from their response to the piercing wail of Medea on the death of her sons.

All this is not to turn the play into any kind of religious tract. It is merely to draw attention to how any work of art has varying meanings for different or even for the same observer. For the Christian theological observer, more important than making explicit any implicit religious references is the art work's capacity to draw the theologian into the creative process itself and still further into creation, in this instance, of a remarkable human being and her remarkable experiences of suffering and loss and her ways of dealing with them. Allowing oneself to be inhabited by Maurya and her encounter with life and death has expanding and even transforming effects of the kind Aristotle suggested and of the kind the Christian doctrines of creation and incarnation also affirm. Without entering the darkness of such experience the theologian remains less human and so less capable of understanding and living the Christian message. The appeal to being 'satisfied' by Maurya at the end of the play may not echo the despair of some Greek counterparts but its pain is unmistakable and its hope as far from established as it was for Mary and the others on Calvary.

Faith Healer

If *Riders to the Sea* is dominated by the conflict between (wo)man and nature, Brian Friel's *Faith Healer* is dominated by a man basically in conflict with himself, but the healer/artist is also in conflict with his gift/craft, his companions and clients. His wife/mistress Grace describes him to her psychiatrist as an artist and many reviewers and critics draw a close parallel between 'The Fantastic Francis Hardy, Faith Healer, One Night Only' and the artist/writer. Hardy himself puzzles over a 'craft without an apprenticeship, a ministry without responsibility, a vocation without a ministry'. It (occasionally) works for him, which is why he got involved, he says, and 'the questions that undermined my life then became meaningless' – for a few hours.

In the four monologues which constitute the play, with Hardy delivering the first and fourth, Grace the second and his manager Teddy (the Cockney) the third, the splits and contradictions within and between characters and narratives abound. Even such a central event as the still birth of Frank's and Grace's son 'in Kinlochbervie in the far north of Scotland, almost as far as north as you can go', differs in significant detail in the accounts of Grace and Teddy while Frank simply 'erases' it as he explains that 'Grace was barren' although he would have liked a son. The 'erasion' of Grace in her view always occurs when he is preparing 'to perform'. Their return to Ireland and to Ballybeg, which climaxes in Frank's death, differs in important detail in the three accounts. These accounts converge most closely perhaps in the great triumph of Glamorganshire when Frank cures ten people of various diseases and disabilities. However, it was failure and death that dominated and divided them.

Friel like Synge is a master of language and the style here that of a kind of prose–poetry if not quite the verse which Eliot thinks appropriate to tragedy. The opening incantation of place names from Wales and Scotland, presumably the names of the towns and villages which the trio visited on their 'healing' journeys, had the effect of 'sedation' on Frank on his way to a 'performance'. The repetition in the course of their monologues by all three gives it the force of lamentation, of Synge's keening women as well as of the Jewish tradition of lamentation expressed in the Hebrew scriptures, and kept alive to this day at the Wailing Wall in Jerusalem. As the play opens Frank's 'incantation' comes out of the darkness and the lights go up at the second line while he continues, eyes closed:

Aberarder, Aberayron,
Llangranog, Llangurig,
Abergorlech,Abergynolwyn,
Llandefeilog, Llanerchymedd,
Aberhosan, Aberporth ...

All those dying Welsh villages. *(Eyes open.)* I'd get so tense before a performance, d'you know what I used to do? As we drove along these narrow, winding roads I'd recite the names to myself just for the mesmerism, the sedation, of the incantation –

Kinlochbervie, Inverbervie,
Inverdruie, Invergordon,

Welsh, Scottish – over the years they became indistinguishable ...

And the settings for the performances, their kirks or meeting houses or schools, are indistinguishably dirty and derelict. In all three accounts the story is of decline in Frank's performance and persona with the rarer results unable to still the internal questioning, the whiskey losing its effectiveness and the relationship with Grace becoming more bitter.

The undermining questions focused on his status as faith healer, authentic gift or just that of a con man, and endless questions in between about faith in what or whom. And the desperation of those who came to him, knowing he could not help and would only reinforce their desperation except on the very odd occasion, as 'in that old Methodist hall in the village of Llanbethian in Glamorganshire in Wales (when) every single person was cured'.

In the darkened secular sanctuary of the Abbey Theatre Frank Hardy as played by Donal McCann was overwhelming, demanding and mysterious. And the mystery remains as it should in relation to any major stage figure, and of course in relation to any living human being. As Frank dismissed those he failed to cure, by Grace's account, we are all tempted to dismiss the personally unattractive or the socially (to us) insignificant. In that Abbey auditorium in the city of Dublin, Ireland, it was impossible to dismiss Frank Hardy, hours, even weeks and months after the play had ended. Teddy's tattered poster, rescued from a dump on his way back from identifying Grace in the morgue: '"The Fantastic Francis Hardy, Faith Healer: One Night Only." A lifetime in the business and that's the only memento I've kept.' And one night only was so disturbing yet one felt compelled to go back to theatre and to text to wrestle with Frank's own questions and still more with that climactic event of his death so knowingly, deliberately and freely accepted at the hands of the wedding guests as he failed to cure, as he knew he would, their crippled friend McGarvey. As Frank McGuinness observes, we are in this play listening to the voices of ghosts at least in the personae of Frank and Grace Hardy. Their stories of the final confrontation and death differ in important detail as nearly all their stories do. But the conclusions tally; Frank in attempting to cure McGarvey is killed for his failure. However it is Frank's telling that brings the play to its powerful, tragic, and yet in speech and on stage, serene conclusion:

It was a September morning, just after dawn. The sky was orange and everything glowed with a soft radiance – as if each detail of the scene had its own self-awareness and was satisfied with itself.

The yard was a perfect square enclosed by the back of the building and three high walls. And the wall facing me as I walked out was breached by an arched entrance.

Almost in the centre of the square but a little to my left was a tractor and a trailer. In the back of the trailer were four implements: there was an axe and there was a crowbar and there was a mallet and there was a hay fork. They were resting against the side of the trailer.

In the corners facing me and within the walls were two mature birch trees and the wind was sufficient to move them.

The ground was cobbled but pleasant to walk on because the cobbles were smooth with use.

And I walked across that yard, over those worn cobbles, towards the arched entrance because, framed in it, you would think posed symmetrically, were the four wedding guests; and in front of them, in his wheelchair, McGarvey.

The four looked ... diminished in that dawn light; their faces whiter; their carnations chaste against the black suits. Ned was on the left of the line, Donal on the right, and the other two, whose names I never knew, between them.

And McGarvey. Of course, McGarvey. More shrunken than I had thought. And younger. His hands folded patiently on his knees; his feet turned in, his head slightly to the side. A figure of infinite patience, of profound resignation, you would imagine. Not a hint of savagery. And Ned's left hand protectively on his shoulder.

And although I knew nothing was going to happen, nothing at all, I walked across the yard towards them. And as I walked I became possessed of a strange and trembling intimation: that the whole corporeal world – the cobbles, the trees, the sky, those four malign implements – somehow they had shed their physical reality and had become mere imaginings, and that in all existence there was only myself and the wedding guests. And that intimation in turn gave way to a stronger sense: that even we had ceased to be physical and existed only in spirit, only in the need we had for each other.

(He takes off his hat as if he were entering a church and holds it at his chest. He is both awed and elated. As he speaks the remaining lines he moves very slowly down stage.)

And as I moved across that yard and offered myself to them, then for the first time I had a simple and genuine sense of home-coming. Then for the first time there was no atrophying terror; and the maddening questions were silent.

At long last I was renouncing chance.

(Pause for about four seconds. Then quick black.)

On stage this closing speech invaded the audience who offered themselves to it and to Frank; no, invade is not the right word because it is an aggressive word. Frank and his speech inhabited the surrendering audience. They too were 'awed and elated' and for a moment 'existed only in spirit'.

For the theologian in the audience, even as reader but more as transcriber, the whole play and particularly its closure is resonant with religious reference. Not that it is a religious play in any conventional sense. *Faith Healer* has a much closer and overt connection with the fictions and factions of art than with the salvific/healing claims of Christian word and sacrament. But readers or theatregoers, however captive to the play, can never completely shed their cultural endowment, including its religious dimension. So while respecting the integrity of play and playwright they inevitably draw on their own resources in responses, positively receptive and negatively critical as they may be. Living with *Faith Healer* over many years and more intensely over recent weeks as I have in the reading and transcription of some sections (a revived entry point to literature for me), in reflection and even prayer made my own theological and biblical connections with Frank, and through him in diminished fashion naturally with Grace and Teddy. (I leave aside here the connections with the ancient Irish legend of Deirdre and the Sons of Ushna to which some critics refer, and the subject coincidentally of Synge's last and unfinished play. I do this not because the connections seem to me unfounded but because they are not relevant to my task.)

As I remarked earlier the recurring incantation of the Welsh and Scottish place names have the effect of biblical and Greek lamentation. The play for all the leavening of Teddy's humour might constitute one long lament were it not for the final lyrical presentation of the tragic and fatal healing of Frank himself. His return to Ireland and Ballybeg had echoes of Jesus setting his face to Jerusalem. The Glamorgan healing of the ten and the short-lived transfiguration of the relationship between Frank and Grace has its own gospel echoes. Indeed the four quite differing accounts of the odyssey of the central character and his retinue may not be very close parallels to the four gospels of Jesus Christ or carry much in the way of 'Good News'. Yet the figure four had at least symbolic significance for one member of the audience and there was the intimation of a healing, a new life of sorts, analogous perhaps to Resurrection in those closing sentences. A new life free of the terror and the questioning through death freely and knowingly accepted at the hands of his enemies.

This is not intended as a rewriting or a restaging of Brian Friel's remarkable play. Quod scripsit, scripsit. And so it will be for actor and audience. But for one reader/audience member the transformative experience opened him up to dimensions of human suffering, failure and mortality which connected with and deepened his personal convictions. As a kind of bonus there was also a healing of his human and Christian faith.

Synge and Friel, in these two plays at least, provide not only for Irish audiences but also for world audiences the sense of tragedy in the human condition which is essential to a healthy psyche and society. The shopping and other addictions which turn so many citizens into consumers only and so many of their leaders into morally indifferent power-seekers, need to be confronted by the Mauryas and Franks of the developed and developing worlds if their sense of their own humanity is to be restored through care and attention to the healing presence of the suffering individuals and masses, from local suicide to distant tsunami.

Writing into God

Remembering Tommy Waldron

In his shimmering essay *Real Presences,* George Steiner rejects aggressive deconstruction of classical texts in favour of their courteous reception. *Per cortesia* is the first manner of the reader–interpreter in seeking to understand and enjoy any artistic work. The critique and further analysis may follow but they should serve to enable the reader/viewer/listener to understand, evaluate and, more deeply, to be more critically as well as courteously receptive of a genuinely artistic work. In a competitive and combative world where high-powered marketing, even with its own brand of creativity, can make it so difficult to distinguish trash from treasure and where critics with a responsibility to discriminate and so to educate are too easily tempted by what might be termed analytic reduction, the call to courteous, critical attention not only to recognised works of art but to interesting and promising newcomers has the ring of sanity. An outstanding quality of Tommy Waldron's approach to life was his courteous attention to and reception of literary and other artistic classics, particularly the Hebrew and Christian Scriptures. All this nourished his courteous attention to and reception of people, his courteous attention to and reception of God.

People before Causes

In meeting, reading and listening to Tommy Waldron one never detected a trace of the ideologue. His commitments to faith and church, to truth and beauty, to justice and peace, were never distorted into uncritical causes or angry campaigning. People in all their weaknesses and ambiguities as well as in their potential and real goodness came first, not causes. This could be interpreted as weakness in the polarised situations of the Irish church and Irish society during his influential years as pastor, preacher and writer. Yet to listen to him or read him in the ranting years of the seventies, eighties and nineties was to recognise a voice of sanity and of strength. In the midst of the divisive debates on law and morality, through the turbulence of the Northern Troubles, during clerical sex scandals, Tommy Waldron concentrated on the people in his constituency who were affected and left the headline elements to others. Not that he thought all the headlines irrelevant, still less untrue, but his sense of people and his gifts of caring for the immediately afflicted and affected determined his priorities. In parish, pulpit and confessional, at baptisms, weddings and funerals, in his regular meditative essays for radio, in his retreats and in his prestigious sermons at the Knock Annual Vigil his attention to real people, with ordinary or extraordinary concerns, in word and image, in story, in inflection of voice and in bodily posture and gesture shone through. The encoded but still vital remains of this devotion to people of all ages and backgrounds constitute the primary value of his writings.

Flesh Made Word

The baby's first words, the child's first sentences, the developing, sometimes riotous vocabulary of the adolescent were all a delight to Tommy Waldron who so loved the words not as dictionary components but as struggling bodily attempts to communicate between body–spirits. The very fleshiness of words was to be savoured like good wine, perhaps sometimes for their own sake, but principally in the delicate and fragile reaching out to the other body–spirit. His care for words was a care of the heart but also a carefully honed skill of the mind and mouth. From his school days to his death days, so cruelly focused on his gradual loss of speech, he exemplified St James's model not just in truth telling but in the beautiful healing way of the telling.

All this caring communication had a history in his own family of course but more formally in his educational interests in languages and literature. He was one of the outstanding scholars of his era in his BA and MA studies in English Language and Literature, had a fluent knowledge of the Irish language and went on to study French to the point of becoming a first class teacher in that subject at second level. His wide reading in novels, drama and poetry extended his mind and sensibility as teacher and pastor. His precise and yet imaginative choice of word and simile, his use of story and parable, his arresting connections between biblical and domestic events as in his reflections on the Mayo woman and the Jewish man, his deployment of the Ugly Duckling fable in a baptismal homily, etc., etc., were all born of a heart, imagination, mind and vocabulary schooled by Shakespeare, Eliot and Heaney as well as by pupils and neighbours, parishioners and penitents in the narrow triangle of his priestly work between Headford, Tuam and Claremorris.

Performance Artist

Readings by major and minor poets are a phenomenon of our time and by and large an enjoyable one. Most good poetry needs to be read aloud at least occasionally and if possible by the poet, who may not always equal technically and aesthetically a Richard Burton but who nevertheless puts his personal and vocal mark on the poem's music and meaning. The 'performance poets' as they are sometimes called belong to a wider range of performance or performing artists, notably of course actors. To this broad category priests as teachers, preachers and celebrants of the liturgy might be loosely assigned, with the liturgical religious ritual background to the development of theatre also to be borne in mind. In Tommy Waldron's case the assignment would be far from loose. In celebrating Baptism and Eucharist as at weddings and funerals he was so often producer/director as well as best supporting actor to Christ and the Spirit, to the marrying and the grieving. The script, partly the church's and partly his own scribbles, was performed with all the skill of his own talent and schooling and all the conviction of his own faith, hope and love. Some of his best work needs to be heard aloud particularly in the voice we no longer enjoy.

Writing and Speaking into God

Writing is a critical part of the human and Christian search, the search for meaning and truth, the search for community and love. So is speaking. They belong together at least for somebody of Tommy Waldron's generation, education and personal gifts. For him they were also human and divine graces of faith and hope and love. To write and to speak were acts of trust in the words and their meaning, in the readers and audience, in the ultimate significance of words and persons resting in the Ultimate Word and Persons of God. The process of writing and speaking led him to that ultimate destiny; it became a writing and speaking into God. The self-surrender in search of the precise and sensitive words to discover and communicate the truth to the audience addressed was a saving act for him and for them. Redeeming the time in one of his favourite Eliot allusions involved as for all wordsmiths redeeming and saving the language and so participation in redeeming self and audience, entering into the creative and redeeming work of God.

For the writer and speaker who was Tommy Waldron the Spirit of God was embracing the performer and the performance all the more in his allowing the scriptural texts to nourish and inhabit him in study and prayer. It is the context of all Christian writing and speaking if only occasionally managed by most. It is costly, as Tommy knew well. Despite his general cheerful demeanour he knew suffering well, that of others as well as his own, and could speak of it authentically and consolingly. One of his favourite books in recent years was *Etty*, a remarkable diary by a holocaust victim. His reading and rereading of that book as reflected in his speaking and writing undoubtedly led him to reading and writing into God, to prayer. Indeed he prayed regularly to her as being certainly now in the company of the saints.

Perhaps it was this companionship with the suffering in life and in death that enabled him to bear so admirably his own painful and lingering death. In earlier times he would quote a phrase of Henri de Lubac to the effect that we all suffer badly. He may well have known a deeper truth of this as he was fatally attacked in his most delicate gift of speech by ravaging mouth cancer but he did not impose the horror of it on his friends. In fact, his courteous reception of them to the end must have prepared the way for God's courteous reception of him.

The Tears of God

Meditating on a Novel by Jerome Kiely

Father Brendan Laide is not your everyday Irish curate. His regular citations of Shakespearian and other literary sources as well as his occasional bizarre behaviour, exemplified in his walking the local village of Kilbroney dressed as an Arab sheikh complete with silver dagger on display, suggest at least an unusual product of the Maynooth of fifteen or however many years ago. And the parishioners of Kilbroney with whom he tangles have their own distinctiveness. And 'tangles' is putting it much too mildly. The first sentence spoken by the narrator, Father Laide, in this novel by priest/poet/novelist, Jerome Kiely, *Heat Not The Furnace*, (Shakespeare, *King Henry VIII*) reads: 'The first nail in my own coffin was driven into it at the funeral of Stephen Burke.'

In summary this novel recounts the differences or rather disputes which the curate has with a series of locals, resulting in an allegation of sexual impropriety on his part with a young boy-visitor whom he befriends. He is removed by his bishop from the parish somewhere in the south-west of Ireland and banished to an island mission. As he tells the story, the incident of bathing naked with the young boy in a mountain lake is grossly misrepresented by one of his major enemies, Sergeant Miller, (renamed because of his wild-life shooting, as Sergeant Killer) and retailed to the bishop by other of the priest's opponents who have already reported him for various misdemeanours.

The structure and mood of the novel are revealed in chapter headings such as 'The First Nail', 'The Yellow Spinster', 'The Day of the Arab', 'Sergeant Killer' and 'First Unholy Communion'. All of these chapters deal with characters and incidents in which the troubles between priest and particular parishioners reach some climax and are presented at best in the style of weekly instalments of a serialised Dickens novel and at worst more like a current television soap. The most charming, charitable, funny and touching of these episodes occurs in the chapter entitled 'Eccentric' which records the friendship between Father Laide and and a very eccentric English resident, Sarah Field, with whom he shares the same love of animals and nature and with whom he soon shares the same enemies.

Although the book is what is usually called a good read, and for some readers may offer insight into the inevitable petty but occasionally destructive squabbling of parochial and clerical life, the point of this comment is not literary or social evaluation but an attempt at Christian meditation on priestly life stimulated by some of the novel's people and events. Over the years in teaching moral theology especially I found novels as well as other artistic productions helpful in opening students to the complex riches of human and Christian living. This essay is intended as a meditative variation on that approach.

Priestly Isolation

It may be how he is or how he tells it, and it may well be the lot of many diocesan priests in rural and urban Ireland, but the priest–narrator seems to have no regular priest – or lay – friends. His parochial contacts are no more than that unless they turn sour, and with the notable exceptions of the two outsiders, the resident but eccentric English woman Sarah Field and the young lad Kevin Warren visiting briefly from England, there appears to be no human warmth in his life. Of course this could and must be true of many people's lives and not just of the lives of priests in remote areas. As a human experience such a friendless existence challenges the validity of Christian community and the possibility of personal growth, challenges confirmed in the final episode in the novel in which Father Laide exacts his revenge on Sergeant Miller.

Isolation and loneliness are recurring dimensions of the human and not just the priestly condition, even if rarely dominant. Contemporary individualism may have exacerbated such difficulties but did not initiate them. In biblical literature they are at least as old as Job and find expression in the alienation of Adam and Eve or Cain and Abel in the early chapters of Genesis. Otherness of each human being provides the basis for isolation and loneliness cuts a person off from real companionship with other human individuals. Without any preceding hostile alienation the very otherness of each human being provides the basis for isolation and loneliness.

The traditional prayer manuals emphasize the value of focusing on particular points for meditation in examining a phenomenon such as loneliness in general and in situations such as those depicted in this novel. An obvious one is that of the busy-ness by which Father Laide and others may not only keep loneliness at bay but conceal it from themselves. The sacred figure and power of the priest may complicate the evasion and concealment further. Celibacy may be another complicating factor. More profoundly it is difficult to know how far a prayer life, companionship with God as it is called, may prove a substitute for the lack of human companionship and a cure for human loneliness.

Prayer and the Companionship of God

There have always been difficulties about the spiritual and prayer life of the diocesan priest. His seminary training and official guide was usually modelled on that of a religious community which might suit seminary life but was not well adapted to parish life. Beyond that confusion there lies a series of other difficulties which might apply to professed religious and to lay people as well as to priests in their parishes. Devotional prayer and a spirituality based on an emotional bonding with God or Jesus, with Mary or particular saints or holy places has played a large and positive part in the history of Christian prayer. It has its dangers, however, in encouraging a sentimentality which can be self-deluding and sometimes breeding an authoritarianism which can be other-abusing. For many priests and laity earlier devotion persists and appears to supply some of the companionship which their isolation demands. It may also move on to a more charismatic phase in prayer and lifestyle. For another group of Christians the intensely devotional no longer appeals as it seems childish although they may not express in that way. Ironically theology, even bad theology, perhaps particularly bad theology, can result in undermining prayer of devotion without necessarily supplying a satisfactory alternative.

In *Heat Not The Furnace* the priest at prayer figures incidentally in the recitation of the breviary although in circumstances of crucial significance to the development of the conflict between Father Laide and his emerging enemies, the opening of the coffin of the deceased 'Yank' to find only his ashes which occurs in the first chapter and the killing of the stranded whale by Sergeant Miller in the chapter entitled 'Sergeant Killer'. The breviary and the Mass (also mentioned) have been the staple diet of the priest's prayer life. However, they are liable to lose some of their spiritual value if they become primarily duties and are too easily regarded as working *ex opere operato*, as achieving their goal solely by technical completion of the work. It is doubtful if many or any priests regard them and especially the Mass exclusively in this light. Yet the development of a eucharistic spirituality for priest and parish which binds the community in loving self-surrender, communal celebration and reconciliation, in sharing and caring, is seldom evident or even attempted. There is little sign of it in Kilbroney. Indeed the Eucharist is another critical point of division there, as the chapter headed 'First Unholy Communion' demonstrates.

Divine Companionship through Human Companionship

To return to the question posed earlier about loneliness, prayer and companionship, the lesson of this story and of real life stories of many diocesan priests at least suggests that, lives of certain saints notwithstanding, there is no divine substitute for human love, friendship and companionship. Indeed there may be no prayer or companionship with God without the experience of such human friendship. 'How can we love God whom we do not know if we do not love our neighbour whom we do know' (1 Jn). To love in the divine context is to pray and to pray is to love.

Both these related engagements and activities require commitment, skills and regular practice. In a pastoral context loving the neighbour is never easy. The preferential option of prayer for the neediest neighbours may be joined to if it does not coincide with prayer for the more difficult. Even private prayer of repentance and forgiveness in such situations can restore that inner calm which may prepare the way for reconciliation but at least will not exacerbate the situation.

More significantly the priest must learn to pray among and with his people. Prayer groups or schools of prayer in a parish are often the target of sharp clerical criticism. Yet if we are to develop a distinctive spirituality for the priest in the parish it must be by praying and caring with and for his people. In the regular exercises of the community of prayer which reach their climax in a well-prepared and well-conducted celebration of Eucharist, the human companionship helps mediate divine companionship and divine companionship transforms and challenges the human companionship. Given the universal presence of the Incarnate God all loving human companionship mediates divine companionship in golf club, in pub, in home visit, at theatre or match and not just in church or prayer group.

Indeed, by neglecting such 'secular' contexts one is unlikely to form the range of human relationships which might lead to deeper and liberating friendships, all the more supportive in a crisis for being outside the immediate church context. More importantly one would be neglecting to follow the example of Jesus as incarnate God in his friendships and socializing, in his vision of community and of nature in 'the lilies of the field' and the sparrow that falls to the ground. In such larger prayer, pastoral, social, friendship and nature settings the companionship with God may be given its authentic expression not as substitute for human relationships and natural beauty but as realised in and through them while prayer may issue in the concrete terms of the Lord's Prayer or on perhaps rare occasions 'catch the heart off guard and blow it open'. As nature did for Seamus Heaney 'along the flaggy shore' in Clare 'when the wind / And the light are working off each other', for Brendan Laide it could happen in 'sailing to Carraig Aonair and back'. Such experience of nature as of people may be prelude to experiencing the painful–joyful presence of God. Contemplation as transforming gift is also possible for parish priest or parishioner.

The Power and the Powerlessness

The story of Father Laide at Kilbroney consists of a series of power struggles between himself and a few parishioners but above all between the apparently major power figures in the locality, Father Laide and Sergeant Miller. It could in its defeats and victories be the story of any other church or civil institution from seminary and university to political party, local council or voluntary association. To Father Laide's credit he never seeks to invoke the wrath of God on his enemies. However, he is clearly engaged in a more human power struggle which can be the fate of many priests in parish or religious community. What the Christian meditator might reflect on is the consideration of how in the interest of truth and justice such power struggles may be necessary in all kinds of contexts but that the Christian priest / leader in issues involving his own 'power' may have to focus entirely on its Eucharistic character as the capacity for self-surrender and forgiveness as modeled on the life and death of Jesus Christ.

In the search for a spirituality for the Christian priest / minister / servant, the self-emptying and surrender of Jesus the Christ constitutes the primary model. That does not preclude resistance and even anger at injustice as his reaction to the money lenders in the Temple or to the self-righteousness and hypocrisy of the religious leaders of his time indicates. There are echoes of all that in Father Laide's reaction to the 'pious hypocrisy' of his new parish priest, and in his willingness to accept his banishment to a remote island by his bishop despite his belief that he has been falsely accused in regard to his trip up the mountain with Kevin. The come-back at Sergeant Miller by starting a whispering campaign with allegations of his practice of voyeurism on the same mountain, if understandable in human terms, strikes a rather different and un-Christian note.

Holy Fools

Most Christians, baptised and ordained, are at best en route to being Christ-like. Self-emptying is never easy or complete. The temptations to 'power over' and to revenge often prove too strong; surrender and forgiveness too weak and foolish. The 'foolishness of God' cannot always replace the wisdom of men. Yet in this novel as so often in life eccentric, foolish, even absurd people, while far from being saints, can convey something of that foolishness of God. They can emerge as 'holy fools' who challenge the conventional structures of wisdom and power. The most obvious candidate for such recognition here is 'The Eccentric', English woman Sarah Field. She and Father Laide are drawn together by their love of birds and animals and consequent opposition to Sergeant Miller. The chapter devoted to the interaction of all three characters is at once the most hilarious and moving in the book. In her passions as in her behaviour, particularly as it deteriorates through alcohol and personal neglect, she seems truly a *duine le Dia* in the older Irish sense and a holy fool in the disregard for herself in protection of God's creatures. Her attempt to burn the dead goat in which action she is joined by her curate friend underlines the innocent foolishness of both of them and the sense of absurdity of life about them which holy fools are called to reveal. Of course, the curate's earlier disguise of himself as the Arab illustrates much the same point and for all his quick temper and lack of pastoral sensitivity at times he shares something of Sarah's holy foolishness.

The Tears of God

In his first call on Sarah Field Father Laide has to struggle through an entrance overladen with fuchsia bushes. He explains to her that its flowers are called *Deora De* in Irish, the Tears of God. And the whole book is marked by the tears of God, sometimes by tears of divine as well as human laughter, as in the courtroom scene and in face of other human self-important absurdities, but mainly by tears of sadness. Jesus weeping over Jerusalem might have regarded the blindnesses and enmities of Kilbroney, on their smaller scale, in much the same way. And he certainly would regard the much greater blindness and division of today's universal church with deep disappointment and sorrow. 'And when he drew near and saw the city he wept over it, saying, "Would that even today you knew the things that make for your peace!" ...' (Lk 19:21). And what of the disciples, the originating church, who could not watch one hour with him while he prayed in Gethsemene in sorrow and near-despair?

Kilbroney, for all its insignificance in church and state, reveals something of their underlying dysfunction and disvalue. However Father Laide might be finally judged in terms of the allegations against him which were never brought to court, he provides a stark challenge to the spiritual condition of the Irish priesthood and its leadership. In another idiom and image, that of Seamus Heaney's 'From The Republic of Conscience':

> At their inauguration, public leaders
> must swear to uphold unwritten law and weep
> to atone for their presumption to hold office –
>
> and to affirm their faith that all life sprang
> from salt tears which the sky-god wept
> after he dreamt his solitude was endless.

The lonely Jesus of Gethsemene and Calvary would abolish the separation and so the solitude and isolation of God and humanity. The people and priests of Kilbroney and their partners around the world have this permanent promise, gift and task in their apparently banal and petty lives.